RELIGION IN ROMAN BRITAIN

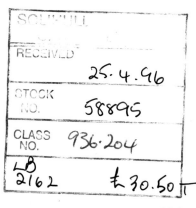

RELIGION IN ROMAN BRITAIN

Martin Henig

B T BATSFORD LTD · LONDON

This book is dedicated to Jo, Leon and Stephen Henig
and also to Lauren, Brian, Theowen, Susannah and Edward Gilmour;
Robin, Alison, Matthew and Helen Taylor;
Philip and Rosanagh Redpath and Julian, Beatrice and Henry Munby

First published 1984

© Martin Henig, 1984
Reprinted 1995

Filmset by Keyspools Ltd, Golborne, Lancashire
and printed in Great Britain by
Butler & Tanner Ltd
Frome, Somerset

for the Publishers
B T Batsford Ltd., 4 Fitzhardinge Street, London W1H 0AH

British Library Cataloging in Publication Data
Henig, Martin
Religion in Roman Britain.
1. Romans—Great Britain   2. Rome—Religion
—History
I. Title
292′.07′09362   BL800

ISBN 0—7134—6047—4

Contents

Acknowledgements

The Author and Publishers would like to thank the following for permission to reproduce the illustrations appearing in this book:

Ashmolean Museum, Oxford for figs 68, 70 and 91

David Baker, F.S.A. for fig 85

Bath Excavation Committee for figs 6 and 7

Brighton Museum for fig 95

Trustees of the British Museum for figs 4, 8, 11, 12, 15, 21, 23, 26, 44, 48, 51, 52, 57, 59, 64, 75, 82, 84, 94, 102, 107 and 108

City of Birmingham Museum and Art Gallery for fig 20

Corinium Museum for figs 28, 30, 47 and 83

Country Life for fig 109

R Downey, Hayling Island Excavation Project for fig 71

Excavation Committee of the Gravesend Historical Society for figs 5 and 76

W F Grimes for fig 41

Grosvenor Museum, Chester for figs 37, 77 and 98

G Soffe, Hayling Island Excavation Project for fig 3

Kent Archaeological Society for fig 97

Lincolnshire Museum for fig 13

Maidstone Museum for fig 99

Julian Munby, F.S.A. for figs 17 and 22

Museum of Antiquities of the University and the Society of Antiquaries of Newcastle upon Tyne for figs 38, 39, 56 and 86

Museum of Archaeology and Anthropology, Cambridge for figs 1, 14, 24, 25, 61, 62, 63, 66 and 96

Museum of London for figs 10, 40, 43 a and b, 45, 49, 50 and 100

National Museum of Antiquities of Scotland for figs 32, and 103

Oxford University Press and R P Wright for figs 2 and 33

A Pacitto for fig 104

E J Phillips for fig 36

Roman Fort and Museum, South Shields, Co. Durham for fig 34

Royal Commission on the Ancient and Historical Monuments of Scotland for fig 101

Royal Commission on Historical Monuments for fig 53

Dr D J Smith, F.S.A. for figs 9 and 42

Society of Antiquaries of London for figs 16 and 78

8 *Acknowledgements*

Society of Antiquaries of Newcastle upon Tyne for fig 27
Dr R S O Tomlin for fig 65
P Turnbull for fig 29
Verulamium Museum for figs 19, 72, 79, 80 and 93
Western Archaeological Trust for figs 18 and 69
R L Wilkins and the Institute of Archaeology, Oxford for figs 54, 55, 60, 67, 74, 88, 89, 90 and 105
Yorkshire Museum, York for fig 46

The Illustrations

Prologue

Uno itinere non potest pervenire ad tam grande secretum
(Symmachus, *Relatio* 3, 9)

Symmachus' great plea for the restoration of the Altar of Victory to the Senate House in Rome, removed by the Christian Emperor, Gratian, is a moving appeal for religious toleration.[1] It also summarises one of the most important facets of Roman policy. Men should be permitted to worship whichever gods they please, for absolute truth is unknowable to mortals – and the unknowable does not concern the State.

During most of the Roman period, pragmatism held sway. Rome's benign neutrality in matters of religion was seriously threatened only by the Jews (in the first and second centuries) because the God of the Jews was a jealous god who refused to co-exist with others; and to a much lesser extent by the Celts whose religion could be used to further unrest against Rome, and whose customs included human sacrifice, an offence against public order, public decency and the *Lex Romana*.

Short-lived religious 'reforms', for instance by Elagabalus who instituted the veneration of an oriental Baal, were soon swept aside after the fall of their initiators. The great change came in the fourth century when Christianity – the faith of Constantine – became the official faith of the Roman Empire.

This book forms part of the same series as Professor Charles Thomas' persuasive *Christianity in Roman Britain*[2] but differs from the approach of this interesting and provocative volume in a number of respects. Some of these are due to the different training and interests of the authors, but others are inherent in the material itself.

Seen from the perspective of the twentieth century, Christianity is clearly a major theme in Roman religion; it was a healthy shoot which flourished through the Middle Ages. Both Medieval Christendom and the religious turmoil of early modern times, the Reformation and Counter Reformation, are consequences of it, and it is clear that Christianity remains a major force to this day.

It is hardly necessary to point out that none of this would have been apparent in third-century Britain, while even in the early fourth century Christianity might have been regarded as no more significant than Aurelian's Sun cult. Was it, indeed, the Sun cult? When the mint of London along with other mints in the Empire struck coins proclaiming Constantine to be 'Comrade of the Unconquered Sun',[3] no-one employed by the mint realised that the Sungod would be subsumed in the person of the founder of an offshoot of Judaism, and that a monotheistic faith derived from this relatively small, relatively isolated religion would sweep through the Empire.

As late as the 360s, Julian's restoration of Paganism was presented simply as a return to 'normalcy'.[4] At any rate down to this time, it is hardly historical to view Roman religion from the standpoint of Christianity. In this book it will shrink to its contemporary importance – as a minor cult in the earlier Empire; later it was one of several significant sects and from the reign of Constantine it was favoured politically. It requires a real effort of imagination and reconstruction to understand cults which vanished, or left only obscure shadows in folklore, in the way that we can with the Christian religion but an attempt must be made to do so, if the past is not to be falsified.

Late Roman and sub-Roman Britain provides us with a few religious texts: Patrick, Gildas and some of the Pelagian writings. All are Christian and little concerned with describing what were taken to be dangerous errors. For contemporary insular Paganism we have merely the inscribed leaden 'curse-tablets' (*defixiones*) from Bath, Uley and elsewhere. Moreover, there was no universal name for Paganism – not, in any case, a single system of belief. The word *paganus* means a countryman, and is suggestive evidence that late Roman urban Christians could dismiss polytheists as country bumpkins. The term *gentilis* (from *gens*, 'a people') seems to have been used in opposition to *Christianus* on a fourth-century tablet from Bath.[5] It is interesting to note that a votary of Sulis Minerva, a pagan, can employ these as contrasting epithets, and this suggests that by the late fourth-century Christianity had gained sufficient ground to be widely regarded as an alternative to everything else.

In order to find out what pagans thought, we have to divide them into categories, study the archaeological evidence, read inscriptions, look at contemporary writings from the Mediterranean world and explore a range of beliefs as different as Hinduism, Lapland Shamanism, peasant Catholicism, Buddhist philosophy, and nationalistic Shintoism today. We shall begin with cults which were old and obscure when Caesar first came to Britain and end with new, dynamic proselytising religions which emerged in the long-civilised lands of the Eastern Mediterranean. In general we shall observe that the simpler cults were concerned with the right ritual, the more complex with right behaviour as well. The former were mainly concerned with success in this world, and the latter also with salvation after death.

The work of Anne Ross and Miranda Green[6] is of great interest and importance. Their hypothesis that the worship of the Celtic gods remained alive and essentially separate from the veneration of Roman gods, and that this is demonstrated by the existence of local iconographic traditions, cannot be dismissed out of hand. The sculpture of the Cotswold region, for example, with its non-Roman nuances, might be taken to indicate a more self-contained native culture than I believe actually existed. The reader must decide whether I have placed too heavy a weight on evidence in written documents such as inscriptions and leaden curse tablets. It must also be stated here that this book does not attempt to discuss the intricacies of temple architecture, except in passing.[7] There is no indication either from inscriptions or from offerings that the usual Romano-Celtic temple plan was in itself a sign that its cult practices were notably different from those prevalent in other forms of temple (notably the standard 'classical' temple) in the Roman World.

In writing this book I have been greatly helped by many friends who have made comments and suggestions to me, amongst them George Boon, Richard Bradley,

Barry Cunliffe, Mark Hassall, Catherine Johns, Harry and Zoë Josephs, Anthony King, Glenys Lloyd-Morgan and Julian Munby. Dr Graham Webster has throughout been a source of help and encouragement as well as a fount of stimulating ideas, and I also owe him a great debt in first encouraging my archaeological studies many years ago. This is also the place to acknowledge my heartfelt gratitude to Ralph Merrifield for long and stimulating discussion on Roman religion in Britain, especially when I worked with him at the Guildhall Museum, London: the germ of this book dates back to that time. At Oxford the classes of Peter Brown (now Professor Peter Brown of Princeton University) made me think hard about what men and women really believed in late antiquity. The visual and artistic evidence is enormously significant in a study of this sort and Professor Jocelyn Toynbee's guidance and interest has been profoundly important to me.

Lorraine Mepham not only typed a very difficult manuscript, but also provided me with useful editorial criticism. Without her assistance and that of Alison and Robin Taylor, the book would have taken very considerably longer in seeing the light of day. I am also indebted to all the museum curators and others who sent me illustrations.

At Batsford, I am grateful to Peter Kemmis Betty for his extraordinary patience. Much of the book was written in two summers amidst the incomparable scenery of the Hebridean Small Isles – and I am very thankful to Mr Julian Ward and Mrs Ann Nimmo-Smith for providing me with refuges in Eigg and Muck respectively. I was able to finish the task at Ashbury, enjoying the quiet of the Berkshire Downs, and stimulated by that wondrous monument of pagan antiquity, the Uffington White Horse, thanks to the generosity of Mrs Mary Munby.

The archaeologist has the obligation while he is writing to be dispassionate with the evidence that he describes, but when he finally puts down trowel and pen, it should be with a sense of wonder at the diversity of belief which is also a sure sign of man's quest for God. The author feels immensely fortunate to have been brought up with love and respect for three gracious and tolerant traditions and faiths: Rabbinic Judaism, the Anglican-Christian culture of England and (through his education) the religion of ancient Greece. He admits to a special empathy with the gods and goddesses of Greece and Rome and points out that, at its best, Graeco-Roman religion was capable of achieving sublime heights. We do well to remember a wonderful passage in Ammianus' work, where the dying Julian chides his friends, 'saying that it was unworthy to mourn for a prince who was called to union with heaven and the stars' (Ammianus xxv, 3, 22).[8] Apart from the personal dedication on the fly-leaf, this book is dedicated to all men, of many religions and of diverse cultures, who have not sought to place their aspirations lower than those of the Neo-Platonic philosopher and Emperor.

2nd February 1983   *Institute of Archaeology, Oxford*

Foreword to the Second Edition

In the ten years that have passed since the book first appeared, there has been nothing to render it significantly out of date or to force me to modify my ideas to any great degree. The keynote of the period has been consolidation, and a number of important excavation reports have been published setting out evidence known to me in 1984, only in briefer summaries. Notable have been *The Temple of Sulis Minerva at Bath* 1 by B. Cunliffe and P. Davenport (1985); 2 edited by B. Cunliffe (1988); *The Uley Shrines* edited by A. Woodward and P. Leach (1993); *Coventina's Well* by L. Allason-Jones and B. McKay (1985); and, for the late prehistoric period, *Excavations in Thetford, 1980–1982* by the late Tony Gregory (1991). In addition, the most important finds from the Walbrook Mithraeum have been fully published in the late J.M.C. Toynbee's *The Roman Art Treasures from the Temple of Mithras* (1986: the full report on Professor Grimes's excavation is in active preparation).

Of course, there have been some new discoveries of which the finds from the temple at Wanborough, Surrey, which include items of priestly regalia (head-dresses, one surmounted by a solar wheel, and sceptres), must take pride of place (see M.G. O'Connell and J. Bird, 'The Roman temple at Wanborough, excavations 1985–1986', *Surrey Archaeological Collections* vol. 82 [1994], 1–168). Another cache of votive bronzes, presumably from a temple, consists of masks (representing deities and/or their worshippers) and of figurines; it was found at Icklingham, Suffolk by robbers and later smuggled out of the country. Two of the masks are illustrated in my companion volume *The Art of Roman Britain* (Batsford, 1995). Personal religion of a highly Romanised sort is represented by another bronze figurine from Suffolk, a herm of Priapus from Pakenham, now in the British Museum (C. Johns and M. Henig, *Ant. J.* lxxi, 1991, 236–9). These years have also seen more work at the temple at Harlow, Essex, the head of a (?)cult statue of Minerva and the establishment of the existence of an Iron Age predecessor to the Roman shrine (R. Bartlett, *Essex Journal* 23 no. i, 1988, 9–13).

Among secondary sources published in the past decade, Batsford has made an important contribution with three works, a general survey concentrating on the sanctuaries themselves in Ann Woodward's *Shrines and Sacrifice* (1992); Graham Webster's *The British celts and their gods under Rome* (1986) which presents a more Celto-centric view of religious practice, somewhat between mine and that of Miranda Green; most fascinating of all is the late Ralph Merrifield's *The Archaeology of Ritual and Magic* (1987) which is by no means restricted to a single period but includes many of the puzzling aspects of ritual behaviour which can be deduced by Roman archaeology.

Other new works are Gerald Wait's *Ritual and Religion in Iron Age Britain* (BAR Brit. ser. 149, 1986) which does something to correct my rather negative bias on this period. On the Roman period proper, Thomas Blagg's paper 'Roman religious sites in the British landscape', *Landscape History* 8 (1986) 15–25, adds a perspective of a sense of place perhaps rather lacking in my book; at the other extreme, Eric Birley takes an epigraphic approach to religion in 'The deities of Roman Britain', *A.N.R.W.* 18.1 (1986), 3–112. Although no new Mithraea have been found in Britain, there have been startling fresh assessments of the cult itself, laying stress on its Roman rather than its oriental nature: see, for instance, Richard Gordon, 'Authority, salvation and mystery' in J. Huskinson,

M. Beard and J. Reynolds, *Image and Mystery in the Roman World* (1988), 45–88, and *idem*, 'Who worshipped Mithras?', *Journal of Roman Archaeology* 7, 1994, 459–74.

It is, indeed, important not to adopt too insular a perspective in studying religious belief. Amongst general books Robin Lane Fox's masterly *Pagans and Christians* (1986), though dealing largely with the Mediterranean, has to be in any bibliography. Three volumes of conference proceedings have appeared, all concerned with religion in the provinces but, as pointed out here, including important papers on Britain. I followed the publication of the present book by organising a conference in Oxford together with Anthony King and publishing the proceedings. *Pagan gods and shrines of the Roman Empire*, edited by M. Henig and A. King (1986), contains contributions on paganism in Late Antiquity by Ernest Black and myself, while a contribution by J.P. Alcock on the concept of Genius in Roman Britain and one by the late Ralph Merrifield on the London hunter-god deserve especial notice. C. Goudineau, I. Fauduet and G. Coulon, *Les sanctuaires de tradition indigène en Gaule Romaine* (1994) contains an admirable survey of recent research on native temples in Britain by Anthony King and Grahame Soffe. Last, C.M. Ternes and P.F. Burke jr, *Roman Religion in Gallia Belgica and the Germaniae* (Actes des quatrièmes rencontres scientifiques de Luxembourg, 1994) includes my own assessment of the Cotswold (or London) hunter-god.

With regard to religious change in Late Roman Britain, the key work on Christianity remains Charles Thomas's *Christianity in Roman Britain to AD 500* (1981; reprinted with new foreword 1985). Dorothy Watts, *Christians and Pagans in Roman Britain* (1991) sees Christianity as having been very widespread in fourth-century Britain, despite some symbiosis with pagan rites and even outright apostasy. More recently K.R. Dark in *Civitas to Kingdom* (1994) sees Christianity as widespread but paganism dominant among the élite and thus responsible for much of the evidence. The disappearance of paganism in the early fifth century can then be seen as the result of social revolution, the replacement of the governing class.

Two series of *corpora* are in progress, those comprising the second volume of the *Roman Inscriptions of Britain* by S.S. Frere and R.S.O. Tomlin and the various fascicules of the *Corpus Signorum Imperii Romani* of which mine on *The Cotswold Region* (1993) contains information on an area which, as I have already hinted, contains a great deal of religious interest. A corpus of a different type is V.J. Hutchinson's remarkable work *Bacchus in Roman Britain: the evidence for his cult* (1986), which fully confirms my surmise that amongst Romanised pagans this god had a key importance.

I have taken the opportunity to make a few simple corrections to my original text. A few other specific comments can be made here. The intaglio (**87**) on p. 182 shows Serapis and the Dioscuri (rather than Isis and Harpocrates) and may have reference to Severus, who associated himself with Serapis, and his two sons. The Mithraic *tessera* (**93**) depicted on p. 189 seems to be a regular Mithraic dedication rather than a magic charm, as the letters **DM** (*Deo Mithrae*) have been discerned on the side (RIB 2408.2). References throughout the book use the Greek form of one deity, Atys, rather than more correctly in the present context, the Latin, Attis.

Martin Henig
February, 1995

1 The Celtic World

I shall not speak of the ancient errors, common to all races, that bound the whole of humanity fast before the coming of Christ in the flesh. I shall not enumerate the devilish monstrosities of my land, numerous almost as those that plagued Egypt, some of which we can see today, stark as ever, inside or outside deserted city walls: outlines still ugly, faces still grim. I shall not name the mountains and hills and rivers, once so pernicious, now useful for human needs, on which, in those days, a blind people heaped divine honours. (Gildas, *De Excid. Brit.* 4, 2–3)[1]

A 'Natural Religion'

In this tantalising passage Gildas alludes to Romano-British paganism while at the same time refusing to tell us anything about it. Neither he nor his readers were interested. However, the connection implied between natural features and the divine world is certainly authentic. Place-name evidence shows that rivers in particular sometimes received their names before a Celtic language was spoken here; the Thames may have been called the Thames in the Bronze Age or earlier. Religious dedications of the Roman period show that such personified natural features were worshipped; thus Verbeia (whose name means 'winding river') is attested as a goddess on a Roman altar at Ilkley in Yorkshire. Apart from such comparatively late evidence, the great number of metal finds of Bronze Age and Iron Age date from the Thames and other rivers and bogs suggests that such places were holy. It may also be noted that the ostentatious disposal of precious objects in dedications to the gods was an ideal way by which men could demonstrate their wealth and so enhance their prestige.[2]

Strabo writes of a great gold treasure dedicated to the gods near Toulouse, but only some of it was kept in temple-enclosures. The rest lay at the bottom of sacred lakes (Strabo IV, I, 13). The earth itself as well as water was sacred – shafts sunk into the ground are known from the Bronze Age. Most, however, are of Iron Age or Roman date. The evidence of sacrifices in these pits, coupled sometimes with the presence of great timbers which could symbolise the sexual penetration of the earth and thus constitute fertility magic, confirms that these are more than mere wells, though doubtless wells too were venerated as they have been in more recent times.[3]

Much of early Britain was forested, and these murky groves were also the resorts of divine powers. The word *nemeton*, related to the Greek *temenos*, means a grove, generally by implication a sacred grove. *Arnemetia*, whose cult centre was Buxton, means 'she who dwelt over against the sacred grove', and was apparently the goddess of the springs of this spa[4] Mars *Rigonementos* at Nettleham, Lincolnshire also presided over a grove.[5] Such evidence may be supplemented by literary accounts. Lucan's account of the grove near *Massilia* (Marseilles) 'untouched by men's hands from antiquity' where the gods were 'venerated with strange rites, the altars piled high with hideous offerings, and every tree was sprinkled with human blood' (*Pharsalia* III, 399ff) is hardly a reliable eye-witness record but it does attest the rough and unwholesome aspect of native religion seen by an outsider. In Britain the groves on Anglesey which were attacked by the army of Suetonius Paullinus (Tacitus, *Annals* XIV, 30) and the grove of Andate (or Andraste) where Boudica's Britons tortured and, in effect, sacrificed prisoners (Dio Cassius, *epitome* of book LXII, 7) conjure up the same feelings of repulsion and mystery.

Alongside veneration of natural features, men would have been impressed by the animals and birds which inhabited the countryside. Their attributes, the swiftness of the deer, the strength of the boar, the high-soaring flight of the eagle suggested divine strength. The migration of birds, perhaps to the realm of the gods, was a great puzzle. Animals were endowed with divine powers, and frequently appear in the post-Roman insular Celtic literature as beings of considerable understanding. Thus the rivalry between two supernatural bulls forms a theme in the Irish epic, the *Táin Bó Cuálgne*. Amongst divine boars are Twrch Trwyth of Welsh legend and Torc Forbartach in an Irish story. Some tribal names, the *Epidii* (horse people) in Kintyre, *Lugi* (raven people) in Sutherland and perhaps the *Orci* (boar-people) of the Orkney Islands, suggest totemism[6] and the fact that Caesar records that the goose, cock and hare were sacred to the Britons (*BG* V, 12), whether or not it was a widespread taboo, shows us that the religion of the Celts was a 'natural religion'.

Although it was so close to nature, it was not without art and philosophy. Celtic art is frequently abstract but, amongst the flowing curves, masks of men and animals appear. Those of beasts include boars, horses and bulls. Whether these ornament objects of daily use amongst the tribal aristocracy (e.g. shields or buckets) or coins handed out by war-lords to their followers, the image always projects a strong idea of the power and beneficence of nature. The horns of bulls on iron fire-dogs and on bronze bucket mounts are emphasised by knobbed ends which may denote the fecundity of the creature. The horns, which are probably an original feature of the Torrs *Chamfron* (similar horns are shown rising from the head of a winged horse on a coin of Tasciovanus), have the same meaning.[7]

It is startling to discover that human heads are treated no differently from the heads of animals. As the great art historian, Paul Jacobsthal wrote, 'The Celts created Man in the image of Beast'.[8] We are so used to naturalistic portraiture that the Celtic mask with its almond-shaped eyes, long nose and slit mouth seems shocking in its complete lack of emotional finesse. The head is a totem of power; it could be severed from an enemy in battle and yet retain life independent of the body. The Welsh hero Bran actually asked his followers to decapitate him and his head became a talisman with the ability to foretell the future. Thus the heads ornamenting the Aylesford, Baldock and Marlborough buckets are not there by chance, but helped to give potency to the wine or beer these splendid feasting bowls contained. Sometimes the human head was provided with horns, notably on the obverse of a silver coin found near Petersfield, Hampshire. Here a facing head is surmounted with antlers 'at the burgeoning velvet stage'. Is this the same god Cernunnos shown on a Roman relief from Paris or has it some other meaning? The wheel between the horns belong to Taranis who is certainly depicted in Roman period art from the Celtic provinces (Chapter 3) and is a solar symbol. Does the coin show two deities conflated or a priest wearing a headdress containing horns and a wheel, or is it merely a conjunction of fortunate symbols? We cannot be sure, but certainly the combination of such powerful elements must have been seen as auspicious. Incidentally, figures who may be priests are associated with heads on coins of Cunobelinus (perhaps adapted from a Roman prototype, Perseus with the mask of Medusa) and also of Verica.[9]

Although the head-cult seem to belong especially to the world of the Celts, it should be emphasised that other ancient peoples including the Greeks and Romans saw the head as the seat of power and energy. The Roman *imagines*, portrait-busts, belong to the same body of belief as does the prodigy of the head of Olus appearing on the site of the Roman Capitol and talking in early Roman legend.[10]

The Organisation of Ritual – The Druids

Our knowledge of how religious ritual was organised in Iron Age Britain is very deficient. Religious officials – masters of sacred lore – commonsense tells us, must always have existed. Certainly it is hard to see how the great stone circles, surely temples, of western Britain like Avebury (c 2600 BC) and Stonehenge (c 2100 BC) operated without such men. However, there is very little evidence, apart from the continuity or at least re-use of a site after a gap of years or even of centuries as at Uley in Gloucestershire or Maiden Castle in Dorset, to substantiate links with the Bronze Age or Neolithic. As Aubrey Burl writes, 'by the Iron Age ... few people came to Avebury' and 'A Roman visitor to Avebury would have found it abandoned'.[11] These sites have been connected with the Druids from at least the eighteenth century, but attractive as might appear to be the connection between our most impressive prehistoric monuments and the one group of pre-Roman holy men all our authorities agree existed, it cannot be substantiated.

Who were the Druids? They appear in many sources as teachers and judges rather than as priests, though they are sometimes said to have been present at sacrifices. The Elder Pliny does write of them as priests and it is from him that we learn that they cut mistletoe from oaks with a golden sickle (*NH* XVI, 251); a story which gripped public imagination from the time of John Aubrey. A *strigil* of Roman date from Reculver, Kent (1) led him to remark: 'Behold the golden sickle with which the Druids used to cut mistletoe.'[12].

If this occasions knowing smiles today the *strigil* deserves to be illustrated as a reminder that any study of a past culture must be at best interpretative reconstruction. For Nora Chadwick, the Druids were philosophers rather than priests.[13] She accepts the tradition of Posidonius followed by Caesar and it must be admitted that both the Greek explorer of the second century BC and the Roman general a century later were in a position to meet Druids and perhaps (through interpreters) to speak to them. When Caesar says that 'the Druidic doctrine is believed to have been found existing in Britain and thence imported into Gaul' (*BG* VI, 13) he may be wrong – Pliny writing after Gaul had been subdued and while

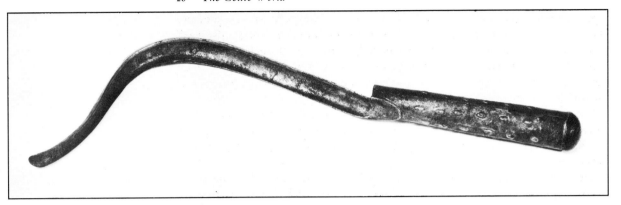

1 The bronze strigil from Reculver, Kent. Length 28.5 cm. *Museum of Archaeology and Anthropology, Cambridge*

Britain itself was being conquered sees it as having been taken there from Gaul (*NH* XXX, 13) – but we must accept the fact that British Druidism already seemed old in Caesar's day. He continues, 'even today those who want to make a profound study of it generally go to Britain for the purpose'. There were, then, cross-channel pilgrimages to Britain.

Even if the Druids were not strictly speaking a priestly caste, it is doubtful whether the exact distinction between Druids and priests would have been apparent to the Roman outsider. As we shall see in Roman sacrifices, the officiant and the man who struck the blow that killed the animal had different functions. Druids may not have slaughtered animals (or people) themselves – but the Romans held them responsible for human sacrifices – drowning, hanging, stabbing and burning are the means cited by ancient writers.[14] Presumably the Druids confirmed that human lives were demanded by the gods, Esus, Taranis, Teutates and others, and this formed part of the reason why they were opposed by the Romans (see Chapter 9).

Temples and Holy Places

Specific sites must have had their own individual rites and ceremonies, for the power of Celtic deities seems to have been very localised. Post-Conquest inscriptions mention names which should go back into the Iron Age, although that does not necessarily mean that we can use Roman-period evidence to understand the cults of Sulis, Cunomaglos, Cocidius or Belatucadrus in earlier times.[15]

Apart from the archaeological evidence, our knowledge of Celtic religion is very sketchy. That there was a calendar of festivals is clear from Irish sources and may be presumed from a bronze tablet found at Coligny in France inscribed with lucky and unlucky days.[16] Augury, a practice shared with the Romans, follows from the deep sympathy felt with the natural world (Diodorus v, 31; Cicero, *De Divinatione* 41). Groves are mentioned and in Gaul at the mouth of the Loire a temple served by priestesses (Strabo IV, 4, 3) implies that women – apart from the redoubtable Boudica – could have a special relationship with the gods.

Archaeological discoveries which relate directly to pre-Roman Celtic religion are still comparatively sparse and difficult to interpret. This is because Celtic temples were timber-built compared to the Roman structures of stone which

replaced them. Even where the quantity of early finds is so great that the presence
of an Iron Age shrine is certain, the massive nature of Roman building activity will
frequently have destroyed, or badly damaged the earlier structure. Harlow, with a
very extensive coin-list but no Iron Age shrine to go with it, and perhaps Bath on
the grounds that the Celts could not have avoided venerating Sulis, the spirit of
the spring, are cases in point.[17]

Where temples have been excavated, and the circular shrines at Hayling Island
and Maiden Castle come to mind, they are really no more than large huts of 'Little
Woodbury' type.[18] At Gallows Hill, Thetford, a group of five huts has been
excavated within a series of three rectangular ditches. Although the site has been
interpreted as 'Boudica's Palace', the extraordinary fact that the huts have two
opposed entrances, which would create through draughts if they were occupied, is
a strong argument against explaining them as dwellings. Surely they could be
shrines, perhaps predecessors of the Temple of Faunus situated only a few yards
away and destroyed when a factory was built, (although it must be emphasised
that the Iron Age site ceased to be used after about AD 60 and was probably
deliberately dismantled by the Romans in the aftermath of the Boudican
uprising).[19]

Large huts (*bruidne*) belonging to the gods of the Other World are mentioned in
the Irish sources. Each of these hostelries contained a cauldron which could feed
any number of guests.[20] A supernatural house with a cauldron of ale and food
(pork and beef) left for the visitor is mentioned in the *Voyage of Mael Duin*.[21] Its walls
were hung with gold and silver brooches, torcs and swords with hilts of precious
metal. These recall the type of offering which might be left in a temple, but it may
be noted that silver was little used in Ireland before the Viking period and in
particular the type of sword described in this and other Irish tales seems to be
Viking. On balance I think we can still use Irish legend as a 'window on the Iron
Age' but we should be aware that there are problems of interpretation.[22] More
idiosyncratic in a land where the predominant tradition of building was the
circular hut is the rectangular temple at Heathrow, Middlesex which with its
central cult-room (*cella*) and porch is sometimes seen as the ancestor to the
Romano-Celtic temple. Other rectangular buildings, generally very small, at
Danebury, South Cadbury and Lancing, are also identified as shrines or temples.[23]
The little Lancing Down shrine is next to a later Romano-Celtic temple of normal
type.

Celtic holy places did not necessarily need a building. The area around the
Roman temple at Uley was sacred in the Iron Age, but it is thought that there was
no pre-Roman building here, merely a boundary ditch to demarcate the land of
the gods from the world of men.[24] Perhaps there was a sacred tree or well in such
cases. Whether a deity had a home in a human sense might be due to a variety of
cult factors. Weather gods were at home under the stars and the rain-clouds, but
some fertility deities perhaps needed private and secret retreats.

The sacred enclosure (*Temenos*) at Hayling Island did have a building on it. The
excavators noted that most of the finds came from the temenos rather than from
the *cella*, thus showing that the cleared space of the enclosure was essential for the
practice of the cult. The actual building, like any other central feature such as a
tree or a pit, was merely a focus for ritual, and was regarded as private to the gods.

It is hard to argue about the names and attributes of deities because inscriptions are unknown in the Iron Age and images virtually never found. Some, probably most, of the Celtic names recorded on Roman inscriptions originated back in the Iron Age but they do not help us to reconstruct anything of pre-Roman ritual. Is the horned head on the coin from Petersfield mentioned above Cernunnos or not? Even if we accept that it is, we are not taken much further in understanding the pantheon of south Britain as a whole. It is true that Caesar writes about images 'of Mercury' in Gaul (*BG* VI, 17), but it is doubtful whether these would have been easily recognised as the Roman god Mercury. The very practice of interpreting native deities to fit them into a classical mould changes their nature. It will be argued in Chapter 3 that the *interpretatio Romana* (Tacitus, *Germania* 43, 3) was a dynamic concept. It did not destroy the ancestral gods but it most certainly changed them. Nevertheless, it is true that a line of continuity in worship and ritual links Romano-Celtic religion with its past. A Briton of the Flavian period must have felt he was venerating the gods of his fathers and grandfathers even though artists from the continent now gave them human (i.e. Graeco-Roman) faces.

To take the case of Uley where the Roman dedication is known to have been to Mercury, the finds of weapons argue that the pre-Roman deity was a warrior. Model spears were still given as offerings in Roman times, and on a Roman curse-tablet the writer is clearly confused about whether he is addressing Mercury or Mars.[25]

At Hayling Island, finds of mirrors and brooches are suggestive evidence that one of the deities venerated was female. Weapons and horse trappings from the site tell something of the nature of her consort. The Romans might well have called him Mars, but as at Uley, they might not have done. An intriguing, if remote, possibility is that as this temple was in the territory of the southern Atrebates, and clearly an important sanctuary site, the cult was in some way ancestral to the veneration of Neptune and Minerva in Chichester, encouraged by King Cogidubnus.[26] Perhaps around the decade AD 43–53 some learned traveller told the tribal authorities that Minerva (Athena) and Neptune (Poseidon) were venerated in the Erechtheion at Athens and that the same combination of deities would surely look after the maritime and agricultural interests of southern Atrebatic/Regnensian lands.

Offerings and Sacrifice

Model weapons and shields from Iron Age levels at Frilford, Berkshire and Worth, Sussex, were only token offerings but might be as effective as real armour and weapons and gifts to warrior gods, invoked against supernatural threats.[27] Model implements such as bows and mattocks are made today by members of a tribe called the Tiv in Nigeria. Here it has been suggested that they are offered at JuJu shrines in order to secure the success of an appropriate enterprise (e.g. hunting or planting crops). Something further may be learnt about the Celtic response to deities if we examine coins found at Hayling Island. The exacavators had at first thought that many of them were of gold, but closer examination revealed the majority to be base metal, thinly plated with gold. The first instinct of a twentieth-century archaeologist is to think of forgery or at least of cheating the gods, but this is not really just. In the spirit world, token-coins and other objects become real.

The substitution of symbolic for real offerings in religious and funerary ritual has a long history, down through the Middle Ages and even until the present day. While some votaries may always have thought in terms of saving precious metal, the motive of others will always have been to let their relatively slight resources make a splendid show. The gods demanded attention, veneration, obedience from the worshipper much more than a simple gift of bullion.[28]

Most offerings were of animals, cereals, fruits, and alcoholic beverages such as mead, beer or even (imported) wine. The principle of life was vital here – the offering which was presented to the god in hope of recompense had to be something that reflected the creative energy of the god and the desire of the giver. Thus we shall find on temple sites the bones of pigs (the favourite food of the Celtic warrior) as well as sheep, goats and cattle. Occasionally the latter are of oxen, while horses, also draught animals as well as the mounts of warriors, were given as special sacrifices. The bulk of the animal bones from the Hayling Island shrine are of sheep or goat and pig, but there are also significant finds of horse skulls. At Uley, the exclusion of pig may not be entirely fortuitous in view of the importance of the animal – were pigs taboo to that deity which the Romans later identified as Mercury?

Human bones are a very small part of total bone assemblages from Iron Age sacred and occupation sites, but examples do turn up with macabre frequency. Pieces of human skull at Hayling, the limbs and torso from a pit at Danebury, and the pathetic remains of a dismembered child from Wandlebury point to the sacrifice of human beings, perhaps of enemies. Possibly cannibalism was involved as well.[29] It is not easy to separate the atrocities attributed for instance to the followers of Boudica from religious activities. The Romans had no doubt that the Druids were involved, and we are in no position to dismiss this allegation. Human sacrifice was something that the Romans found repellent.

It does not follow that because Romans sometimes acted as though the lives of 'barbarians' were of little worth, or because Romans enjoyed gladiatorial displays which had originated in funerary ceremonies for notables that there could not possibly have been strong objection to human sacrifice or that the 'persecution' of the Druids arose simply from their political role. Apart from the fact that the atrocity stories show that the cruelty of the Druids and their political disaffection were connected, the Roman state could not condone the sudden death of subjects under their protection at the hands of judges operating under non-Roman custom. Besides this, the sadism of the amphitheatre was only one side of the Roman character. Another which lived uneasily with it was an instinct for tolerance, justice and compassion. Men like the Emperor Claudius were avid to extend the privileges of citizenship to provincials; in return, it was expected that the provincials would adopt Roman ways. Of course the Celts, and specifically the Druid priesthood, must have seen things differently. The gods demanded blood and sometimes human blood. There is a little evidence to show that human sacrifice may have continued (as an illegal aberration from Roman practice), especially in rural areas. Infant exposure was allowed in most societies – infants were without rights when newly-born, and parents who could not afford to rear them might give them to others or even expose them. Such infant exposure (or very high infant mortality) is represented by the sad remains of infants buried in the courtyard of the Hambledon villa.[30] However, when at Springhead, for example, infant skeletons were found under the foundations at the corners of buildings, we may allow ourselves to suspect ritual infanticide. There is an alternative explanation, in that the babies could have died naturally and have been presented to 'mother earth' or have been buried in a shrine associated with a healing goddess associated with childbirth (like the Roman Juno Lucina).

Adult sacrifice is more problematic. At Bourton Grounds (Thornborough), an adult was apparently buried under the path leading to the temple. It is most likely that this was disturbed from an earlier burial. There is a barrow nearby.[31] Many skulls have been found in the Walbrook, London as well as in wells from London and elsewhere. Some may be offerings to the gods by Boudican insurgents, though not all can be. Were some the trophies of head hunting preserved from Iron Age times or the result of illicit action taken against malefactors by the inhabitants of Roman London? Deposition in water is suggestive of a religious practice. Skulls preserved in oil from the site of the Wroxeter basilica are of particular interest. They may have been kept there from an early date and been dispersed after the basilica went out of use c AD 300, or they may have belonged to a subsequent shrine. Perhaps they are best regarded as war trophies rather than sacrifices.[32]

Nationalism and human sacrifice apart, native religion was well adapted to be merged with the Roman rites and to be interpreted in accord with Roman beliefs. Celtic religion was not abolished, but nor did it stay the same. Romanisation was pursued with energy and determination by the ruling power. It had profound effects on how men envisaged the gods and the shape of a new world, so much expanded from that of a local community. Before we can understand what happened to the native religion of Britain, we must turn to look at Roman beliefs.

2 The Roman Gods

In the summer of AD 43, the independent Celtic kingdoms of Britain were confronted by an invasion force of some forty thousand armed men together with their various camp followers.[1] Apart from various political and military factors this force was the cultural spearhead of a process we call 'Romanisation', and it would thus be very interesting to know something of the religious attitudes prevalent amongst the troops massed at Boulogne (Dio LX, 19). Unfortunately we are not well-informed, but the fact that the troops mutinied at the idea of crossing the sea is significant, for it sets the limits of their horizons, literally.

Oceanus was the great river surrounding the earth – beyond it was nothing except the chill and sombre realm of the dead. Even although Julius Caesar had visited Britain in 55 and 54 BC the fear of the Ocean lived on – indeed when some soldiers in Germanicus' army, attempting to navigate the Dutch coast in AD 16 were swept across the North Sea, not a man returned who did not have his tale of wonder to tell (Tacitus, *Ann.* II, 24). Incidentally, the story of Britain being at the end of the world or even beyond it was remarkably persistent and, as late as the sixth century AD, Procopius was writing of fishermen and sailors on the continent carrying dead souls across Ocean to the Isle of Brittia (*De Bello Goth.* VIII, XX, 42–58).

Nevertheless, the attitude of the braver and more heroic spirits among the Romans was capable of rising to the challenge. Here we see Rome as heir to the Greek tradition of Alexander the Great who reached the very boundary of Ocean to the east in India. It was a Greek, Demetrius, probably the *grammaticus* Demetrius of Tarsus (Plutarch, *de defectu oraculorum* 410A) who dedicated a bronze plaque in York c. AD 80 to Ocean and Tethys, the consort of Ocean (2); a dedication recalling that of Alexander at the mouth of the Indus in 325 BC.[2]

The Hellenistic and Roman world view, then, had moved beyond the Platonic image of civilised men, sitting around the Mediterranean 'like ants and frogs around a marsh' (Plato, *Phaedo*, 109b), but not by much. The religious beliefs of the legionaries remained rooted in the soil of west Mediterranean lands. The AD 43 mutiny was not brought to an end by exhortations to emulate Alexander, but by the incongruous sight of an Imperial freedman – an ex-slave – Narcissus, mounting the tribunal to harangue the troops. The world must have gone topsy-turvy when ex-slaves reminded free-born Romans of their duty; indeed it was just like the midwinter festival of the Saturnalia, and *Io, Saturnalia* is what the legionaries called out.

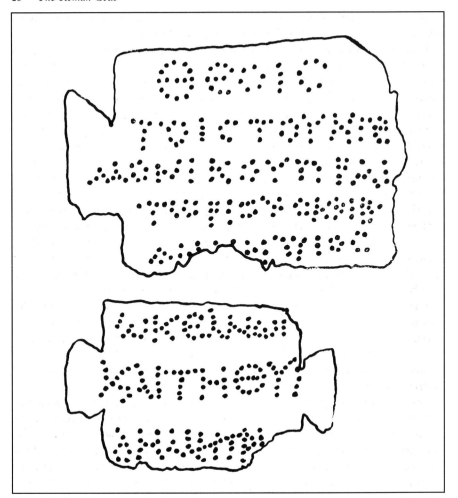

2 Bronze plates dedicated in Greek to the gods of the Governor's Residence and to Ocean and Tethys, by Demetrius. From York. Lengths 8 cm and 5 cm. *Yorkshire Museum*

The Calendar and Festivals

The Romans shared with the Celts an agricultural and pastoral heritage, but we know far more about their calendar as they were literate. Indeed for the first half of the year from January until June, we have Ovid's lovely poem, the *Fasti*, which describes festivals in verse. After the poet's exile to Tomi in AD 8, possibly on a charge of moral turpitude involving no less a person than Augustus' daughter Julia, Ovid was unable to complete the poem to his satisfaction and for the second half of the year we are left with simple calendars like that written out by the palaeographer Filocalus in the fourth century which survives in a seventeenth century copy.[3] These all list the festivals. Further information about some of these is found in the writings of antiquaries such as Macrobius in his *Saturnalia*.

Incidentally, Ovid was a widely read poet in the Imperial period and it is likely that some of the senior officers – even Aulus Plautius or the antiquary-Emperor Claudius – had packed *Fasti* in their luggage.[4] In any case we may be certain that the correct sacrifices and supplications would have been made from the very start of the invasion, probably on the lines of the military calendar found at Dura Europos on the Euphrates, much later in date but containing instructions that could well have been laid down by Augustus himself.[5]

There are three key aspects of the Roman calendar which together explain the main characteristics of Roman religion. At its heart are the rustic and family festivals which correspond to such seasonal Celtic feasts as *Imbolc* (lambing season), *Beltine* (spring − purification by fire), *Lugnasad* (late summer) and *Samain* (end of autumn − harvest). The annual cycle was a wonderful thing; its continuance was secured by rituals performed by specialists in divine lore (i.e. priests), who in time might be regarded as indispensable for satisfactory harvests or increase of flocks and herds. Such primitive ideas were partly overlaid by Greek or Graeco-Italian religion replete with gods and goddesses and young human heroes. The stories told about them were not only intensely fascinating but gave a warm, living soul to a world which could have been regarded as gripped by impersonal forces. It is this central aspect which seems to me to justify the epithet 'religious', in a description of the Roman year. At its heart is the proposition that man must live his life in harmony with the will of the gods. Primitive man may on occasion have felt that he could *control* the heavens by magic; the Roman *knew* that the co-operation of the gods bestowed of their own free-will was vital to every enterprise.

A final element in the calendar consisted of the veneration of dead rulers. This may also have had a Greek origin but developed in a distinctive Roman manner under the influence of ancestor-worship and the desire to hallow the memories of the Great Men of the past. History was a very important study in Rome. It is not always easy to separate these three elements, but they should each be kept in mind as strands in the composition of a religiosity, which the Roman called *Pietas*.

The admixture of primitive and more sophisticated notions is to be seen in ceremonies honouring Mars. One of the most famous was the sacrifice of the 'October horse' on the Ides of October (15 October).[6] A chariot race was run and the near-horse of the victorious team was sacrificed and decapitated. Then a game took place rather like the Eton Wall Game when the inhabitants of the Via Sacra and the Suburra fought over the grisly trophy and the side which won affixed it to the wall of the *Regia* or the *turris Mamilia*. This may have been an end-of-harvest fertility rite comparable to the display of corn dollies in more recent times, associated with the important fertility god Mars. The priests of Mars, the *Salii*, had very primitive rituals. In the spring, their leaping dance was believed to help the corn grow. When the Elder Cato wishes to give an example of a prayer to be recited by a farmer for purifying his land (*De Agri Cultura* CXLI) he invokes 'Father Mars', Mars Pater.

We think of Mars as a warrior deity akin to the Greek Ares, but he presumably acquired this familiar aspect as a protector of the Roman people. As the paramour of Rhea Silvia and the father of Romulus and Remus he was intimately connected with the Lupercalia, one of the most rustic of all Roman festivals, on 15th February, though the central figure on this day was, or at least was assumed to be in Ovid's day, Faunus (*Fasti* II, 267−452) − the goat god.[7]

Mars, as god of the Roman people was harnessed to political ends. The temple of Mars Ultor stood centrally in the Forum of Augustus, an invitation to him to destroy enemies abroad and root out corruption at home, while in the Roman military calendar found at Dura Europos on the Euphrates, it is clear that Roman troops everywhere celebrated the birthday of Mars Pater Victor on 1 March with the sacrifice of a bull.[8]

Many Roman deities are simply names to us, and belong to a primitive aspect of belief. Every object, every action had its divine *numen*. The priests of Ceres, whose name itself is connected with the word meaning 'to create', *creare*. invoked Vervactor (associated with the first ploughing of the fallow land); Redarator (literally the 'second plougher'); Imporcitor (harrower); Insitor (sower); Obarator (top dresser); Occator (hoer); Sarritor (raker); Subruncinator (weeder); Messor (reaper); Convector (sheaf-binder); Conditor (storer) and Promitor (distributor) (Servius, *Comm. Vergil Georgics* I, 21). If this were all there would be little to say indeed, but Ceres was equated with Demeter, the Greek goddess venerated at Eleusis, and took over her mythology.[9] Moreover there was a quasi-political aspect, for Ceres was especially worshipped by the Roman Plebeians while the Patricians venerated a goddess imported from Pessinus in Asia Minor, the *Magna Mater* (Cybele).

To follow the Roman religious year was, as Varro, Ovid and others realised, to explore the anthropological roots of Rome. A few pages in this chapter can do no more than encourage readers to make their own exploration of the Calendar. The First of January (*Kal. Ian.*) was dedicated to Janus, the double-headed god of entrances who looks back at the old year and forward into the year ahead. For friends and relations and especially children it was a happy day on which small presents of fruit, toys and other little gifts, especially clay lamps to light one's path through the year, were given. Also at this time the Consuls entered office and army units made vows so that the gods would preserve the Roman nation for all Eternity.[10]

As in the Celtic world the means by which men parleyed with the gods was through sacrifice. If a god accepted a sacrifice, he could be trusted to keep his side of the bargain. The central religious ceremonies of Paganism sound more like the dealings of the market place than what is understood by religion today, but they were hedged about with law and taboo. The sacrifices made by army units throughout the Roman world for the Eternity of Rome read 'to Jupiter Optimus Maximus, an Ox; to Juno Regina, a Cow; to Minerva, a Cow; to Jupiter Victor, an Ox; to Mars Pater, a Bull; to Mars Victor, a Bull and to Victoria, a Cow.'

Thus we see that gods like to receive male animals; goddesses, female animals. Then too, deities need to be addressed by their correct cult names. Jupiter appears both as 'Greatest and Best' and as 'the Victorious', Mars as 'Father' and 'Victorious'. To all intents and purposes, the sacrifice treats them as different deities, and to neglect the correct cult names can well negate the efficacy of the sacrifice. This legalistic aspect of Roman religion has a strong bearing on cult practice in Britain and we shall have to return to it.

The early months of the year were connected with sowing and the sprouting of the seed. The *Sementivae* in January (Ovid, *Fasti* I, 657–704) and the *Lupercalia* on 15 February are both connected with farming practice. The famous race at the latter event when young men dressed only in the skins of sacrificed goats struck bystanders, especially women, with thongs made from the victims, is an example of fertility magic. This was a good time to propitiate and honour the family dead. Most Roman tombstones carry a dedication analogous to the dedication on an altar, but whereas the latter might read *Deo Invicto Herculi sacrum* or *Deo Neptuno*[11] gravestones are usually inscribed *DM* or *Dis Manibus*, 'To the gods, the Shades' – in other words the friendly dead. Ovid tells us that 'the *manes* ask but little; they value piety more than a costly gift' (*Fasti* II, 535–6). Attention paid to the grave, offerings and perhaps a feast at the tomb of one's kin, would also protect one's ancestral land.

The growing season proper begins in March, and was dedicated to Mars whom we have already met as a vegetation-god. The fiddle-shaped shields (*ancilia*) of Bronze Age form carried by the Salian priests help to emphasise his primitive nature in Rome; the Salii danced and chanted a hymn which nobody could understand, though equally it was essential to continue to sing it year after year.

In contrast, the *Megalensia* on 4 April demonstrates the ease with which completely foreign deities and religious rites could be absorbed into the fabric of Roman religion if there was a need for them.[12] Cybele, the Great Mother (*Magna Mater*), was a powerful Mother Goddess from Asia Minor, where her chief cult site was Pessinus. At the end of the third century BC she was brought to Rome to lend her power to the desperate fight against Hannibal, but her cult remained, together with its eunuch priests, mainly oriental (Ovid, *Fasti* IV, 179 ff) – although her worship spread through the provinces and became to some extent acclimatised, in the west.

A sacrifice to the earth on 15 April (*Fordicidia*) involved sympathetic magic of a primitive kind. Pregnant cows were sacrificed, the calves burnt and their ashes used for purification on the feast of the *Parilia* or *Palilia* which followed on 21 April (Ovid, *Fasti* IV, 629–76; 721–806). This was dedicated to an ancient and very obscure pastoral deity called Pales, whose celebrations included leaping through flames. There is here a reminiscence of the Celtic Beltine ('Bel's Fire') celebrated on 1 May, when cattle were driven between fires as a protection against disease, and of the bonfire-leaping current in many parts of Europe from Easter to Midsummer.[13]

The day came to be kept as the birthday of Rome, and was celebrated as such throughout the Empire. We even have post-conquest evidence of its being celebrated in Britain, at High Rochester.[14] Rome had to have a birthday at some time of the year, but presumably a day of exceptional purity, after the stains of ritual pollution had been washed away, was especially attractive to Romans of the Early Republic – rather as Easter and the period after it, especially May Day, have seemed auspicious to modern secular states for their national celebrations.

Ovid digresses in his account of the year to tell us of the digging of a ditch in which Romulus made a foundation sacrifice to the gods of the underworld (*Fasti* IV, 807–62), which parallels the digging of sacred shafts, discussed in Chapter 1. A furrow was then ploughed around the site of the city by a team consisting of a cow and a bull; such a team might not be the most suitable for agricultural purposes, but it emphasised the fertility element. The city of Rome must be capable of reproduction through its citizenry. Evidence from Britain consists of a little model of a plough-team from Piercebridge, Co. Durham; the fact that one animal is a cow and the other a bull shows that this is no genre-bronze but probably a religious ex-voto connected with fertility and very probably alluding to the foundation of Rome or another city.[15]

Very soon after the *Palilia* and Rome's birthday, momentous events in the calendar, we find the sacrifice of a sheep and a red dog in the grove of *Robigo* (red-mildew).[16] This sacrifice on 25 April may not have been very important; *Robigo* clearly belongs to a very primitive stratum in Roman religion, and Ovid's account suggests that he was very localised (*Fasti* IV, 905–42). However, the fact that he had a grove like other Roman deities and, as we have seen, many Celtic ones, shows a point of contact between countryside cults in Italy and the Celtic world; furthermore the hound sacrifice which may in part be connected with sympathetic magic, could suggest a sacrifice to the earth itself. Hounds were other-worldly animals in Britain (e.g. the hounds of Arawn of Annwvyn in the *Mabinogion*) just as they were in Roman Italy, where they were creatures of chthonic deities, such as Hekate, shown in art on lamps and on the bezels of rings sleeping. Darkness and sleep are in themselves allusions to death.

The *Floralia* between 28 April and 3 May (Ovid, *Fasti* v, 183–378) corresponds to our May Day.[17] Ovid makes the goddess Flora pronounce, 'Perhaps you may think that I am queen only of dainty garlands, but my divinity has to do also with the tilled fields. If the crops have blossomed well, the threshing-floor will be piled high.' It was far more than a flower-festival. In the army, when the standards were decked with flowers through the month of May, the soldiers' thoughts were on the success of their arms. The *Rosalia Signorum* in particular, marked on the Duran calendar both on the 10th and 31st of the month, was an important event.

May was a time of anxiety to both farmer and soldier. The year was well-advanced and hostile forces both natural and supernatural could level their powers against mankind. Amongst supernatural powers were ghosts. The *Lemuria* on 9 May was not merely a repeat of *Parentalia*. To the Roman mind, the dead might be conceived either as ancestral spirits and benign, or as a terrifying crowd of malevolent ghosts, which needed to be expelled or bought off (Ovid, *Fasti* v, 419–92).[18] Rational distinctions were not always made, which is why we shall find in discussion of funerary rites in a later chapter (Chapter 9) some ceremonies which were designed to comfort the dead and others to ensure that they did not leave their graves to trouble the living. It is true that offerings were brought to graves at the *Lemuria*, but more characteristic was the ceremonial in which the head of the family (*Pater familias*) rises at midnight, with bare feet and makes the *mano fica* sign 'with his thumb in the middle of his closed fingers', a fertility charm as we can see from its presence on amulets including a magnificent example from the first-century fort at the Lunt, Baginton.[19] He washes his hands and casts black beans over his shoulder, all the while saying, 'These I cast out; with these I redeem me and mine.'

The *Lemuria* ritual was private and obscure; it reminds us of the vast weight of superstitious practices which only occasionally surface in gestures like cursing enemies (Chapter 6). Another primitive ritual, more public but of uncertain meaning, took place on the 14 May when puppets made of straw called 'Argei' were thrown into the Tiber. Did these represent merely a spell to obtain rain, by wetting images of men, or was this a purification ceremony – casting out demons – or did the straw figures take the place of human sacrifices? The last suggestion is attractive, and in the Celtic world we recall the deaths by drowning of the victims of the Celtic Teutates and also Caesar's account of wickerwork *simulacra* filled with men and set on fire (Caesar, *BG* vi, 16). Against this is the strong opposition of Roman writers to human sacrifice, never regarded as a Roman rite.[20]

Two other events should be mentioned in May. The first, the festival of Mercury on 15 May, was taken over from the Etruscans who had equated the god with the Greek Hermes. Guilds of merchants would meet to feast on this occasion; Ovid's merchant prays, 'Only grant me profit, grant me the joy of it and make sure that I enjoy cheating the buyer' (*Fasti* v, 663–92). Here, then, an imported ceremony takes root because there is a demand for it.[21]

The other, the *Ambarvalia*, a movable feast at about 29 May, was a ceremony of beating the bounds, more appropriate to the countryside than the town; a persistent rite which still has its parallel in the Rogationtide boundary-beating. In the Roman ritual, agricultural deities especially Mars, Ceres and Bacchus were invoked, and a *suovetaurilia*, the sacrifice of a pig (*sus*), sheep (*ovis*) and bull (*taurus*), all young and healthy animals, was a central ceremony at this *lustratio* (literally, a purification ceremony conducted by moving around something).[22]

The *Vestalia* on 9 June was another ancient ceremony;[23] if the fields had to be purified, so did the home, symbolised by the hearth. Vesta, goddess of the hearth, was not envisaged in human form until late and under strong Greek influence, but in one sense she was the most omnipotent of all deities. Every time the family congregated in front of the fire and ate a meal cooked on it, they would be grateful to Vesta, and would be sure to pour a libation of wine onto the flames. The hearth of Rome was the circular *aedes* of Vesta, served by virgin priestesses who had to ensure that the fire was never extinguished. The shrine was like many Celtic shrines, a reminiscence of a primitive hut while the enforced celibacy of the priestesses like those of some other cults (and of such goddesses as Diana) was actually seen to be appropriate for a goddess of fecundity. On the days before and after the *Vestalia* while the Vestals purified the *aedes*, no public business was allowed in Rome.

The lack of Ovid's *Fasti* after the month of June (whether the poet finished the poem or never wrote the second part is unknown) means that our knowledge of the later months of the year is rather thin. We may note the same mixture of aboriginal and imported cults. The *Lucaria* on 19 July (or 21st) was certainly native; the name, which is connected with the word *lucus*, a grove, suggests a woodland cult and close links with the veneration of groves in the Celtic provinces. It has been suggested that the festival originated at a time when the Romans were clearing forest and scrub around the City, and wished to propitiate the angry spirits dwelling therein.[24] Among such wood-sprites were the *fauni*, who were specifically worshipped on 5 December (Horace, *Odes* III, 18).

Amongst imported rites, the games of the Greek god Apollo between 6 and 13 July stand out. Apollo fulfilled a need for a Sun-god to care for the ripening crops.[25] Harvest festivals included the *Vinalia* on 19 August, connected with the Vintage, and the *Consualia* on 21st, in honour of a deity whose name is derived from the verb *condere*. Consus is the god of the storing up of the harvest.[26] Harvest festivities continued until October, when the rite of the October-horse on 15th ended the active period of the year. The *Ludi Romani* in September which were celebrated in honour of Jupiter from early in the Republic and especially the *Lectisternium* on 13th of the month when images of Jupiter, Juno and Minerva were feasted would have been a graphic way of recording the beneficence of the gods to the Roman people.

Now began the last part of the year, a time of rest culminating in the December holiday of the *Saturnalia*.[27] Although no doubt holidays, large meals and presents appealed to the hedonistic tastes of many a Roman, it is doubtful that the Saturnalia was ever as completely secularised as Christmas is for many people today. On 17 December, those cries of *Io, Saturnalia* (which resounded in jest at the end of the Boulogne mutiny in the summer of AD 43) recalled the mythical golden age of Saturn and gave men of all ranks a yearning for an ideal world when men and gods were in concord. Later the unifying cult of the Sun-god whose birthday was on 25th, and after that of Christ, born on the same day, kept that message alive.

Dimly we perceive in acts of purification and propitiation a shape to the year and of divine intervention in nature which would have seemed as true to the British Celt – or the Christian medieval peasant – as to the Roman. The theology was clearly different, but an outsider might have found that what distinguished Roman religion from medieval religion and the wilder effusions of the Celts was a precise legalism. In this we can see the genius of the Romans as legislators, applied to religion; a genius which relied on the appreciation that legal language must be exact and phrased without ambiguity, and one which relied on literacy. The Celts could not, and (despite the growth of Canon Law in the Middle Ages) western Christendom would not, become so involved in defining the precise obligations of man to the divine.

Prayer, Sacrifice and the Gods

However, we find something of the Roman attitude in both Orthodox Judaism and Orthodox Christianity, whose prayers have to be correctly pronounced and whose ceremonies must maintain traditional means of observance down to the smallest word or gesture. Not surprisingly both were moulded in the Graeco-Roman Mediterranean world, and draw their natures in part from the Talmud on the one hand and the Early Church fathers on the other.

The Roman Festivals provided a framework within which man could approach the gods. Relations between man and the gods was regulated by means of prayer and sacrifice (see Pliny, *NH* XIII, 10; Cicero, *de Haruspicium responso*, 23).[28] The former had to be couched in the form of precise formulae, which had to be scrupulously correct or they might not work. As in Orthodox Jewish and Christian practices today, if the officiant made a mistake, even a very tiny one, he had to go back to the beginning of the prayer or even the entire ceremony. In some cases invocations had to be repeated; thus the early prayer of the Arval priests addressed to the Lares, Mars and the gods of sowing consisted of invocations repeated three times.

Furthermore the form of words must contain the correct name of the god or goddess. No deity wrongly addressed would respond to prayer. This explains such qualifications in prayers as 'to Jupiter' or 'to the Nymphs' followed by 'or whatever name you wish to be called'[29] or the altar seen by St Paul at Athens dedicated 'to the unknown god'. It was however better to know (as in the Dura Calendar) when to invoke Mars Pater and when to address Mars Victor.

Of course, the actual subject of prayer was important. Two factors must be kept in mind. First, prayer is not magic. Magic is not religion but rather a debased offshoot from it which assumes that the gods can be controlled by man. Religious prayer is addressed to gods who are free agents, not obliged to answer it. Roman gods, however, were more likely to do so if you gave them something in return. The devotee would make a *nuncupatio,* or declaration, promising to set up an altar and sacrifice an animal to the deity *if* he received the divine aid which he requested. Only if the god answered his prayer need he fulfil his vow, with the *solutio.* Votive altars were generally inscribed *V(otum) S(olvit)* [*L(aetus)*] *L(ibens) M(erito)* – 'Paid his vow [gladly], freely and deservedly.' It was important not to grudge one's contribution or give it under restraint.[30]

The process may be illustrated in the so-called curse-tablets from Roman temples where a sheet of lead is inscribed with a *nuncupatio*. E G Turner published one from Ratcliffe-on-Soar, Nottinghamshire, where 'the god (Juppiter Optimus Maximus) is to work on parts of the thief's body … force him to repay, and is thereby to enjoy a tithe of the sum recovered. The curse is therefore in a sense a prayer for justice addressed to a deity … .'[31] This and other curse-tablets will be discussed in Chapter 6.

The *solutio* generally involved a blood sacrifice (though other items of value such as grain or fruit and votive gifts ranging from silver plate to clay figurines might also be dedicated). Life symbolised by blood was the most fitting gift for the gods. Most ancient peoples of Europe and the Near East killed animals for their gods and the Celts were no exception as we have seen. Even today, animal sacrifice is widespread, and is theoretically accepted in Judaism though in the absence of the Temple no sacrifice has taken place since AD 70 – an interesting case of sacrifice belonging in a particular sanctuary. Sacrifices are readily performed in India to Hindu deities, of course, as also by other peoples in the Old World.

Such comparative examples and a wealth of literary texts allow us to enter into the spirit and practice of sacrifice to some extent. Before describing what happened, two points should be made, the first religious and lying at the centre of ritual, the second secular and explaining something of the nature of sacrifice in everyday life. The killing of a living creature arouses feelings of guilt, for life belongs to the gods; it can only be expiated by the use of an elaborate ritual, and even then the circumstances have to be right. It was essential that the beast was a willing victim, and that no signs of bad omen were observed during the ceremony.[32] In contrast to the solemnity of the event was the fact that this was a major source of meat for the populace – the gods were given token and often inedible portions, entrails and fat cut from the haunches. The rest was consumed either in a feast after the sacrifice or through the butchery trade. Thus, if the idea of blood-sacrifice revolts us, we should compare it to twentieth-century factory farming – the mere raising of animals for meat without that reverence for life which was implicit somewhere even in the most lavish animal sacrifice in antiquity.

No two sacrifices were the same – there were state sacrifices and private sacrifices; and in some there were dramatic departures from normal practice. Thus the fear of pollution through blood has been mentioned and in most Roman ritual this is symbolised merely by the action of sprinkling flour mixed with salt (*mola salsa*) between the beast's horns and cutting a few hairs, but at the *Lupercalia* two youths were first smeared with blood from the sacrifice and then cleansed with wool dipped in milk, and it is possible that the *Regifugium* also in February was the day on which the priest known as *Rex Sacrorum* sacrifices and flees. If so it recalls the famous Athenian *Bouphonia* (Pausanias I, 24, 4; Porphyry, *De Abstinentia* 2, 29–30) when the sacrificial axe was tried for killing the ox.[33]

In most Roman sacrifices, the officiating priest, his toga drawn up over his head to drive out sights and sounds of ill-omen, with musicians to assist further in keeping unlucky sounds at bay, performed the necessary preparation of the beast, the sprinkling of the *mola salsa* etc. and awaited the *popa*'s felling of the animal with a pole-axe in order to plunge in the knife.

The ox would have been garlanded and its horns gilded; garlands would hang around, and the air was sweet with incense. But for the killing, the reverential piety and the colour of flowers, and hangings and of silver-gilt vessels, including the invariable patera and jug used in pouring libations of wine to the gods, would have reminded us of joyous religious and public ceremonies today.

The killing was a climax but not the end of the sacrifice. It was important to remove the liver, and those skilled in the art, 'gut-gazers' or *haruspices*, who had been trained in the art of hepatoscopy (perhaps by studying model livers, such as one that has survived from Piacenza) were able to interpret the liver of the sacrificial animal as a map of the sky, and to see in the variations and imperfections of that organ the will of the gods.[34] There were confraternities of *haruspices* in many parts of the Empire including the Rhineland, and a *haruspex* set up a statue base at Bath.[35]

The sacrifice was generally followed by a feast in which the participants could feel a kinship with the god(s), with whom they shared the victim. In some cases the carcases of beasts which had been slain at the altars might be sold at the market; in others they had to be consumed within the sacred enclosure. Not even rubbish might be taken away.[36]

Sacrifice was thus not just a gift to the gods but helped men to understand the divine world. Alongside the craft of the *haruspex*, however, was that of the more usual type of *augur*. Bird-flight across the sky was mysterious – especially, no doubt, the great migrations from Europe, south to Africa each autumn, and the return flight each spring. The true explanation of these movements was not, however, known. Surely they were part of some divine plan, messages sent by the gods who after all did themselves take avian forms at times, Jupiter as an eagle, Minerva as an owl, Mars as a woodpecker. Venus was associated with the dove and Juno with the peacock.

The gods could make their wishes known to mankind through many kinds of portent. It is easy to dismiss freak phenomena as natural and disregard dreams, as Caesar did on the night and morning of 15 March 44 BC, before falling victim to his enemies' daggers, but not many people in the Roman world were so foolhardy as to ignore signs from the heavens.

Dreams might be interpreted by experts at temples or the private individual could consult a Dream-book.[37] Insofar as dreams were regarded as religious phenomena, they can be equated with oracles. Some, like the oracles of Apollo at Delphi and Claros operated through a medium, who in a trance-like state, possibly in part induced by drugs, could pass on messages from the gods.[38] Another form of oracular response was provided in the consultation of sacred books. The Sibylline Books, traditionally purchased by King Tarquinius Priscus from a prophetess, were consulted in time of emergency by the priests at the request of the Roman Senate. The means by which passages were selected and interpreted is not known, but many of the actions which flowed from their consultation – including the introduction of foreign cults (such as that of Cybele in 204 BC) – were intelligent and far-reaching, articulating the true needs and best interests of the community.[39]

The *Pax Deorum*, the good relations between the Romans, chosen people of the gods, and the heavens, was reflected in festivals, sacrifices, signs and wonders. Its contractual nature was an expression of the legalism of the Roman people.

As the invasion force neared the shores of Britain, 'a brilliant flash of light appeared in the East and shot across the sky to the West – the direction of their course' (Dio Cassius LX, 19). With this Roman omen the story of religion in Roman Britain truly begins. As we have seen, there were many parallels and resemblances between Celtic and Roman religion; the seasonal calendar, sacrifices, masters of divine law, and of course sacred places, whether buildings or groves or springs, as the homes of deities. Political and military events were now to produce a merger of the two religious systems, as far-reaching for Britons of at least the upper classes as the adoption of Latin, the Roman dress and the Roman house (Tacitus, *Agricola* 21).

3 The Romanisation of the Celtic Cults

The first two chapters of this book have treated of Celtic and Roman religion as separate, even though related, systems. Despite the establishment of a *colonia* at Colchester, a city of settlers from Italy and the western provinces, and the building of the great altar and temple dedicated to the Imperial cult which incensed nationalist feeling in Britain (see Chapter 4), there was no large-scale clearance of Britons from the Province, as was to happen in Dacia (Romania) some seventy years later.

A Celtic-speaking population was subjected to Roman culture. The result was compromise and fusion between the systems. However, the compromise was not sought; it happened largely by chance. The government's policy for Britain was to spread Latin culture as widely as possible. Tacitus (*Agricola* 21) tells us that Agricola assisted communities to erect temples and *fora*, and encouraged the upper classes to adopt Roman ways, including the speaking of Latin and the wearing of the *toga*. Roman-style houses (*domus*) were built, with their dining-rooms for banquets. Baths and porticos replaced the simple buildings of the Iron Age.

This should not be underestimated. It is ironic that most modern writing on religion in Britain should take as its starting point a passage in Tacitus' *Germania* about a German tribe called the Nahanarvali, living far beyond the Imperial frontiers (*Germania* 43). The tribe venerated twin gods called the Alci, 'but according to the Roman interpretation the gods so recorded are Castor and Pollux'. A Roman readership is thus told something about completely foreign deities so that it can understand them. In Britain, by contrast, Roman culture was able to play an active role in the religious development of the province. It was only limited by Roman antiquarianism which insisted that traditional rites were to be preserved, and by the tolerant attitude of the Roman government towards practices which did not conflict with the interests of the state. We may be sure that the conservatism of the local peasantry remained a factor throughout the period, but that need not concern the historian of religion. Sculpture and inscriptions were set up only by Romans and by articulate Britons who sought to adopt Roman ways. The beliefs of the countryman, the *paganus*, are inevitably harder to understand for they were not articulated, and by their nature defy the methods of historical research. An early result of the Conquest was that British religion shed its nationalist character. Clearly, the priestly class which had directed opposition to the Romans could not be allowed to survive as an organised force, nor could certain practices such as human sacrifice to be tolerated. However, the rooting out of Druidism, *as such*, was not part of Roman policy. We hear of no trouble in the

South for instance in the Regnensian Kingdom. Peter Salway points out, that when Suetonius Paullinus and his men invaded Anglesey eighteen years after the conquest the wild Druids and women reminiscent of Furies (terrifying mythological beings) were a shock and a surprise. A priesthood, submissive to the Roman Law was no threat and might be safely tolerated. Long centuries of toleration and social acceptance would allow a respectable fourth-century university professor to claim descent both from the Druids and from Roman priests of Apollo (see below).

Continuity of Ancient Sanctuaries

The treatment of sacred sites during the Roman period follows the same conservative approach, very much in the spirit of a ritual prayer cited by Macrobius, offering foreign gods shelter and games in their honour (Macrobius *Saturnalia* 3, 9, 7–8). Shelter generally took the form of a temple (*fanum*), either replacing an earlier structure or enhancing a holy place where no building yet existed. The plans of such temples generally made concessions to local traditions and probably to pre-Roman liturgical practice. The ambulatories around square and polygonal temples of Romano-Celtic plan were probably designed for

3 Air view of temple on Hayling Island, Hampshire

processions around the inner room (*cella*) where the deity lived. They recall the fact that prehistoric houses of any size had to have an interior circle of posts to support the roof and that screens between these posts created a private room surrounded by a corridor.[3]

An example of a circular Roman period temple (3) has been excavated on Hayling Island, Hampshire.[4] Technically, its stonework belongs to the Roman tradition exemplified by the Fishbourne palace and first-century official and public building in London and elsewhere in the province. No doubt foreign masons (from Gaul) were involved. However, the temple replaced an Iron Age circular temple, itself based on the standard dwelling-house of the time. It is possible to see the change as merely one of better materials and so conclude that the Celtic worshippers rejected Roman culture except in externals. This is, however, not the only explanation here. Indeed, the only votary recorded by an inscription (unfortunately his name is not completely preserved) was a soldier of *Legio IX*, in other words part of the influx of Roman and Romanised newcomers to Britain.[5] To him and his kind, a round temple would not symbolise cultural defiance, but a respect for traditional custom (*mos maiorum*). Circular temples, notably the temple of Vesta in Rome, were not unknown to Graeco-Roman cults, and they too are thought to be descended from huts.

As we have seen, square and rectangular temples are recorded in the Iron Age at Heathrow, Danebury and South Cadbury. The tradition may have evolved in north-western Europe, perhaps as early as the fourth century BC, though convincing dating evidence is not available as yet. Translated into stone in the Roman period, the type became widespread and certainly presented the onlooker with a temple of strikingly different appearance from temples in Rome. However, although British and Gaulish *deities* were housed in tower-like *cellae* with clerestory lighting, while gods in Italy and Greece were normally expected to dwell in long, dark, rectangular rooms, it is not at all clear that the differences between the 'Classical' and 'Romano-Celtic' *fanum* went very deep. There were many regional traditions in the Empire, elaborate temple structures of attached, axially related courts in the East, leading the eye on to a Holy of Holies, and tall buildings in North Africa, for the Semitic gods were no more Roman than Romano-Celtic ones, and yet the temples at Baalbek and Dougga are often cited as the quintessence of Roman provincial architecture.[6] It is essential for us to keep an open mind on whether Romano-Celtic temples were necessarily un-Roman in cult until we have examined the deities and individual sites.

Meanwhile, we should remember that temples did not stand alone; at the very least they had precinct walls to demarcate a sacred enclosure for which the Greek word *temenos* seems appropriate. An altar in front of the temple was necessary for sacrifices; subsidiary altars, provided by worshippers who wished to embellish the shrine, as well as screens and arches would also be in evidence. Free-standing columns like one from Springhead in Kent,[7] statues, sacred bushes and trees should also be considered amongst the 'furniture' of shrines. Associated with many temples were offices and houses for priests and inns for visitors, hospital-like buildings for those seeking cures and baths for refreshment – and perhaps ritual purification (at Uley and Lydney Park, for instance).

The theatre or theatre-amphitheatre used for entertaining the crowds and addressing them but also for honouring the gods must not be forgotten. The

tradition that theatres were sacred and linked to temples is found in Greece and
Rome. It spread to the Celtic provinces, perhaps fulfilling a need already perceived
for a place of congregation at festivals. The low, flat-topped plateau of Dragon's
Hill below the White Horse and the hillfort at Uffington, Berkshire, makes a
suggestive setting for such ceremonies, though neither here nor at Iron Age
temple sites are arrangements for *spectacula* provable. However, the scouring of the
White Horse, which was accompanied by festivities in recent times, must go back to
the origin of the figure or it would have become grassed over and lost. A theatre is
associated with a temple at the Gosbecks Farm site near Colchester. The Frilford
(Noah's Ark) temple was associated with an amphitheatre. In the words of its
discoverer, 'its presence may indicate that the temple complex represented a major
religious centre in the Roman period which would have accommodated
worshippers from far afield.' Almost certainly the temple and baths complex at the
great sanctuary of Sulis Minerva, at Bath, was completed by a theatre. A 'Romano-
Celtic' temple in Verulamium was placed on the same alignment as a theatre-
amphitheatre. Other towns where temple and theatre probably comprise a group
include Colchester and Canterbury, but many theatre structures were doubtless
flimsy and have not been recognised.[8]

Finds of theatrical masks at Harlow (Holbrooks), Baldock, Catterick, Dover and
London attest performances of plays in both town and country.[9] These spectacles
had a religious aspect and in each case it is likely that a temple lay nearby. Many
masks have been found at the Trier Altbachtal, where a simple theatre was used for
sacred dramas – to entertain the gods, no doubt, though the primitive and often
grotesque nature of the masks may be suggestive of a secondary function: to drive
off evil spirits. All these are features which are common to Graeco-Roman shrines
everywhere: they give weight to Ramsay MacMullen's suggestion that Paganism
may be studied as a coherent system throughout the Roman Empire.[10]

The Romanisation of Ritual

Already we can imagine the scene at such a sanctuary on a festival day; the
seasonal nature of both Celtic and Roman religion will suggest that activity was
not constant or equal throughout the year. At the inn travellers arrive and refresh
themselves. Some of the visitors seem to be ill; for them, more than rest and
medicine is required, and the god or goddess may help to effect a cure; others are
more distressed in mind, seeking to avert domestic tragedy or to punish an enemy
by asking for divine assistance. On the day of festival, a play may be performed in
the theatre by masked actors, or there may be bear-baiting, acrobats or a
gladiatorial spectacle. All would in some way honour the divine powers, who are
believed to participate in the pleasures of mortals.

A procession now wends its way through the open *temenos* gates, led by chanting
priests accompanied by temple servants with animals to be sacrificed. Behaviour
within the *temenos* is probably regulated by a special *lex sacra* inscribed on a stone at
the entrance, informing visitors that certain offerings are required by the deity
while others are taboo. This could explain variations between bone 'assemblages'
from temple sites in Britain: in one instance, most of the bones are of sheep or goat,
and in others pigs and bovines are more in evidence (Chapter 6).[11]

Our visitor can feel a sense of community, and will not begrudge a few coins to

4 Silver-gilt votive plaque dedicated to Mars Alator from Barkway, Hertfordshire. Height 9.5 cm. *British Museum*

buy some little trinket at a temple stall, either to keep as a souvenir of his journey, or to present to the god(s) in the sanctuary. Some people will be paying more than a few coins. A local farmer's servants carry in a large stone altar to be erected near the main one; a rich merchant hands the priests a silver dish; the bronze-smith places a small figurine on a ledge in the temple ambulatory, and a wealthy peasant is holding a very large leaf or feather of silver. Closer inspection reveals that it is worth far less than the merchant's offering for it is almost paper thin (4).

The doors of the temple are open and there in the half-light, upon a low platform (*suggestus*) flanked by columns (5) stands the god, or rather a stone figure of the god enriched with paint and holding a sceptre of gilded bronze, candles on candelabra gutter around him, and the fragrant incense wafts out of the holy place to give our imaginary onlooker the illusion that he is actually on the threshold of the divine world.

The procession has stopped in front of an altar on which a fire burns. The officiating priest pulls his toga more firmly over his head and intones a prayer which is in Latin though not always pronounced as it would have been in Rome. The epithets of the god are also strange and foreign, but the instruments of the musicians – double-pipes, cymbals and little bells – are similar to those that could be heard in Mediterranean lands. The jug and *patera* are indeed Italian, made at Capua, but the wine for the libation is Spanish (and not of the highest quality!).

The ox's horns are gilded and hung with a garland of seasonal flowers. The beast hardly notices the priest sprinkling flour and salt on its head and cutting off a few hairs. The skilled attendants distract its attention while the *popa* fells it with a pole-axe, and the priest immediately stabs it with an ancient bronze knife with an inlaid handle. Blood flows over the ground. More incense is burnt and our onlooker senses that the ceremony has achieved a sacramental union with the gods. His feelings have little to do with moral excellence – though no doubt he pays his taxes, honours the emperor, is mindful of the horrible fates of Tantalus and Sisyphus (or alternatively is haunted by Romano-Celtic images of man-eating monsters like that represented by a figurine from Woodeaton). It is based on a realisation that man and the gods are at peace with one another.

The person who has paid for the sacrifice will have remained a little anxious until the *haruspices*, experts in interpreting the meaning of heart and gut and liver, point out that all is well. The *viscera* are pronounced to be whole and not diseased, and can be burnt on the fire together with the thigh fat. As the smoke from the burnt offering ascends to the heavens, the cooks are busy preparing the ox for roasting on another fire. Temple servants scurry around setting up couches and trestle tables in the courtyard and filling in a few rubbish pits which remain from previous festivities. As we have seen (Chapter 2), it might well be forbidden to remove even rubbish from the sacred enclosure. Soon samian bowls full of oysters and jugs of wine, eggs, poultry and fish are produced from the kitchen area (outside the *temenos*) and the religious ceremony ends in a delightful alfresco party whose *pièce de resistance* is the consumption of the sacrificed ox.[12]

This scene, it must be readily admitted, is fanciful, but there is evidence for all the features mentioned. Many of them can be supported from archaeological evidence. In general outline there is nothing that a Greek or Roman need have found surprising. The shrine itself belongs to the same ancient world as those of Delphi or Dodona; so does the ritual of sacrifice. A common fallacy is that the

5   Temple I at Springhead, Kent

Romanisation of the gods was simply a matter of dressing Celtic deities in *togae*. Beneath a very thin veneer they remained uncorrupted by Rome. However, it is clear that the Britons were not superficially Romanised; they became Romans. To stress the point, consider the king of the Regni, Tiberius Claudius Cogidubnus, made a citizen perhaps by Claudius and possibly taking his title *Rex Magnus* 'Great king' from Herod Agrippa I who, it is pleasing to think, was a fellow exile in Rome. The one certain known act of his reign (apart from Tacitus' comment that he 'remained most loyal down to our own time', *Agricola* 14) was to allow the guild of smiths to erect a temple to Neptune and Minerva. He may well have lived in the palace of Fishbourne, more probably in the earlier Neronian 'proto-palace'. If so, his heirs would have continued to live at Fishbourne in the enlarged Flavian building, no longer as kings but as Roman gentlemen.[13] In the same way a god or goddess might find name, home and mythology transformed by the influence of Rome. More depended on the status of the worshipper than the status of the god. This chapter depends largely on inscriptions and must therefore be qualified by the proviso that it deals only with the beliefs and aspirations of the Romanised (i.e. those who could read Latin).

The most extreme case of Romanisation appears to be that of *Sulis*. The name is certainly Celtic and it seems hardly possible that the hot springs beside the Avon at the place we call Bath and the Romans *Aquae Sulis* could have been ignored in the Iron Age. Water cults are well-attested amongst the Celts and the phenomenon of hot springs, unique in Britain, must have excited veneration.[14] Nevertheless, only a few native coins from the spring are dated to that period. Roman engineers transformed the spring into a great ornamental pool, probably embellished with statues and enclosed it in a grand building. Beside it they built a temple of Mediterranean type (**6,7**). Its pediment was sculpted with tritons and a male Medusa conflated with a water-god (perhaps Neptune). The Medusa mask belongs to Minerva who wears it on her breast-plate, and Sulis was of course equated with that goddess.[15] A magnificent suite of baths lay contiguous to temple and spring, and there was almost certainly a theatre both for ceremonies and for entertainment.

The names Sulis and Minerva were used together and interchangeably. Thus, while the Roman writer Solinus suggests that the shrine was called *fons Minervae* (*Collectanea Rerum Memorabilium* 22, 10) a recently deciphered leaden tablet shows that *fons Sulis* was equally (or more usually) employed.[16] Inscriptions call her Sulis or Sulis Minerva, indiscriminately, with people of Italian origin (the *haruspex* Lucius Marcius Memor, for instance) and Greek freedmen (e.g. Gaius Javolenus Saturnalis and Marcus Aufidius Maximus) just as likely to use the Celtic name alone – as did Priscus, the stone-mason from the Chartres region.

It is worth pointing out that, for a visitor from Italy, the cult would differ little from that of *Minerva Medica Cabardiacensis*, whose temple was situated near Piacenza (ancient *Placentia*) in Cisalpine Gaul. Amongst the votaries of this thoroughly Romanised sanctuary was L. Naevius Verus Roscianus, prefect of *Cohors II Gallorum Equitata*, who made his vow (*nuncupatio*) before going to Britain (or while in the province) and thankfully paid it to the goddess (*solutio*) on his return to Italy.[17] A spring and sanctuary of Minerva, of characteristic Roman type, is shown on a patera handle from Capheaton (**8**). There is no way of telling whether it depicts Bath or some other site.

THE PRECINCT OF THE TEMPLE OF SULIS MINERVA

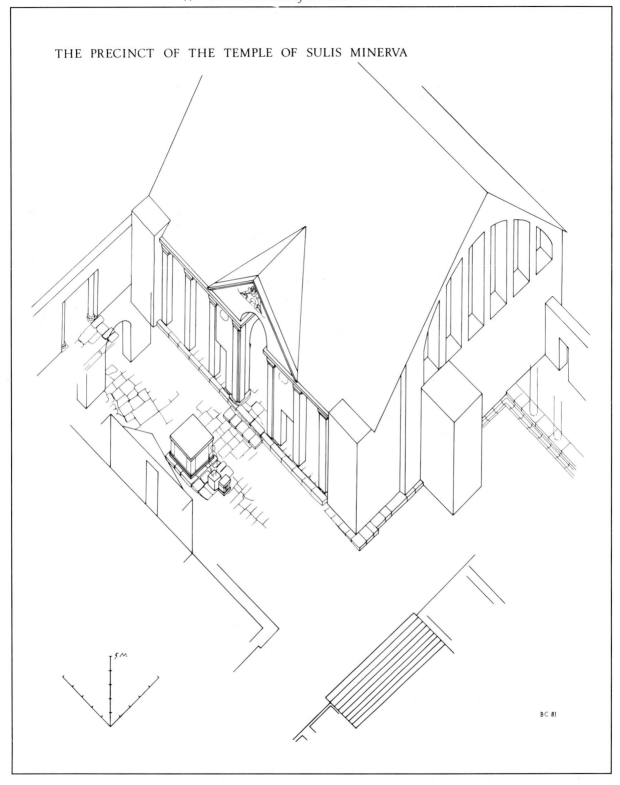

5M

BC 81

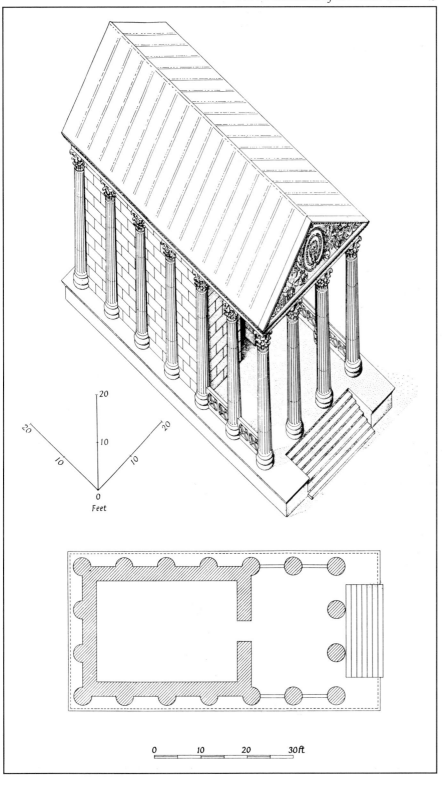

6 *Opposite* Precinct of the Temple of Sulis Minerva at Bath, showing steps of temple, altar and the building over the sacred spring (reconstruction)

7 *Left* Temple of Sulis Minerva (reconstruction). Recent excavation has shown the steps to be wider than is shown here

8 Minerva presiding over a sacred spring. Silver patera handle from Capheaton, Northumberland (incomplete). Length 8 cm. *British Museum*

Bath is frequently singled out as a special type of sanctuary, where official involvement in the cult was greater than usual. Certainly the temple was of more regular Roman form, and the sanctuary was larger and richer than usual, but there was no difference in kind. This is virtually proved by comparing the altars of Bath with those from other sites, and above all from a study of the form and content of the curse-tablets with those from smaller temples such as Uley.

Another water-goddess was Coventina. Her name, like that of Sulis, is Celtic, but she was not conflated with one of the great deities of the Roman state. On one inscription she is addressed *Deae Nimfae Coventine* and on another as *Nimphae Coventinae*[18], while artistic representations show her as a nymph. She was not below the notice of army officers of equestrian rank such as Titus Cosconianus, prefect of *Cohors I Batavorum*, although the majority of her other worshippers were less distinguished. Quantities of coins, small bronzes, pots (including incense-burners 73) and other finds have been found in the spring at Carrawburgh.[19]

Nevertheless, Coventina did not possess a monopoly of worship here. Apart from a Mithraeum, a very specialised type of temple, there was a little open-air shrine to the nymphs and the *Genius Loci*, set up by another prefect, Marcus Hispanius Modestinus, who cannot have seen the nymphs as a precise equivalent of Coventina (9).[20] What was his attitude? We have several clues. One is the Younger Pliny's description of the source of the River Clitumnus, where apart from the main temple there were 'many other shrines around, each for a separate deity with his own title, his own ceremonies and very probably his own spring' (*Ep.* 8,8). Extreme localisation, such as this, came about because people were anxious that the shrine of every divine power received its due. Indeed anxiety seems to have invaded the sleep of quite ordinary people, and an altar found near a spring at Risingham is inscribed in verse, 'Forewarned by a dream, the soldier bade

9 The Shrine of the Nymphs and the *Genius Loci*, Carrawburgh, Northumberland

her who is married to Fabius to set up this altar to the Nymphs who are to be worshipped';[21] no wonder that the legionaries of Chester, noting the streams emptying into the River Dee as well as the great river itself, were right to set up an altar to the nymphs and water-sprites.[22]

While water-cults of Italian and of British origin would have been hard to tell apart, Mother-Goddesses have a far more north-western European aspect. An Italian fertility cult would probably have concerned itself with Juno Lucina or perhaps Venus, although the appearance of *Terra Mater* on the Ara Pacis may be noted as, in effect, a single Mother Goddess.[23] Nevertheless, although the Mothers, often worshipped in a triad, were Celtic, they seem to be newcomers to Britain, 'imported representationally into the British Isles in Roman times'[24] probably from the Rhineland.

It is certainly true that Celts were involved in their worship; the sculptor Sulinus, son of Brucetius (or Brucetus), set up dedications to the *Matres Suleviae* at Bath and Cirencester.[25] The sculptor was, in all probability, named after the goddess Sulis and although the name *Suleviae* is not derived from the British deity as well – it is presumably Rhenish in origin like other epithets of the *Matres* – that

10 Relief portraying four *Matres* found at Blackfriars, London. Height 90 cm. *Museum of London*

does not mean that Sulinus himself was not impressed by the similarity between the names.

Time and again the *Matres* were 'appropriated' by Roman officers and officials who seem to have found a need for them – and sometimes to have invested them with power over areas not previously noted as centres of a mother-goddess cult. This is demonstrated by an inscription from Dover, set up by Olus Cordius Candidus, transport officer to the Governor of Britain, who set up a shrine to the Italian *Matres*.[26] Communications with Italy must have been especially important to Candidus and veneration of the supposed guardians of his homeland may have appeared to be a logical piety. An altar from Winchester, restored by Antonius Lucretianus, was dedicated to the Italian, German, Gallic and British *Matres*.[27] Another, found at York, was dedicated by Marcus Minucius Audens, a specialist officer (ship's pilot) of the Sixth Legion, to the African, Italian and Gallic Mother Goddesses.[28]

On the one hand, the numbers of divine mothers are multiplied and given a geographical range which alters the original conception; on the other, we may suspect that they were re-interpreted as household or regional deities (rather comparable with *Lares Compitales*). A well-cut plaque from Chichester was set up to the *Matres Domesticae*, originally a cult from the Bonn region analogous to the *Matres Aufaniae*.[29] Chichester was not a military centre after the mid-first century, but a highly Romanised civilian city, and I suspect that the *arkarius*, or guild treasurer, and his guild were borrowing a name to apply to goddesses of the locality.

The wealthy, Romanised background to the cult of the *Matres* is demonstrated by its presence in London, which was a new foundation of early Roman times, with many of the inhabitants drawn from abroad and hardly a trace of indigenous native deities.[30] A fine group of three seated *Matres* from near St Olave's Church, Seething Lane, may have been associated with a temple, but unfortunately the circumstances of discovery are rather imperfectly known. The sculpture was found on a pavement. A temple is certainly implied by a silver plaque from Moorgate Street, with repoussée relief decoration of a triad of Mothers within *aediculae*. This is a good example of one of the most characteristic categories of ex-votos from Roman shrines. A stone showing four seated goddesses (**10**) was found re-used as foundation material in the late Roman riverside wall at Blackfriars.[31] In northern Britain, Caius Iulius Cupitianus, centurion in command at Castlesteads, rebuilt a temple to the Matres, while the votive treasure supposedly found near Backworth includes a gold ring inscribed for the *Matres* and a magnificent silver gilt skillet, dedicated to them by Fabius Dubitatus (**11**).[32]

Although this book is essentially concerned with the religion of Britain, considerable light is thrown on the religious beliefs of the merchant-class trading with Britain by the great cache of altars and sacred reliefs from the mouth of the River Scheldt and also at Domburg (Walcheren). Here the goddess was *Nehalennia*, an Earth Mother presiding over the fecundity of the soil and perhaps with other-worldly functions. She is usually shown with her hound. No doubt she is localised on the North Sea coast, as the existence of two shrines dedicated to her strongly suggests,[33] but the remains no more tell us about the Celtic religion of the Roman Netherlands than do those connected with Sulis inform us about Iron Age Somerset. Let us meet two of her votaries; Lucius Viducius Placidus came from Rouen and was engaged in trade with Britain as a *Negotiator Britannicianus*. He does not seem

11 Silver-gilt patera dedicated to the *Matres*, said to have been found near Backworth, Northumberland. Length 24 cm. *British Museum*

to have confined his attentions to Celtic deities, for an inscription dedicating an arch and a shrine which he erected at York was probably set up to the Asiatic god Jupiter Dolichenus, as well as to the *genius loci* and the *numina Augustorum*.[34]

Another merchant, Marcus Secund(inius?) Silvanus was a trader in pottery with Britain (*Negotiator Cretarius Britannicianus*) and presumably came from the Rhineland.[35] Neither he nor Placidus would have been worshipping Nehalennia if they had not been beneficiaries of the Roman trading system. Direct comparison may be made with the case of another merchant M. Aurelius Lunaris, who set up an inscription of millstone grit (brought from Yorkshire!) at Bordeaux to the *Tutela Bourdigalae*,[36] the local city goddess, perhaps descended from a Celtic deity but now in Roman times equated with the Phrygian goddess, Cybele. As we shall see in Chapter 4, Lunaris was a priest of the Imperial Cult (*Sevir Augustalis*) at York and Lincoln and he had probably grown wealthy as a wine-shipper.

The Roman god Mars was conflated with a large number of native deities, but although the names are legion, he functions as in Italy as a warrior and fertility deity. The Berne Scholiasts on Lucan, commentators who certainly wrote before the tenth century AD (the date of the manuscript in question) equate *Teutates*, whose name appears to mean 'God of the Tuath (tribe)' with Mars, and the name occurs on silver rings from York and other sites and on a silver dedication from Barkway in Hertfordshire. Another Barkway plaque uses the epithet *Alator* (4), also obscure.[37] In truth we can only hope to understand the character of the god from his *Roman* personification. A fine bronze figurine from Barkway portrays the type of a youthful dancing Mars (12) who brings to mind the annual ritual leaping of the

Salian priests described by Ovid (*Fasti* III, 387).[38] No name is attached to the figurine, but like the Salian rites, his actions may be connected with the coming of spring, the growing of the crops.

It is easier to understand this, and other obscure and local cults in their Roman guise, if we are not concerned too much about epithets. For most of the Roman period, lowland Britain was at peace and would have had no need for a warrior deity. Despite his helmet, armour and spear he must have been venerated as a fertility god. Unlike the regular Italian Mars he is frequently mounted. A relief from Stragglethorpe, Lincolnshire (**13**), shows him spearing a reptilian monster (some evil power) while a bronze figurine of Mars Corotiacus from Martlesham, Suffolk, also depicted him riding over a prostrate foe.[39] Bronze figurines of horses and armed riders have been found in the circular temple at Brigstock, Northamptonshire and there are other examples of such figures in a cache of cult bronzes unearthed at the Hempsals, Willingham Fen, Cambridgeshire (**14**).[40] It can be no accident that this conception of Mars occurs in a part of Britain which is predominantly flat, with lush pastures suitable for horse-breeding. Mars was a suitable deity to preside over this activity.

This does not mean that other activities were forgotten. The well-known figurine from the Foss Dike was dedicated to Mars by the Colasuni brothers with the co-operation of a bronze-smith Celatus (**15**).[41] Nor is this the only association of Mars with craft in our area, for the inscribed silver ex-votos from Barkway and Stony Stratford include dedications to Mars and Vulcan, the smith god.[42] Above all, of course, the fields and wild places were his. Q. Neratius Proxsimus, who was almost certainly a settler or descendant of a settler from the Samnite country south of Rome, set up an arch near Lincoln to *Mars Rigonemetos*.[43] The name Rigonemetos is Celtic like the other epithets cited here, combining the words for 'king' (*rigon*), and 'sacred grove' (*nemet*). For Proxsimus, however, the sanctuary would have appeared similar in kind to the grove at Tiora in central Italy where, incidentally, there was an oracle with responses given by a sacred woodpecker (Dion. Halic., *Rom. Ant.* I, 14). Indeed, it is quite possible that this rather unusual cult associated with *Martius Picus* may have had a part in transforming an Iron Age sacred site near Thetford (dedication unknown) into a sanctuary of Faunus, the son of Picus either in the late Roman period or earlier; a theme which must be pursued later in this book (Chapter 10).

Mars was widely worshipped elsewhere in civilian Britain (leaving aside for the moment his veneration in the military camps of the Highland zone, see Chapter 4). Three examples will show the diversity of his appeal. Mars Nodons or Nodens possessed a major temple at Lydney in Gloucestershire. He is equated with Mars on two votive plates from the site[44] and also on the bases of two statuettes found near Lancaster where perhaps there was another shrine.[45] The name Nodens is philologically related to the Irish *Nuada Argat-lam*, 'Nuada of the Silver Hand', but in order to find out about his cult in Britain we must turn to archaeology. Despite recent questioning of the dating evidence, the excavation and report on Lydney Park are amongst Wheeler's most interesting. Here was a sanctuary of the type envisaged in our account of an ideal Romano-British shrine. Admittedly, no theatre has yet been found, but there was a large guest house, baths, and a long building, perhaps an *abaton* for sacred sleep (as existed at Asklepieia in the East) (**16**). A healing function is strongly suggested by the find of a votive arm, and an

12 Bronze statuette of Mars from Barkway, Hertfordshire. Height 20 cm. *British Museum*

13 Relief sculpture of Mounted Mars from Stragglethorpe, Lincolnshire. Height 74 cm.

14 Bronze figurines showing horsemen (? Mars), from Willingham Fen, Cambridgeshire. Height of complete examples 7 cm; 8 cm; fragment (rider) in middle, 4.5 cm. *Museum of Archaeology and Anthropology, Cambridge*

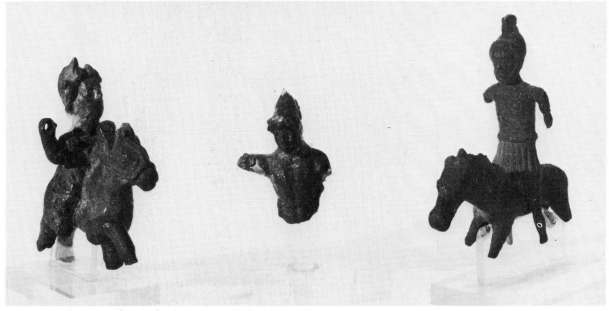

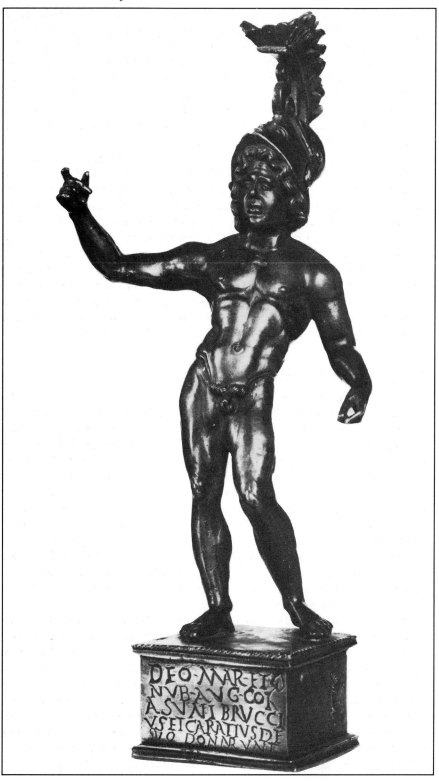

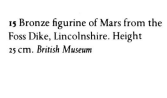

15 Bronze figurine of Mars from the Foss Dike, Lincolnshire. Height 25 cm. *British Museum*

anatomically explicit bone plaque showing a woman. Hound figurines (17) are reminiscent of the hounds of Nehalennia; they may be other-worldly creatures or have had a healing role, perhaps by licking the wounds or withered limbs of those afflicted in body. A hound is also shown on a votive plaque dedicated to Nodens by Pectillus. The temple is a strange hybrid, basically of Romano-Celtic plan with central *cella* and ambulatory but rectangular in the Roman style. The back wall of the *cella* is divided into three, perhaps in order to house a triad of statues. The clientele must have been both diverse and wealthy; the range of cult buildings and their embellishment with sculpture and mosaic shows that.[46]

In the Cotswold region of Gloucestershire were other shrines of Mars, at King's Stanley, Bisley and Custom Scrubs.[47] At the last-named site, a relief depicting Mars was accompanied by an inscription which describes the figure as the Roman hero Romulus. Gulioepius was certainly a Celt, and he surely belonged to a lower level in society than the Lincoln citizen, Q. Neratius Proxsimus, but this relief as decisively, and indeed more touchingly, demonstrates the change of outlook that Roman culture brought. So do curse-tablets from Uley, addressed to Mars-Silvanus and Mars-Mercury.[48] The site at West Hill was as we have seen sacred in the Iron Age. Although the pre-Roman name of the deity is of course unknown, finds include weapons. In the Roman period, votive spears are present, but the overwhelming quantity of material, bronze figurines, *caducei*, altars, a cult statue and curse-tablets, shows that he was generally considered to be Mercury.

The dynamic of Religious change

We can guess what happened, and in so doing see *interpretatio romana* as a living, active force. A Roman trader or soldier visits the hill, clearly the dwelling of some god, for the hill is surmounted by an ancient mound and has on it a sacred grove in an enclosure. He asks the name of the god, probably at first unsuccessfully, for names are powerful things and might give him power over the god of Uley. Yet whether the natives are friendly or unfriendly to him, our visitor must wish to venerate the god. Perhaps he owns land in the vicinity or is going on a hazardous expedition; surely the god will help if he can only offer him a gift. One way out would have been to call him the *Genius Loci*. Gods of place with names unknown to man are found widely in the ancient world. A famous passage in the *Acts of the Apostles* (17, 23) concerns an altar at Athens inscribed 'To the unknown god', and the same uncertainty may be read on a pedestal from the Wall dedicated *sive deo sive deae*, either to the god or the goddess, and on an altar from Risingham, inscribed *Dis Cultoribus*, to the gods who dwell in this place.[49]

This may have been quite enough for some earlier visitors. The elder Cato's prayer and sacrifice of a pig (*De Agri Cultura* CXXXIX) begins with the formula *Si deus, si dea es* – 'Whether thou be god or goddess to whom this grove is dedicated, as it is thy right to receive a sacrifice of a pig for the thinning of this sacred grove, and to this intent, whether I or one at my bidding do it, may it be rightly done . . . .'[50]

Real religious enthusiasts often lacked both the time and the self-discipline to make exhaustive enquiries. The second-century satirist Lucian of Samosata provides us with an amusing account of the fraudulent oracle of Alexander of Abonuteichos. One of his dupes was the Proconsul of Asia, P. Mummius Sisenna Rutilianus who had once in his youth been legate of the Sixth Legion based at

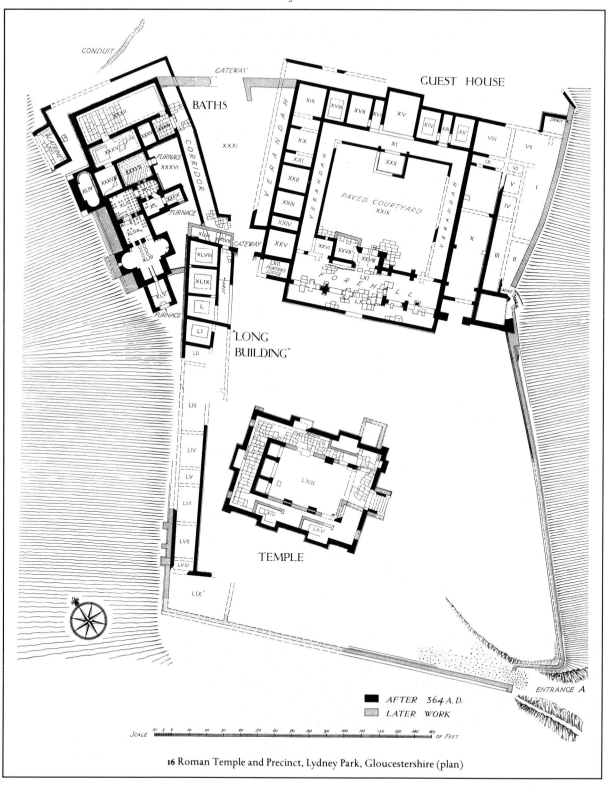

16 Roman Temple and Precinct, Lydney Park, Gloucestershire (plan)

York. Lucian says that 'though he was a man of birth and breeding ... in all that concerned the gods he was very infirm and held strange beliefs about them ... If he but saw anywhere a stone smeared with holy oil or adorned with a wreath, he would fall on his face forthwith, kiss his hand, and stand beside it for a long time making vows and craving blessings from it' (Lucian, *Alex.* 30).[51] Did he behave in the same way as a young man? There was a large number of Romans for whom the concept of deity itself was quite enough – the Christian convert Arnobius tells us that before he saw the light he was equally uncritical (see Chapter 7).

Our visitor does observe a few things about the Uley cult. The cult offerings include weapons, and these point to the god being Mars; on the other hand a grove could equally be the preserve of the wood-god Silvanus. All ancient authorities from Caesar onwards are agreed that Mercury was the most widespread of gods amongst the Celts, and at some point a decisive change in the nature of the cult came to be made by the act of presenting a large limestone statue of Mercury accompanied by his cult animals – a ram and a cock (**18**). The sculpture which we call the cult image is after all itself only an expensive ex-voto. It replaces the simple herm-like wooden idol which our visitor might take to be Mercury. Perhaps the new work was purchased in the studio of Sulinus, a sculptor whose clientele stretched from Bath to Cirencester. Whether or not the sculptor of the Uley Mercury was a Briton or a Gaul, his work copies the work of the great master of late Classical Greece, Praxiteles.[52]

The same image of the god was later carved in relief on at least two votive altars found at Uley and was also employed for bronze figurines. Mercury is shown as a youth (*ephebe*) holding in one hand a herald's staff (*caduceus*) and in the other a moneybag. His animal familiars are likewise a cock and a ram (or goat). This conception of Mercury-Hermes is widespread throughout the Graeco-Roman world. A limestone relief at Cirencester is so similar to one of the Uley reliefs that we can probably assign it to the same studio; it can be taken to illustrate the key importance of towns as centres of Roman ways in disseminating religious ideas. A bronze statuette found at King Harry Lane just outside Verulamium (**19**) was

17 Bronze hound from Lydney Park. Length 10.2 cm. Site Museum

apparently associated with burials (and hence introduces Mercury in one of his other functions as herdsman of the dead). This figure has two additional attributes which are in marked contrast one to the other and illustrate the influence of both the Mediterranean and Celtic custom in the art and religion of Roman Britain. Mercury is here accompanied by a tortoise, not a native of Northern Europe, and wears a silver neck torque which for the Celts was a symbol of divine authority. This is by no means the only instance of the god being given a local aspect.[53] In the Roman *colonia* of Gloucester, a community of Roman citizens, he is represented on reliefs with a young woman who is much more likely to be the Celtic Rosmerta, than his mother in Roman mythology, Maia. Here we have a graphic illustration of the way in which Romans were prepared to venerate the divine powers of the surrounding countryside.[54]

The artist had a key role in rendering regional religious beliefs acceptable in the wider Empire. He owed his success ultimately to the spread of literacy and hence of

18 Head of Mercury from Temple at Uley, Gloucestershire. Height 35 cm. *British Museum*

standard Graeco-Roman myth. At the heart of the concept of *interpretatio romana* is language. Anyone who could read Latin literature was a potential 'convert' to the classical mode of the Uley cult, just as we — beneficiaries of classical culture since the Renaissance — are able to respond to the names of the gods of Greece and Rome in a way that we are unable to do, to those of other peoples. Offerings of model *caducei* and of bronze figurines at Uley demonstrate how the classical concept of deity prevailed, although the presence of miniature iron spears and of little metal rings (presumably stylised torques) reminds us that a local, British element survived as a subsidiary element in temple ritual here.

It is obvious that our best evidence for religious practice in Roman Britain comes not from the bottom of society but from men of some rank and social consequence. In order to be able to 'interpret', one must first be articulate.

Vinotonus' two shrines on Scargill Moor near Bowes may stand for many personal dedications scattered around the countryside, wayside shrines commissioned by the pious native and foreigner alike. One of the shrines of Vinotonus was dedicated by Lucius Caesius Frontinus, prefect of the First Cohort of Thracians. He came from Parma in Italy. The other shrine has an altar set up by the centurion Julius Secundus, which equates the god with Silvanus, a god of groves as we have seen, but also of hunting.[55] The two shrines bring to mind one of the best-known altars from Roman Britain, set up by Gaius Tetius Veturius Micianus, prefect of the Sebosian Cavalry, on Bollihope Common in Weardale; it is dedicated to Unconquered Silvanus because Micianus had been able to bag a remarkably fine boar which his predecessors as prefect had hunted in vain: *ob aprum eximiae formae captum quem multi antecessores eius praedari non potuerunt.* The language is exultant and boastful.[56] Micianus had not, perhaps, been in the area long enough to learn Silvanus' local name; Frontinus' enquiries had been more thorough, but we have no reason to doubt that the religious concepts in the mind of either were anything other than Italian.

Antenociticus, whether a British deity or imported from the continent, had a temple at Benwell. Tineius Longus, not only prefect of cavalry but having been adlected into the Senate by Marcus Aurelius and Commodus, a man of considerable future consequence, set up a dedication within it, as did Aelius Vibius, a centurion of the Twentieth Legion.[57]

Tanarus or Taranis or Taranus is represented with a wheel, a symbol of the sun and hence of the sky which is his element. Amongst indications of his worship in Britain are a pre-Roman coin from Hampshire (see Chapter 1) and the figure holding a wheel included in the frieze upon the Willingham Fen mace or sceptre. We can see how he came to be envisaged if we examine the cast-bronze head of a bearded man found with a model wheel and other objects at Felmingham Hall, Norfolk (**64**). The head is clearly not a Mediterranean import, but it nevertheless displays the transcendant nobility of Jupiter Capitolinus, his iconography based on Pheidias' Olympian Zeus whose 'beauty can be said to have added something to traditional religion' (Quintilian, *Inst. orat.* XII. 51f.) A syncretistic image of Jupiter with the symbols of sun and moon in the cache shows how easily Taranis could be incorporated into the Roman concept of a sky-god. We can illustrate this from an altar dedicated at the legionary fortress of Chester to *Juppiter Optimus Maximus Tanarus* in the year AD 154 by a senior centurion of the Twentieth Legion, Lucius Bruttius(?)

19 *Right and opposite* Bronze figure of Mercury from King Harry Lane, Verulamium, Hertfordshire. Height 8.2 cm. *Verulamium Museum*

Praesens, who came from Clunia in Spain. Although he could have found the name Tanaris mentioned by the Roman poet Lucan (*Pharsalia* I, 445–6), it is highly unlikely that he conceived of Tanarus as a wild, barbarian god; for him the name was simply the correct local epithet for his own familiar Jupiter.[58]

Finally we may cite the nymphs of the stream, certainly worshipped in some form from very remote times as riverine offerings suggest. They attracted Roman patronage from the beginning. At Bath the river-goddess was evidently conflated with Minerva as Sulis Minerva, although a more conventional fountain-figure pouring water from a vessel appears with other deities on the Great Altar (**54**). An altar from Ilkley demonstrates that Clodius Fronto, prefect of the Second Cohort of Lingonians, knew that the nymph or goddess of the River Wharfe was Verbeia while at Carrawburgh votaries of Coventina included Titus Cosconianus, prefect of the First Cohort or Batavians. Cosconianus' relief shows her reclining by a flowing urn and holding a water-plant in the normal manner of Greek and Roman nymphs.[59]

Class differences and the spread of Roman ways

It is generally realised that those who resisted the material blandishments of Rome in distant places within the island, far to the north or far to the west, remained materially impoverished. There was no question of their keeping the vitality of Iron Age culture alive. Only in Ireland, where the leaders of society remained both wealthy and free of Roman power, could it continue as before. So in religion we may suspect that fully 'native' beliefs were only strong and relatively pure amongst remote communities and, as we have seen, the illiterate and backward lacked rich offerings to give or ostentatious means of giving even what they had. How can we tell what was in the mind of a poor peasant visiting a shrine with a tiny coin, or a small votive pot clutched in his hand?

A very few clues remain – a first-century shrine at Wall in Staffordshire, destroyed when the Roman *mansio* was built, contained at least nine carved stones which were incorporated in later structures.[60] Representations of heads in niches show the survival of the head-cult into Roman times. Another stone shows two pairs of warriors, one pair standing and the other lying horizontal, surrounded by a single-line border. Are they dead and is this a mythological scene (**20**)? Some of the carvings from the Cotswolds, where the oolite is soft and readily workable, are very simple. As instances we may take the simple triad of *genii cucullati* from Cirencester, three cloaked scurrying figures carved in an almost abstract manner.[61] Other *genii cucullati* are shown in two reliefs from a well at Lower Slaughter, while another relief shows three armed men and somewhat recalls the Wall carving mentioned above.[62] Two altars from Chedworth Roman villa depict male figures in simple outline, but one is inscribed Lenus Mars, and we sense that it stands near the beginning of the process by which religion becomes Romanised.[63]

There are more inscriptions from the frontier region than from southern Britain. For our purpose those dedicated to the *Veteres* in the Carvoran region are especially significant, for these deities are invoked largely by people low in the social scale. At first sight the name seems to be Latin, 'the old gods' but Anthony Birley has commented that 'the number of forms, especially the rarer ones with *hv-* (or *vh-*) indicates . . . that the deity's name could not readily be expressed in the

Latin alphabet'.[64] In the region of Brougham and old Carlisle, Belatucadrus also appears to have had a strong appeal to the indigenous population, as the poorly-cut inscriptions and uncertain spellings often suggest.[65] We would like to know more about these cults which may have remained more primitive and less affected by Roman ways than others, but for that very reason their worshippers lacked the means of communicating theology or ritual to future ages.

Most of the leaders of British society, Tacitus' 'sons of chiefs', accepted Roman ways and thus the province was for almost four centuries part of a Mediterranean world. Britons aspired to be citizens of the Empire, and their supra-national ideals were reflected in their religious outlook. However, here as in other aspects of life in antiquity there was a local aspect.

The Graeco-Roman gods were themselves of very mixed parentage; at their various cult sites they had absorbed into themselves many local godlings while at the highest level we know that the Greek Zeus was identified with the Roman Jupiter; Athena with Minerva; Hermes with Mercury. *Interpretatio* was not a concept confined to north-west Europe by any means.

The mythological tradition of the poets and the skill of artists created some order from this anarchy. We know that Olympian Zeus and Jupiter Capitolinus were both represented as mature and bearded males, enthroned and holding sceptres (**21**), and each accompanied by an eagle, the king of birds. Following the tradition of antiquity we generally regard them as a single god. Whether Delian Apollo and Delphian Apollo were originally two separate deities or one need not concern us either. Apollo's sister Artemis went under many names and was worshipped in widely different ways. Her rites ranged from that at Brauron in Attica, associated with the bear as totemic animal (the Bernese *Dea Artio* might have been a distant relative to her) to those of Patrae in Achaea, where Artemis Laphria was venerated with primitive rituals involving the sacrifice of living creatures on a vast bonfire (Pausanias 7, 18, 11–13). Artemis' Roman equivalent, Diana, had a famous grove at Aricia, where her priest was a runaway slave who had obtained his position by murdering his predecessor. Her cult name *Nemorensis* recalls that of Mars near Lincoln, *Rigonemetos*. The same idea of deities as rulers of

20 Low relief sculpture from Celtic shrine at Wall, Staffordshire. Length 36 cm

21 Bronze figurine of Jupiter from West Stoke, Sussex. Height 8.5 cm. *British Museum*

woodland, emphasised by linguistic similarities which betray a common Indo-European heritage, demonstrates the ease with which Celtic and Roman religion could merge. However, the gods of Asia, for all that they might look different (Diana of the Ephesians with her many egg-like breasts; Jupiter Dolichenus standing on his bull, and the Baal of Emesa who was finally merged with the Roman Sun-god as *Sol Invictus*) were equally acceptable to worshippers from the west.

The images in the figural arts of Roman Britain which differ from strictly classical conceptions of deity betray the power of tradition in ancient religion and the zeal of men and women who had inquired of the priests what was required of them in their sacrifices, gifts and prayers. A silver figurine (a rich offering) showing a bull with three feathered harpies from the temple site on Maiden Castle must represent *Tarvos Trigaranos*, 'The Bull with Three Cranes' whose name appears on the Monument of the *Nautae* at Paris, but the use of an iconographical type for the 'Cranes' drawn from Greek mythology (i.e. showing harpies instead of cranes) tells us to be on our guard against assuming that the cult was now simply a survival from pre-Roman Celtic Britain. Similarly, the ferocious wolf eating a man, from Woodeaton (**22**) was an appropriate image to offer to Mars (if he was the chief deity venerated there). Similar figurines have been discovered at Chartres and presumably also came from a temple. Like the lion killing a stag in Roman art, the image evokes the idea of sudden death. In the extraordinary Southbroom (Devizes) cache of figurines (**23**) some of the deities are shown with unexpected attributes; thus Mars holds two horned serpents (iconographically there is surely a

22 Bronze figurine of wolf-like monster eating a man. Probably from Woodeaton, Oxfordshire. Height 6.8 cm. *British Museum*

reminiscence of the myth of the infant Hercules strangling serpents here); and Mercury, a *patera* and a rattle-like object, which, does not look at all like the traditional purse. Perhaps it is meant to be a rattle like one recently recognised by George Boon in the Felmingham Hall cache. It is an unwarranted assumption that even such curiosities give us an easy access to pre-Roman Celtic belief. As Stephanie Boucher has shown, figural bronzes were essentially associated with the upper Romanised strata of society and had little place in native art, and very few are anything but conventionally Graeco-Roman. Where their iconography is more interesting, they reflect the intellectual ferment of the Empire. The same might be said of the better and thus more informative sculpture; it belongs, just like inscriptions, to the Roman tradition.[66]

The crux of the matter was that, to approach any god, the *local* cult title and the *established* ritual were essential. The Greece of Pausanias is full of different religious rituals which that urbane writer takes in his stride. It is a pity that we have no such guide-book to the temples of Roman Britain, but at least the inscriptions we have tell us a little of how people approached the gods, not just Celts but anyone. Thus Q. Terentius Firmus from Saena in Etruria and Aelius Antoninus from Melitene on the Euphrates erected altars to Apollo Maponus at Corbridge and Ribchester respectively.[67] They were legionary officers, not theologians, but presumably they thought that simple dedications to Apollo or ones giving epithets from their homelands would be at best useless, at worst unwise – Apollo needed to be invoked with his *local* epithet. Even artistic differences arise from the antiquarian zeal of priests (who might well fabricate a traditional image if none existed in order to express the various attributes of gods and goddesses). This process was syncretistic, and indeed most scholars are used to the religions of the ancient East combining with Roman cults in this way. Here it is suggested that the same dynamism was used by priests and artists under their lead, as well as Romano-Britons in general, to make their gods fully Roman. Sometimes people looked beyond the simple contractual relationship with the gods in their local aspects to venerate them as great powers which ruled the world. This, as we shall see in Chapter 5, was a dynamic force in mystery religions, but it may also be found amongst the adherents of the more popular cults. Ausonius's friend Attius Patera claimed Druidic ancestry. Ausonius says he was 'sprung from the stock of the Druids of Bayeux' and that he traced his line from the temple of Belenus. His name recalls the libation dish so often depicted on the sides of altars, and used in temple ritual –

23 Bronze figurines of deities from Southbroom near Devizes, Wiltshire. Heights between 10.4 and 12.8 cm. *British Museum*

not surprisingly because his father was a priest of Apollo Belenus. Belenus is of course Celtic (we may recall our own Catuvellaunian Cunobelinus) but the priest's name was *Phoebicus*, derived from the cult of Apollo at Delphi (*Phoebus*). Patera's own son was called *Delphicus*, which makes the connection even clearer to us (Ausonius, *Comm. Profess. Burdigalensium* IV, 7–14). This is the same world of antiquarianism; the veneration of classical deities and symbiosis with the local Celtic gods revealed by the Thetford Treasure (Chapter 10.)

Romanisation was no doubt in large part a matter of example; it would have happened in any case, but the governing classes from the time of Augustus decided that religion was a useful basis for demonstration of loyalty to the Roman State. In many of the inscriptions dedicated to Romano-Celtic deities, these gods and goddesses are linked to the divine spirit (*numen*) of the emperor, while temples were built in the cities and altars were erected by the roadsides and outside military camps, which reminded soldier and civilian alike that in the final analysis, the great gods were protectors of the Empire. It is to these 'Official' aspects of religion that we must now turn.

4 The Roman State and Religious Practice

The idea of State Religion is associated today with monolithic systems of belief, whether a variety of Christianity or Islam, Buddhism, Shinto or even Communism. Such faiths may be imposed on subjects of the State and at the very least they are privileged. In no society have the acts of politicians been so circumscribed by religious regulation as they were in ancient Rome. It has been demonstrated above that many aspects of this Italian religion – or conglomeration of cults – were taken to the provinces. Temples were certainly built with State encouragement. But was there a state religion in the medieval or modern sense? There was certainly no exclusive body of belief which encompassed all man's emotional and ceremonial needs, but the stories of Christian martyrs which show them being punished for refusing to sacrifice to idols or to the Emperor's *genius* should warn us against too hasty a dismissal of 'State' or 'Official' cults, even if they are not always easy to define.[1]

It is possible to isolate five areas of veneration which appertain to the State. First, there was the partly Hellenistic idea of the deified Emperor caring for the State, which may also be defined as an extension of the Roman cult of ancestors writ large. To it is joined the veneration of the *genius* or *numen* of the living Emperor and his various attributes – a vast magnification of the honour due to a private individual. Second, the political organisation of the Empire produced personifications which were recorded on coins and monuments. Only *Dea Roma* was particularly important, as loyalty to Rome (conjoined with loyalty to the *numen* of the Emperor) bound the individual to obey the rulers of the Empire and to maintain its laws. The third aspect of official interest concerned the cults which preserved concord with the gods. In the north-western provinces, though not always elsewhere, the principal cults of the cities were modelled on those of Rome – just as the temple forms were of Mediterranean type – but they certainly shaded into the ordinary Romano-Celtic beliefs of the provincials. Jupiter and Minerva were too real to be reserved for State ceremonies. A fourth manifestation of official religion in Britain lay in the cults of the army; there is some evidence that certain ceremonies were imposed on the troops alongside secular duties, as service discipline. However, as well as dedications to Jupiter Optimus Maximus made by military officers on behalf of their men, we find the same commanders sacrificing to local deities. This warns us not to see a rigid demarcation between official cults and everyday beliefs. At the same time, Professor MacMullen clearly goes too far in denying the existence of State cults.[2] A fifth aspect of the subject, the special favour shown by specific emperors to particular cults does, however, substantiate one of

MacMullen's points. Emperors could act as private individuals with the one difference that they had vastly greater resources of power, influence and money at their control. Those activities belong with other aspects of the interplay of religion and politics such as the suppression of political Druidism, and will be discussed in Chapter 9.

The Emperor

'Vae,' inquit, 'puto deus fio.' (Suetonius, *Divus Vespasianus* XXIII, 4). 'Alas!' he said, 'I believe I am becoming a god.'

With these words the dying Vespasian, former commander of *Legio II Augusta*, and one of the heroes of the Roman battle for Britain, expressed a half-humorous cynicicism about the nature of the Imperial Cult. He might have been voicing the doubts of many thinking Romans. The gods, for them, belonged to the supernatural world; the Emperor was a man, a magistrate with enhanced authority (*auctoritas*), the chief-citizen (*princeps*) assuredly, but still an ordinary human being. In the Eastern Mediterranean, it is true that Hellenistic kings claimed divine honours in their lifetimes, adopting titles such as 'Saviour' (*Soter*), or 'god made manifest' (*Epiphanes*), but officially at least the victory of Octavian (Augustus) over Cleopatra VII in 31 BC had ended the danger of absolute monarchy being imposed by an oriental despotism. In fact the Julian house found some of the trappings of eastern kingship very useful, and the Imperial Cult as it emerged under Augustus owed much to Hellenistic custom and practice, although it also took full account of Roman Republican sensibility.[3]

The Emperor was brought into religion, but he was not worshipped in his lifetime, though sacrifices might be made on his behalf rather in the way that Anglican church services today include a prayer for the Queen in the liturgy. He was regarded as possessing a spiritual power or *numen*, and this Imperial *numen*, which might be defined as 'such divinity (which) doth hedge a king' (**24**), was frequently associated with dedications to deities of all sorts. After death, emperors were frequently deified. Such an apotheosis came to be symbolised at the cremation of a deceased ruler by the liberation of an eagle (Dio Cassius LXXV, 5, 3–5), the bird of Jupiter, from the pyre.[4] However, although dead emperors were divine, it is notable that vows were not made to *Divus Claudius* or *Divus Vespasianus* as they were to the Olympian gods or their Celtic avatars.

The greatest public monument of the Imperial Cult in Britain was the temple at Colchester, whose massive podium, measuring 32 by 23.5 metres, later served as a platform for the great Norman keep. Unfortunately, nothing of the super-structure of the temple remains but contemporary practice demands that this be a sumptuous temple, with columns in the Corinthian order. It has been suggested that it was octastyle in front with eleven columns down its long sides. We may compare it in general form with the smaller temple of Augustus and Livia at Vienne and the *Maison Carrée* at Nîmes, also dedicated to the service of the Emperor.[5] In front of the Colchester temple as at other temples was a great altar, and both temple and altar were enclosed by a boundary wall.

This is one of those rare instances where literary evidence is of direct use in the interpretation of archaeological remains. Seneca implies in his satirical *Apocolocyntosis* ('Pumpkinification') that a temple of *Divus Claudius* was dedicated – the Latin word is *constitutum* – at the beginning of Nero's reign in AD 54.[6] However, the Britons were apparently venerating the Emperor even earlier, because the altar in front of the building was intended to be equivalent to Augustus' great altar of the Three Gauls at Lyon (*c.* 12 BC) and the German altar, *Ara Ubiorum*, at Cologne (*c.* 9 BC) where Augustus had allowed his name to be associated with the goddess *Dea Roma*.

At Lyon and Cologne the altars were the centres of provincial assemblies which, while they did allow the opinion of aristocratic provincials to be mobilised against the abuses of individual governors and procurators, were basically *foci* of loyalty where the priests (*flamines*) of the Emperor could sacrifice on his behalf. There certainly was a provincial council in Britain, as is shown by an inscription from Rome set up by the *provinciae Brittann(iae)* which could only have been incorporated as a body in this form, and by two inscriptions mentioning *patroni* of the province.[7] The Colchester altar presumably dates from between AD 43 and Claudius' death.

However, it was the temple, newly erected in Nero's reign, and clearly very expensive to the provincials, which aroused real indignation. To the Britons it was the *arx aeternae dominationis* (Tacitus, *Ann.* XIV, 31), and fittingly it was the place where the Roman colonists made their last stand against the Boudican rebels.

After the revolt, the temple was rebuilt as a symbol of Roman rule in the province. There are no further references to it, and it is sometimes supposed that the cult-centre was moved to London; this theory is without substance, depending on an inscription now lost but said to read *Num(ini) C(aesaris) Prov(incia) Brita(nnia)*, which in fact only tells us that the Imperial Numen was invoked in London by the Council; and a tombstone set up by a certain Anencletus to his wife. Anencletus was a *provincialis*, a slave serving the provincial cult, but he may have worked in

24 A dedication to the *Numina Augustorum* flanked by figures of Victory and Mars. From Risingham, Northumberland. Length 144.8 cm. *Museum of Archaeology and Anthropology, Cambridge*

Colchester and in any case his presence in London does not mean that the Colchester altar and temple had ceased to function.[8]

It is certainly a mistake to see the Imperial Cult as being tied to any one centre. Rather it was the Empire-wide expression of spiritual loyalty to the state. Apart from the Colchester cult-centre, its most prestigious manifestation would have been found amongst the wealthy merchant class of the cities, who frequently provided priests called *augustales*, organised in colleges of six men (*seviri*) to sacrifice to the Emperor's *numen*. They were normally freedmen, a class which owed everything to the imperial system, and whose loyalty was unimpeachable. Trimalchio and his friends in Petronius's *Satyricon* were *augustales* (see Petronius, *Satyricon* 71).

Evidence pertinent to Britain is slight. As we have seen in Chapter 3, M. Aurelius Lunaris, a merchant trading with Bordeaux (and a *Sevir augustalis* at Lincoln and York) set up a fine altar made of Yorkshire millstone grit to the *tutela* of Bordeaux and to Health (*Salus*), at the end of a voyage from Britain. Another *sevir* rebuilt a temple in Lincoln on account of his appointment to the priesthood. Whether or not this too was a temple of Jupiter or otherwise associated with the Imperial Cult is not known, but it certainly demonstrates the system whereby the wealthy were supposed to demonstrate their worthiness for public office by erecting works of public utility, such as temples.[9] An inscription from London shows a *libertus Augusti*, surely an aspirant for the Sevirate if in fact he was not one, involved in the restoration of a temple probably dedicated to Jupiter Optimus Maximus, an officially sponsored cult often linked to that of the Emperor.[10] This is in the spirit of the encouragement given to individuals to erect *templa* recorded by Tacitus in *Agricola* Chapter 21, though Tacitus did not approve much of freedmen. Two sarcophagi from York introduce us to a *Sevir* and his wife.[11] Marcus Verecundius Diogenes has a Greek cognomen, but he describes himself as a citizen of the Bituriges Cubi (from Bourges). He married a Sardinian lady, Julia Fortunata, probably also a freedwoman and incidentally bearing the same cognomen as Trimalchio's wife. The tragedy of enslavement in both cases had given way to wealth and the possibility of a distinguished career for their heirs as *honestiores*; a lot far better than if they had been born the children of peasants or mere artisans. It was only right that men like Diogenes should support a system which had brought them such success, and indeed venerate the powers which guarded the Empire.

The Sevirate may have been particularly well-established in large cities like London and in the coloniae, but the practice of invoking the Emperor's *numen* in association with deities spread far beyond the greater centres of Roman influence. It in no way displaced established forms of worship, for *numen* is a quality, not a god.[12] An emperor can only have one *numen*, although several emperors can share a *numen*. However, by including the Emperor's *numen* in a dedication, the worshipper made a declaration of loyalty to the Empire. The refusal of Christians to sanction the incorporation of the Emperor's *numen* or *genius* in their worship of God was doubtless an irritant to many pagans, confirming the insufferable inability of these 'atheists' to live at peace with the gods and their fellow men, but Jews also desisted. More surprisingly, perhaps, Mithraists also did no more than ask for divine protection to be given the Emperors.[13] Provided, then, that one was trusted, the cult of the *numen* was voluntary, to be observed or not as the individual thought fit. Most people were happy enough to invoke the Emperor's *numen* or *genius* in

25 Bronze sceptre-head portraying Antoninus Pius from Willingham Fen, Cambridgeshire. Height 9.7 cm. *Museum of Archaeology and Anthropology, Cambridge*

association with gods of all sorts – the great State deities, Oriental gods, especially Jupiter Dolichenus and local Celtic gods. The following examples are typical.

A Roman officer on policing duties (a *beneficiarius consularis*) was stationed at the small town of Dorchester, Oxfordshire. He set up a small shrine consisting of an altar with screens, and dedicated it to Jupiter Optimus Maximus *and* to the Imperial *numina*. The inscription reminds us of official religion, very much at home in the Roman army, where the most important ceremonies of the Roman religious year were kept conscientiously as long as the pagan Empire lasted. Marcus Varius Severus was 'showing the flag' – this was not Rome, not even a cavalry parade ground, but a one-man dedication to the highest of the Roman gods, and it is not surprising to find the spirit of the rulers of the State remembered alongside him.[14] Jupiter was also invoked at Benwell by a centurion of *Legio II Augusta*, but here in a form equated with the thunder-god of Doliche in Asia Minor. This was not an 'official dedication', nevertheless the formula used was very similar – 'To Jupiter Dolichenus and to the Imperial numina'.[15] The Imperial *numina* were in fact frequently associated with deities of local, Celtic origin. The range is vast, extending from Antenociticus, whom we have met already at Benwell, Mars Ocelus at Carlisle and Mars Thincsus with the German goddesses known as the Alaisiagi at Housesteads, to civilian dedications in southern Britain: Mercury Andescociuòucus at Colchester, where the freedmen Imilco was probably a Celt, and Mars at the Foss Dike in Lincolnshire, where Bruccius and Caratius, who commissioned a figurine, certainly were.[16]

It is from eastern Britain that the most striking ritual or votive objects connected with the *numina* have been found. These are small bronze heads of emperors, which in one case certainly and in three others probably came from shrines. The certain example is a head of Antoninus Pius from Willingham Fen, originally mounted on a sceptre (**25**). Other finds include a mace head, including in its detailed iconography a representation of the Celtic wheel-god. A bronze club and figurines of Mars were also found. The cult was clearly poor and local, but at religious ceremonies which might in some respects be very different to festivities in Rome, the presence of an image of the Emperor on a sceptre-head would have been a sign of Romanisation, highly gratifying to the authorities.[17]

Portraits scarcely strike us as religious objects, although no doubt images of Queen Victoria in many parts of the nineteenth-century British Empire were regarded in a religious light by her native subjects. To the Romans, a person's head, and especially his features, enshrined his personality, and the Imperial personality, his *numen*, was too powerful to be viewed in anything other than religious terms. A Roman knight called Falanius once had a very nasty shock when he was prosecuted for selling land on which an Imperial statue stood (Tacitus, *Ann*. I, 73). Conversely, the *damnatio memoriae* consisted very largely in destroying the power and persona of a dead Emperor by smashing his image.

Even in Britain, portrait-statues would have been thoroughly familiar to the populace, to judge from the large number of fragments which have been found. Only a few actual heads survive. The most impressive is the enormous marble head of an emperor, too battered for certain identification but possibly Trajan, found at Bosham and now in Chichester Museum. Its original setting is unknown – it could have come from Fishbourne – but it may be associated with the loyalty of the area as a client kingdom (and afterwards) to the Emperor, demonstrated by King

Cogidubnus and his subjects in inscriptions and recorded by Tacitus (*Agricola* 14).
We may note, incidentally, a small marble head from Fishbourne, but this does not
appear to be an Imperial portrait.[18]

A cast-bronze head of Claudius (three-quarter size), hacked from a statue, was
found in the bed of the River Alde in Suffolk. It *may* have been looted from the
colonia at Colchester by Boudica's tribesmen, anxious to take into their own hands
the power of the ruler of Rome; the desire to take a trophy here vies with the
primitive superstition of the head-cult.[19]

No Flavian portraits are known from Britain, but Suetonius (*Divus Titus* IV, 1) tells
us that statues of Titus were numerous here – information acquired in all
probability from Agricola, who may have inspired such dedications: it is indeed
possible that Titus served in Britain as a military tribune at the same time as
Agricola, during the Boudican revolt and that there was a personal tie of friendship
between the two men.[20] Agricola was certainly a Flavian protegé. In any case the
policy of Romanisation which it was his duty to foster must have included
encouragement of the cult of the Emperor's *numen*.

Hadrian was, no doubt, well represented by commemorative statues in Britain
as in many other provinces, for he was a great traveller, determined to bind the
disparate provinces of the Empire together, and he had, of course, come to Britain
in AD 122. The great bronze head from London is one of only two *certain* bronzes of
the Emperor to survive. The other, of even better quality, comes from a Roman
fort near Beth Shean (Scythopolis) and shows the Emperor wearing a cuirass with
relief decoration of Aeneas' victory over the Latin tribes[21] – perhaps a reference to
the Roman victory over the Jews in AD 135. We do not know whether or not the
London statue was similarly ornamented, perhaps with a reference to victory in
north Britain and the construction of Hadrian's Wall. It is very likely to have been
dressed in armour, as was the statue of an emperor which stood in the basilica at
Silchester. This is represented by an overhanging flap or lappet (*pteryx*) from the
ceremonial kilt, decorated with a lion-mask in relief to scare away evil forces. The
type of lappet may well be early second-century, and the statue could well have
been of Hadrian. Other lappets from the headquarters of the fortress at Caerleon
and the fort at Caernarvon (*Segontium*) emphasise the close relationship between the
veneration of emperors by the army and their veneration by *civitates* and other civil
bodies.[22] The statuette of Nero from Baylham Mill exhibits this element in Imperial
military dress very clearly (**26**).

The stone head of Constantine from York shows that the Imperial image had
lost none of its potency in the fourth century. Even after paganism was replaced by
Christianity as the State religion, the Emperor continued to be a man unlike all
other men – God's deputy on Earth. There are no portraits of later emperors from
Britain, but coins circulated in the provinces of Britain as elsewhere, a few of them
displaying the Hand of God (*Manus Dei*) descending from the heavens to bless his
servant, the Emperor.[23]

The veneration of Imperial power, insofar as it was a religious activity, had both
a formal and an informal aspect; these were often mixed, as we saw in the case of
the bronze from Israel, where a formal portrait is combined with a commentary in
the form of a myth portrayed on the breastplate. This is illustrated here in the two
bronze plaques dedicated by Demetrius at York in the Flavian period (Chapter 2).
One of them is dedicated 'to the deities of the governor's headquarters'. A F

26 Statuette, bronze inlaid with silver and *niello* showing Nero in the guise of Alexander the Great. From Baylham Mill, Coddenham, Suffolk. Height 55.9 cm. *British Museum*

Norman, in an excellent study of Roman religion in York, comments that this 'combines the concepts of . . . ruler worship, since the governor's headquarters are *ex hypothesi* so maintained under Imperial auspices and of service discipline'. In other words the governor's headquarters, whether at York or on the Cannon Street site in London, was a provincial extension of the Sacred Palace, and also a little Rome within camp walls presided over by the deities of the State protecting the Legatus as the deputy for the Emperor. So much for the correct and formal public attitude. Privately, the language used about the Emperor went further. Demetrius' second dedication 'To Ocean and Tethys' (2) recalls Alexander the Great's altars set up at the end of his long eastward progress to India. Norman rightly comments that this 'combination of formulae reveals Demetrius' confidence in Rome's destiny in the West', but we may surely press the point further. Not only was Rome 'the heir and successor to the greatest conqueror and civilizer of the ancient world', but the Emperor was himself an Alexander, hero and demi-god.[24]

Most emperors displayed a certain reticence in adopting what was, after all, the forms of Hellenistic divine kingship. After all, the last of the Hellenistic monarchies had been defeated at Actium in 31 BC by Octavian in the name of the Roman Republic. Although engraved gems distributed to friends and supporters show Augustus as Alexander, Achilles, Theseus or even various deities – Mercury or Jupiter[25] – the public face of Imperial power remained (as we have seen) correct: Nero flouted these conventions. The very fine, bronze statuette (ornamented with silver and niello) (**26**), showing Nero in the persona of Alexander, now in the British Museum, was probably found at Baylham Mill near Coddenham, Suffolk, the site of an early fort. Of all the early Roman emperors, Nero was the most obsessed by Rome's Greek (ie Hellenistic) inheritance, but he lacked the political acumen to see how damaging his behaviour was to his reputation in the West. Dr Graham Webster suggests that the figure was discarded and perhaps deliberately damaged at the time of Nero's death and *damnatio memoriae* in AD 68.[26]

Personifications

Between the Emperor and the gods stood various personified virtues, of which the *numina* may be regarded as specialised examples. Most of them are qualities which we still recognise today, and although we would not think of sacrificing to them in church, they are invoked by clergymen in sermons as well as by their congregations in secular contexts. Amongst them are Virtue, Victory, Discipline and Fortune, and in Roman times these were often linked to the power of the state in the person of the ruler.

VIRTUS

Virtue was personified as an Amazon, wearing a helmet and a tunic which did not cover her right breast. Reliefs from Duntocher (Antonine Wall)[27] and Chesters (Hadrian's Wall)[28] dated respectively to the second and third centuries show the *Virtus* of the Emperor(s) holding a vexillum. Both were made on behalf of military units, but an individual altar to the Emperor's Virtus was set up by a woman called Hermione, daughter of Quintus, at Maryport.[29]

VICTORIA

Victory was a popular attribute in the army, a proud battle honour of certain legions (e.g. *XX Valeria Victrix*), and her personification in art as a winged maiden generally holding a palm branch and a wreath is very familiar. Victory was naturally an attribute of the Emperor. Thus a dedication from Maryport commemorates the Victory of the Emperor and figures two of these winged beings.[30] A very fine sculptured slab from Risingham, part of the Cotton Collection assembled in the sixteenth century and now in Cambridge, is dedicated to the Imperial *numina* by the Fourth Cohort of Gauls (**24**); on either side of the inscription stands a figure, in one case Mars and the other Victory.[31] As in the case of Virtus we find civilians making similar dedications. A bronze tablet from Colchester was dedicated by Vepogenus, a Caledonian, to Mars Medocius and – instead of the *numen* – to the Victory of the Emperor Severus Alexander.[32]

The Emperor's own Victory could be linked to the prowess of his army units. A statuette of *Victoria* found near Rochdale was dedicated to the Victory of the Sixth Legion by a soldier called Valerius Rufus, as the *solutio* of his vow.[33] Regiments and parts of regiments had *genii*, and Rufus was simply attributing a divine quality to his own legion.

We need not always think of Victoria as a personification. She has an equal claim to be regarded as a goddess, the Roman equivalent to the Greek Nike. If on the Risingham relief cited above, Mars is a god, Victory has every right to be considered as a goddess, his consort. Certainly Victoria seems more alive, for instance, than *Disciplina*, because she – or rather her Greek equivalent, Nike – had been envisaged as a real deity for so long by artists and poets. Symmachus' defence of the Altar of Victory in his Third *Relatio* warns us not only to beware of dividing Roman religion into rigid categories (for Victory was clearly defended by these late Roman senators as a being whose reality was deeply felt); it also tells us that we cannot always divide the divine world into neat categories, however convenient it might be for the modern scholar to do so.

DISCIP(U)LINA

Discipline was a quintessentially military attribute who first appears in Britain during the reign of Hadrian. Indeed Hadrian, who reformed army discipline and abolished certain luxurious excesses (*SHA Hadrian* x) was probably responsible for her actual creation. The earliest known altar to *Discipulina* comes from Chesters and is dedicated to the Discipline of the Emperor Hadrian Augustus by the *Ala Augusta* (**27**), but such altars continued to be set up in the *aedes* of Roman forts down to the reign of Severus as stern reminders to the troops that divine sanction backed the orders and punishments meted out by officers.[34]

FORTUNA

Discipline, Virtue, and even Victory were rather cold attributes. Insofar as the attachment of ordinary people, soldiers and civilians, to the Emperor's *numen* excited real enthusiasm – and no doubt it really did when crowds were seated in theatres and amphitheatres, assembled on parade grounds or in the temene of temples – it was the Emperor's (good) Fortune they would acclaim. The Fortune of the ruler was the fortune of all – and there is plenty of evidence in inscriptions, statuary, coins and gems that many people in Roman Britain were very attached to Fortune. In their daily lives, good fortune meant success in games of dice and other forms of gambling; she presided in bath houses both for this reason, and because naked men were vulnerable to mischance. She was assimilated to the Greek *tyche* and in art her *cornucopia* and the rudder with which she steers Fate had long been familiar. Her association with rulers goes back into Hellenistic times and she is shown for example on faience jugs used in offerings to the deified Ptolemaic queens of Egypt.[35]

The horn of plenty which she held might be assimilated to that of *Annona*, the corn-supply, but as in all probability London (unlike Rome) had no corn-dole and Britain was a corn exporter rather than a corn importer, this aspect may not have had much importance. Nevertheless the rudder of Fortune was a literal symbol of the steering of the Ship of State. The distinction between Imperial Fortune and Fortuna as she affected the individual in the chance of life, when far from home he wanted a homebringer or in the bath-house felt vulnerable in his nakedness, feared for his business dealings or his crops, was by no means absolute. Titus Flavius

27 Altar dedicated to the *Discipulina Imperatoris Hadriani Augusti* by the *Ala* called *Augusta* for valour. Fragment measures 79 cm in height. *Chesters, Northumberland*

Secundus, prefect of the First Cohort of Hamian archers, dedicated an altar to *Fortuna Augusta* in the bath-house at Carvoran *ex visu* just as, for instance, Julius Severinus, a tribune at Risingham made a much more personal dedication to *Fortuna Redux*, the homebringer.[36] Together with Caecilius Donatianus' poem to Julia Domna as Cybele-Caelestis, also from Carvoran (see Chapter 5), this shows that even the apparently official and ceremonial aspects of Roman religion might shade into the private, emotional faith of the dedicator. Fortuna may be seen in another traditional role as the protector of Imperial property, in this case provisions for the Severan campaigns in Britain, as a lead sealing from London impressed with her image and inscribed *For(tuna) Aug(ustae)* shows.[37]

In concluding our discussion of 'Emperor worship', it may be said that the forms it took – the veneration of the dead (deified) emperors, of the *numina* of living emperors, and of various Imperial virtues – were much less aberrations from Roman tradition than might have been expected. Cicero had placed Scipio Africanus amongst the stars in the *Somnium Scipionis*, a fictional dream of his descendant Scipio Aemilianus who is advised by his sainted forbear. All men had *genii* and it required no great shift in thought to raise special men, such as emperors, to the heavens after their death. As for personifications, were not the most primitive manifestations of deities, such as the gods of sowing, of latch-keys, of the hearth, little more than these?

That most wise and conscientious Emperor, Hadrian, calls himself 'son of all the deified emperors' on an official dedication near Hadrian's Wall; in other words he has acted in the best traditions of his ancestors in building the Wall. Further, he claims that 'the necessity of keeping the Empire within limits had been laid on him *by divine precept.*' His outlook is not essentially different from that of Scipio Aemilianus or rather Cicero, and has nothing to do with the dangerous claims to godhead entertained by Gaius or Elagabalus.[38]

By association, whatever touched an Emperor could not help but obtain the grace of his *numen*, and this was particularly true of his family, the Divine House. Several inscriptions, including two from Chichester, in the client kingdom, honour the *Domus Divina*, but we would be wrong to think that the Emperor's wife was worshipped in the normal course of events. A statuette from Well in Yorkshire and the Hutcheson Hill distance slab (both mentioned below) may conflate a *deified* Empress with a province, Roma or another personification. Similarly Septimius Severus' wife, Julia Domna, did associate herself with oriental goddesses, especially Caelestis and Cybele in her lifetime, but here an eastern style of monarchy is in evidence.[39] Generally, Caesar's wife was above suspicion, worthy of respect, not worship. Nevertheless, as the human world could be held to mirror the heavens, so the Empire grew more absolute (a process which Christianity did nothing to halt), and the Emperor and Empress came to be vital elements in the natural ordering of society. It was easy to see the Emperor as the deputy and companion of Jupiter or Sol or ultimately Christ upon earth. The doctrine of the Divine Right of Kings certainly has a Roman pedigree.

Nevertheless, the Emperor was not be be confused with the gods, however much he and his family symbolised divinity. As Duncan Fishwick has written, 'Genuine piety, expressed in the form of ex-votos, seems hardly to be attested in connection with the ruler cult, for in time of sickness or peril one turned not to the Emperor but to the gods.'[40]

Rome and the Provinces

The altar at Lyons and in all probability, the altar in front of the great Colchester temple as well, were dedicated both to *Dea Roma* and to Augustus. As a personification, Roma was comparable with such figures as Eutychides' Tyche of Antioch; she epitomised the power and good fortune of the city. In Republican times, the rulers of Rome fancied her to be a city state on the Greek model. Her citizens were indeed formally attached to city (voting) tribes even if they came from afar. By the later first century BC, the Roman Empire claimed supra-national dominance. Virgil expressed it as a mission 'to crown Peace with Law, to spare the humbled, and to tame in war the proud' (*Aeneid* VI, 852–3).[41] Thus when we come to see her position in Roman Britain, *Roma* appears at the summit of a pyramid under which is the provincial goddess, Britannia; next regional deities, principally Brigantia; then city 'tyches'; and finally local deities of particular places, Sulis (equated with Minerva) at Bath, Arnemetia at Buxton and *genii loci* everywhere Rome's birthday was celebrated (on the *Parilia*, 21 April) as the *Feriale Duranum* attests. An altar was set up by the *duplicarii* of a *numerus* stationed at High Rochester, to Rome on her birthday.[42] Another altar, from Maryport, tells its own story. G. Cornelius Peregrinus was a tribune of a cohort, but his dedication shows him in his civil capacity, for he had served on the town council of the colonia of Saldae in Mauretania Caesariensis (North Africa) and longed to go home. He makes a vow to the *Genius loci* (of Maryport), and to *Fortuna Redux*, Fortune, the homebringer who will guide him to Spaldae. *Bonus Fatus*, good Fate, is also a necessary concept. However, *Rome Aeterna*, Eternal Rome, linked to these, is a reminder that as a citizen of the Empire, Peregrinus could expect this great *Tyche* to transport him from one place in *her* Empire to his home. It is interesting to find *Roma Aeterna* and *Fortuna Redux* similarly linked on another inscription from the fort.[43]

28 Nicolo intaglio showing *Dea Roma* from Cirencester, Gloucestershire 1.4 × 1.2 cm. *Corinium Museum*

Actual figures of *Roma* personified are rare in Britain, apart of course from those depicted on coins. She is normally shown as a seated goddess, like Minerva in appearance, but wearing a short tunic – the type is heavily influenced by representations of *Virtus*, discussed above as an Imperial Virtue. There are several representations on gems; from the York fortress, the *colonia* of Colchester and the major towns of Cirencester (**38**) and Silchester. The findspots help to confirm that the appeal of *Roma* was to the most Romanised members of the population.[44]

Two figures in stone are more controversial, and other explanations may be proposed. The first is a statuette from Well in North Yorkshire. A female figure stands with her right breast bare (**29**), Amazon-fashion (like *Virtus*). She wears a long chiton. This is a miniature version of a type represented by a full-size statue from the temple of Rome and Augustus at Ostia, which is presumably to be identified as *Roma*. Although much of the head is missing, a bun of hair at the back above the nape of the neck suggests that the features may have recalled a deified Empress. However, she must be conflated with some personification for no Roman lady in life would have appeared in public improperly dressed. The wreath that the figure holds shows that she is a bearer of Victory, either an attribute like *Virtus* or more probably the goddess *Roma* or one of her provinces, in this context *Britannia*.[45]

The best parallel in Britain is on a relief from the Antonine Wall at Hutcheson Hill where a similar figure (with breasts, however, covered) hands a wreath to an eagle on a standard held by a standard-bearer. The relief has been fully discussed in the context of her personifying Victory, a deified member of the *Domus Divina*,

29 Sculpture from Well, North Yorkshire, probably *Roma* or *Britannia*. Height 65 cm

30 Altar from Cirencester dedicated to the *Genius Loci*. Height 137 cm. *Corinium Museum*

Britannia or all three. However, Roma is another possibility. She was intimately concerned with Imperial Victory, and many representations of Roma show her holding a victory while on the intaglio from Cirencester she grasps a wreath.[46]

The relations between Rome and her Empire were complex, and this complexity is reflected at a symbolic level. The case of Britannia is typical. The earliest appearance of the goddess is at the time of the conquest. A relief in the Sebasteion, centre of the Imperial cult at Aphrodisias in Asia Minor, shows her as a young woman humiliated by Claudius. She is no more than a stage-prop to emphasise Claudius' triumph, not a goddess to be worshipped.[47]

A statuette was, however, dedicated to Holy Britannia at York by an Imperial freedman with a Greek name, Publius Nikomedes, and Quintus Pisentius Justus, a prefect of the Fourth Cohort of Gauls, stationed on the Antonine Wall at Castlehill, seems to have set up an altar to her (if it is interpreted correctly – it is possible that it mentions British Mother Goddesses). As Britain and the Britons came to be regarded with greater sympathy, Britannia begins to appear in a divine role. Hadrian probably took a leading part, for Britannia (amongst other provinces) appears on coins in his time. Hadrian envisaged the Empire as a commonwealth of peoples, and his propaganda would not unnaturally emphasise the enduring, divine aspect of this (Chapter 9). His successors maintained his programme. The statues of provinces in the Hadrianeum demonstrate Antoninus' *pietas*; so do his coins, including a large issue of bronze, perhaps struck in Britain, showing Britannia. As we have seen, the type is hard to distinguish from *Roma*, and we cannot be sure which the Hutcheson Hill distance slab and the Well statuette actually portray.[48]

The goddess Brigantia, whose veneration was encouraged by the Imperial house (see Chapter 9), appears on a number of inscriptions. She should be regarded as the deity of a large area in Britain and perhaps the personification of Britannia Inferior.[49] Each town had its *Tyche* (i.e. Fortune), embodying the personified presence of the divinity of the place; the battered head of a *Tyche* from Silchester was perhaps venerated in the basilica, while on a fourth-century mosaic at Brantingham in Yorkshire, a female head surrounded by the *nimbus* of deity, may represent the city of York, or else *Brigantia* the eponymous goddess of the region whose centre was York.[50]

Genii might aspire to be territorial deities. The *Genius Terrae Britannicae* to whom Marcus Cocceius Firmus set up a parade-ground altar at Auchendavy is one of them (see below), but so is the *Genius loci* with his mural crown shown on a large altar from Cirencester (30). The one belongs to Roman military religion, the other to the cult-life of a flourishing town. While none of these deities may have inspired the deepest emotion, a sense of place was important, and a god or goddess to look after that place, whether it were a province, a city or a spring, would have been comforting.[51]

The Great Gods of the Roman State

The third aspect of official religion in Britain is harder to evaluate, for it had connections far beyond the interests of the state. Public sacrifices to the Capitoline triad – Jupiter, Juno and Minerva – took place on altars in front of the major temples (*Capitolia*) in the *coloniae* and some other cities, presumably because their calendars and foundation statutes were modelled on those of Rome. Nevertheless, in North Africa Saturn was venerated as chief deity, and in Ostia, Vulcan was the most important god. The place of Athena as city goddess of Athens was presumably unassailable. This diversity has led Professor Ramsay MacMullen, as we have seen, to deny the concept of a state religion altogether, but all that we really need is to adopt an attitude of flexibility towards it. The great powers of nature were altogether above the dry formulae of government regulations; human beings owed to Jupiter, Juno and Minerva as also to Mars, Apollo, Venus and Diana, deep and passionate prayer.

For instance, to take one example, a curse-tablet found at Ratcliffe-on-Soar, Nottinghamshire, is addressed *Iovi Optimo Maximo* – to Jupiter Greatest and Best, not only because he was the Father of the gods but because he was the most powerful of them, and the one most associated with Justice. A suppliant approaches him to recover stolen coins, but he might under other circumstances have approached Minerva or Mercury.[52]

Jupiter, Juno and Minerva were not special because they stood apart from supposedly fuller-blooded and more personal Celtic deities; indeed they were frequently conflated with such gods. However, in addition to looking after individuals, they were especially charged with care for the health and security of the Roman State. Thus, whether they were venerated in the administrative centres of the towns or in those special strongholds of Roman custom and tradition, the forts (see below), a solemn sacrifice to Jupiter would have been an awesome sight.

Evidence for the cult of Jupiter Optimus Maximus in the towns of Britain is all too slight. The Forum of Verulamium had two temples added to it, one of which could have been that of Jupiter. A very small temple beside the earlier forum of London may have served the same purpose, although we might have expected a much more impressive building. Nevertheless it has been suggested that 'it was sacred to the Imperial House and that the temple would therefore have contained Imperial statues and other official civic dedications'. An altar re-used in the riverside wall of London concerns the restoration of a temple, very probably of Jupiter Optimus Maximus, in the third century. In some ways the most significant evidence for the State cult in the chief town of Britain is part of a contract written on a wooden tablet, including an oath sworn in the names of Jupiter Optimus Maximus and the Genius of the Emperor Domitian.[53] At Silchester, a bronze eagle may at one time have been associated with a statue of Jupiter (or of the Emperor in the *persona* of Jupiter). Such statues, whether in temples or in public places, *basilicae* or *fora*, were eloquent reminders of the *Pax deorum* – the peace with the gods, by which the Empire survived.[54]

Religion certainly played a part in Romanisation. When Tacitus speaks of Agricola encouraging the building of *templa*, he is probably thinking predominantly of temples of the State gods. The process reached beyond the frontiers of the Empire into the client kingdoms. A most interesting statue-base or base of a Jupiter column at Chichester is carved in relief with figures of Minerva, Mars and two nymphs on three sides; the front is inscribed *I(ovi) O(ptimo) M(aximo) in Honorem Domu(s) Divinae*.[55] The monument stood in the great square which corresponded to the forum of a Roman city; strictly speaking the name 'forum' should be reserved for the centre of a city under full Roman government, though no doubt the Romanised inhabitants of first-century Chichester would have called their public square the Forum. We do not know whether or not Jupiter had a great temple, but Neptune and Minerva certainly did. This temple was dedicated to them in order to ensure the health of the Imperial family (*Domus Divina*), with the express authority of the local client king, Cogidubnus. While it is easy to see why Neptune and Minerva would have been suitable patrons to a Guild of Shipwrights, the dedication hints at far more than a private shrine. Neptune and Minerva were suitable guardians for a city dependent on both land and sea for its livelihood; Poseidon was venerated beside Athena on the Athenian acropolis for this reason. The Temple seems to have occupied the next *insula* to the 'forum'; it could have been, in fact, the most important temple in the city. At Sulis Minerva's shrine at Bath Neptune may be represented in the mask (conflated with that of a Medusa) set within a wreath in the centre of the temple pediment. Here was a centre of Roman culture, patronised in particular by the army, and the Athenian precedent may also have been in the mind of the founders.[56] A local nymph, Sulis, was combined with Minerva, and hence brought into the ambit of official religion, just as at a later period Brigantia was Romanised in the North as the regional deity of the Severan province of Lower Britain.

The State Religion and Christianity

There was hardly any attempt to impose religious orthodoxy in paganism; the religious calendar of Rome, though widely influential, would not have been followed to the letter everywhere. Certainly intolerance had no place, and the State only expected and required the gods to be venerated; all gods were acceptable because the diversity of religious expression in the Empire meant that nobody could be sure of the real names of the deities. The *passio* of the martyr Albanus, outside Verulamium and probably on the site of the later Abbey, at some time in the third century, demonstrates that the hand of government could fall heavily on 'atheists', *i.e.* those individuals who appeared to insult the gods and threaten mankind's contract with them. St Alban was executed because he refused to make an offering or pour a libation to an idol, possibly an image of Jupiter, no doubt in the vicinity of the Forum temple(s).[57] His offence seemed commendable to later Christians, and still appears heroic to us, for did not Alban refuse consent to tyrannical power? The authorities were not, however, arbitrary tyrants; on their own terms 'atheists' (such as Christians) denied the sustaining power of the divine world to the Roman State. The Christian advocacy of spiritual disarmament should be seen as analogous to present-day suggestions of immediate unilateral disarmament by the West, with the difference that even critics of nuclear disarmament will concede that the *motives* of many of the disarmers are right and not a few would say that such disarmament has a chance of working, but that it is too dangerous to take the risk. No pagan could expect anything but ill from discourtesy towards the gods – the wrath that 'atheists' would bring down on the Empire was certain and terrible. Furthermore, the words of Christians who spoke wildly of the Fall of Babylon (i.e. Rome) scarcely reassured them.

When Christianity suddenly and unexpectedly became the religion of the State, pagan official observances, that is those paid for with public funds, were stopped at once. Revival could only come with a restoration of paganism, which in fact occurred in 360 when Julian became Augustus. Probably at this time, Lucius

Septimius, governor of Britannia Prima, restored a Jupiter column to the *Prisca Religio* (Former Religion) at Cirencester.[58] Such restorations did not last, for all future emperors were Christian; even at Rome, where the pagan aristocracy maintained a position of considerable influence, all the polished oratory of Symmachus failed to return the altar of Victory to the *curia* in AD 382.

Paganism was no more killed by the adoption of Christianity as the State Religion than Henry VIII ended Catholic piety in England, but in both cases the replacement of public encouragement by public hostility removed vast reserves of patronage. In late Roman Britain, the majority of temples functioned as before; silence only reigned in the *Capitolia* of the cities, though recent research suggests that a century of urban decay, at least with regard to public buildings, may have masked the effect of the State's seizure of temple treasures (mainly, one suspects, the treasures of large urban temples – the very ones, which, it is suggested in Chapter 6, drew least in the way of real devotion).

Ceremonies of the State Cult

The relation of man to the gods, as we have already stated, was regulated by sacrifice. Our only illustrations of state sacrifices from Britain do seem to have a military context, but as they also relate to civil ceremony they are mentioned here. Indeed they are a vital link with the subject of official religion in the army, the subject with which this chapter ends. A terracotta cake-mould from Silchester depicts a scene suggestive of a celebration in the town after Septimius Severus' northern victories. Severus, Geta and Caracalla each wear tunic and *sagum* (military cloak) and pour a libation onto a tripod. This is a preliminary to sacrifice. Also from Silchester is an intaglio showing Caracalla dressed in a toga and boots (31). He wears on his head the corn measure of the Egyptian god Serapis, whose worship was especially encouraged by the Severan dynasty (Chapter 9). He is conflated with the *Genius Populi Romani* and is figured pouring a libation on an altar. A vexillum and military trumpet depicted in the field suggest that the reference is again partly military.[59]

The scene shown in relief on the right side of a distance slab from Bridgeness on the Antonine Wall (32) also shows the pouring of a libation, but here certainly as a preliminary to a sacrifice.[60] The *vexillum* of *Legio II* indicates a legionary setting but every other aspect of the sacrifice could have taken place in the forum of a city, and indeed the presiding chief celebrant is in civilian dress; he wears the toga, although he has not yet veiled his head with it. Normally the officiant would cover his head as a sign of humility before the gods and as a shield against sights and sounds of ill-omen, but that solemn moment may not yet have been reached. A flute-player (*tibicen*) provides the solemn music that accompanies all such ceremonies. Below, an attendant crouches, perhaps the *popa*, although the boar (*sus*), ram (*ovis*) and bull (*taurus*) which will be offered in the *Suovetaurilia* are as yet unharmed by either pole-axe or knife. The identity of the priest is uncertain; it is very likely that he is not a professional but the governor of Britain or the Legionary legate in a priestly capacity. He is making an offering on behalf of his men, in order to confirm the *Pax deorum*, just as a private sacrifice regulated the contract between the individual and the gods. The sacrifice is symbolised by the altar; hence, whenever a Roman altar is found, the inscription upon it should be read not as a dry-as-dust document but as

31 Green plasma intaglio showing Caracalla as the *Genius Populi Romani*. Silchester, Hampshire. 1.55 × 1.05 cm. *Silchester Collection in Reading Museum*
32 *Opposite* Distance slab from Bridgeness, West Lothian on the Antonine Wall. Height 86.4 cm. *National Museum of Antiquities of Scotland*

a record, however terse, of one man's attempt to make contact with the powers above, for himself as well as for his family, friends, military unit and nation.

Religion and the Army

In addition to the evidence already discussed, sculptures and inscriptions from forts and fortresses confirm what we might well have guessed – that, even in the most distant garrisons, the Roman army maintained Roman ways. A copy of a Roman military calendar of festivals, dated to the third century, was found at Dura Europos on the River Euphrates. It demonstrates that the *Cohors XX Palmyrenorum* followed the traditional usages of the city of Rome and laid particular stress on the most ancient and traditional gods as well as on Imperial anniversaries. The calendar 'connected the troops to Rome by the simultaneous celebration of festivals. It connected them to ancient festivals and therefore to tradition.'[61] The fort or fortress was a religious microcosm of Rome or a Roman *colonia*. In the centre was its headquarters building, with its shrine of the standards called, indeed, *aedes principiorum*, 'Shrine of the Headquarters' on an inscription from Reculver.[61] This corresponded to the *Capitolium* in a city. The *pomoerium*, the sacred boundary of a town frequently represented by the city wall was here replaced by military fortifications.

In theory at least, only such religious expression thought appropriate to a Roman community belonged inside the walls; temples of Jupiter Dolichenus, Mithras, Antenociticus or Coventina were built outside and their cults were excluded from the camp. In practice this isolation had little importance and far too much ink has been spilled by scholars in constructing a rigid demarcation between

33 Altars dedicated to Jupiter by the Cohors I Hispanorum at Maryport, Cumberland. Heights 109.2 cm, 109.2 cm, 99 cm, 78.7 cm. *Netherhall Museum, Maryport*

official and non-official cults in the army. Just as the towns might accord a major place to deities other than Jupiter and Minerva, or even to gods with native epithets (even if more in the Eastern than the Western provinces) so do we find commanders of units sacrificing to a host of deities both privately on their own behalf and that of their families, and also for their units. We should not forget that Dura Europos has yielded a fresco showing the tribune Julius Terentius with his men sacrificing to a triad of Syrian gods. The scene could have been in North Britain, save that there the Palmyrene gods would have been replaced perhaps by mother goddesses (at Old Penrith, milecastle 19 near Halton Chesters and Cramond), Antenociticus (at Benwell), Cocidius (at Birdoswald) or the Eastern god Jupiter Dolichenus (at Old Carlisle). This is merely a random list of deities receiving dedications from military units.[63] A group of altars set up the legionary centurion M. Cocceius Firmus at Auchendavy, Dumbarton, probably on the parade ground of the fort, invoke the *Genius Terrae Britannicae* together with a number of deities included in the Dura calendar, notably Jupiter, Mars, Minerva, Hercules and Victory. Diana and Apollo are both listed on the altars (although they do not appear in the calendar), not surprisingly as they were Roman deities, but the presence of the Celtic horse-goddess Epona and the Campestres, Mother Goddesses of Rhenish origin, should surprise those who make a rigid division between official and unofficial (foreign) army religion.[64] Even within a fort, it is startling to find silver ex-votos to *Mars Cocidius* in the strong-room below the *aedes* at Bewcastle, where the fort may have been placed at or beside the major sanctuary of the god, if *Fanum Cocidi* was here.[65]

Admittedly, most officially sponsored religious activity in the forts had a highly Roman stamp. In his classic paper on religious cults in Corbridge, Sir Ian Richmond was able to illustrate veneration for the gods and goddesses named in the Feriale – Jupiter, Juno, Minerva, Mars, Vesta and Neptune, Victory, Salus and Roma, very largely from sculptural and epigraphic remains from that one site. If we turn elsewhere, this evidence is duplicated and strengthened, especially in the case of Jupiter.[66]

Perhaps the best-known ceremony in the army is the annual January sacrifice when Jupiter and other deities were invoked to care for the Roman state in the coming year. It had its counterpart in Rome, and probably in most cities of the Empire. A large number of altars have been found on what is presumed to have been the parade-ground of the fort at Maryport (33). Most are dedicated to Jupiter, but Juno, Minerva, Mars and Victory are also represented.[67] It is sometimes said that the previous year's altar to Jupiter was buried on the renewal of vows, but there is no real evidence for this. Indeed, had this been the case, we should have expected to recover even more altars on the sites of fort and fortress parade-grounds. It is perhaps more likely that altars were buried, if they were, when a fort was abandoned either totally or to another unit. Burial in the ground was the established way of disposing or of storing objects charged with divine power – in other words *sacri* (sacred). Alternatively, the burial of the altars may have been a native ritual performed in the absence of the Roman garrison, as is possible at Newstead, where both an altar to Jupiter and human bones were found in a pit in the *principia* courtyard, and where a number of other pits containing skeletons and other objects were excavated.[68] A well in the *praetorium* at Bar Hill which was full of Roman stonework including altars could also have been filled by superstitious

Caledonians after the withdrawal of Roman forces as well as by Romans. The burial of objects which could still exercise power and yet needed to be treated with respect is found again in the disposal of a head of the cult statue of Mercury at Uley (Chapter 10).

It may be difficult for us to find genuine religious feeling in the apparently stereotyped language of inscriptions, but we should not assume that even the religion of the *Feriale Duranum* – the most conservative and formal aspect of military cult – was empty of meaning. In the first place there was an *esprit de corps* which was fostered by the act of sharing in a sacrifice, especially at the party which followed, when the ox or boar was consumed. At such times we may imagine many a soldier felt very close to the deities of Rome. A fragmentary wooden writing-tablet from Vindolanda includes the words *ad sacrum* and may be concerned with victualling such a (sacred) feast. Even more tangibly we find soldiers wearing openwork roundels on their belts inscribed with a prayer: *(Juppiter) Optime Maxime, conserva numerum omnium militantium* – 'O Jupiter Greatest and Best, succour this band of fighting men all!' while the parade-armour of cavalry *alae*, commissioned from armourers, was ornamented with images of Jupiter, Mars, Minerva and the Dioscuri (Castor and Pollux) – protecting deities. Evidently the men who wore these helmets and greaves had a deep trust in the gods (even if the armour was standard army issue).[69]

The standards find a place again and again in this military art (34) because they were regarded as holy icons – the very personifications of individual units, and their loss was the greatest disaster imaginable. The Romans were not the first, nor were they the last, people to treat standards as though they possessed supernatural power. In Christian Europe it is still customary to hang up captured enemy ensigns and also those of one's own disbanded units in cathedrals and churches, despite the fact that in origin Christianity was an anti-militarist religion. The author was present at a most interesting ceremony in the City Church at Oxford where the standard of the veterans' association of the 'Old Contemptibles' was handed over to be kept by the church, thus to some degree preserving their spirit for ever.

Standards were not gods in the Roman army, but it is not in the least surprising that they – or the standard-bearers – had *genii*.[71] For many they were the means by which the power and goodwill of the gods was made visible. The famous story of the standard-bearer of the Tenth Legion who took the initiative as Caesar's fleet landed in Britain in 55 BC makes the point – he called out 'Leap down, unless you wish to betray your eagle to the enemy' (*BG* IV, 25). In that instance the legionaries would have been guilty of sacrilege if they had not followed the sacred standard ashore. Standard-bearers were, it need hardly be said, very important in the army, and not simply for their strictly military function of relaying commands through signals; they were also bearers of icons. The resemblance of military standards to certain standards carried in religious processions, for example the 'enseign' of Serapis from Flobecq (see Chapter 6) was not fortuitous. Both were emblems of supernatural power.[72]

Both, too, were housed in special places. The shrine (*aedes*) of the standards was situated at the inmost part of the inmost building, the *principia* of a fort. It was approached with awe by soldiers delegated to sprinkle the standards with perfume, though Pliny the Elder found this a bit incongruous; 'the eagles and the standards, dusty as they are and bristling with sharp points, are anointed on holidays'. He also suspected that many men abused the honour by dousing themselves (*NH* XIII, 23). Incense, dim light and an atmosphere of solemn mystery characterised many a temple in the ancient world, not only those of the mystery cults, and with regard to the *signa* they may have helped the soldier to feel genuine religious awe as though he were visiting the shrine of a god. In May the standards were taken out and garlanded with roses for *Rosaliae Signorum* which corresponded to the *Rosalia* or *Rosaria*.[73] The *aedes* might contain, as we have seen, statues of the Emperor, and perhaps figures of deities. Below the *aedes* was the strong-room to deter would-be thieves from stealing with the fear of committing sacrilege, and also because the gods would surely defend such a spot with the greatest vigilance.

The presence of Mars Cocidius in the *aedes* at Bewcastle can be explained in two ways. It might reflect laxness of discipline, which we have seen was considered a problem in Hadrian's time, hence the invented cult of *Disciplina*. More probably it shows that, in a world where syncretism and religious diversity became ever more powerful, few people were concerned with which aspects were 'official' and which were not. Mars, for instance, was a central deity in military cults. Even the rather unattractive concept of Mars as the Avenger (*Ultor*) had its place in taking care of the soldier's anger, just as for the Emperor Augustus Mars Ultor had pursued both the Parthians who had humiliated the Roman army by capturing her standards, and also the murderers of Caesar. Soldiers invoked Mars under all sorts of aspects —

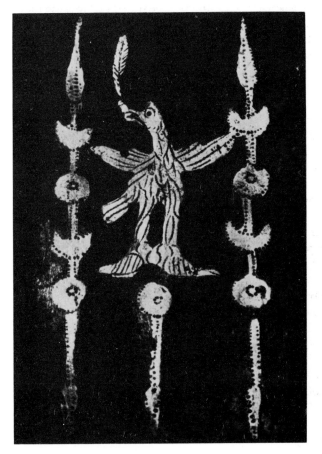

34 *Left* Gilt bronze inlay from iron sword-blade showing Eagle and Standards. South Shields, Co. Durham. Height 4.45 cm. Roman Fort and Museum, South Shields

35 *Below* Shrine of Minerva in a quarry face near Chester, *in situ*. Height 144.8 cm

Victor, Militaris, Ultor and Pater. That this veneration was heartfelt is shown by the frequent appearance of the god Mars on signet rings which soldiers wore, partly for use in signing documents and partly as protective amulets (see Chapter 7). It was not far from here to the many local epithets which were used by irregular formations, auxiliary regiments and even by legionaries, who do not appear to have been constrained in this by any rule-book.[75]

Much that we think of as official may not have been imposed by law but by custom. A clerk wherever he came from, finding a new home in the camp and especially in the office, might have turned quite naturally to the goddess who presided over writing and learning, Minerva. Minerva, indeed, was the goddess of crafts, as we saw when discussing the Chichester temple dedication. It was thus natural for soldiers of *Legio XX* engaged in quarrying near the Chester fortress to carve a little shrine for her in the rock face, where it still remains (**35**). This need have been no more an official act than the erection of a shrine to Vinotonus Silvanus by the prefect of the auxiliary unit stationed at Bowes (Chapter 3). Indeed, huntsmen responsible for producing a supply of fresh meat for their unit would also invoke Silvanus; Roman officers saw in Hercules, the mighty hero (who laboured under the protection of Minerva) and god, their exemplar in prowess and self-discipline (**36**). Fortuna guided Augustus, and sustained the triumph of the Roman armies, while as *Fortuna Redux* she brought the officer safe home to his Mediterranean birthplace. And of course, there were all the specialised *genii* of units, offices and military installations.[76] The religion of the army was not immune from change, outside the ceremonies listed in the Dura calendar. The influence of the East brought in Sol Invictus, who arrived in Italy at the battle of Bedriacum (AD 69) when legionaries from Syria are recorded as greeting the rising sun (Tacitus, *Hist.* III, 24). The Sun god became ever more important in the army as elsewhere during the third century. He, like Hercules, was *Invictus*, a bringer of Victory. Other foreign deities, too, especially Jupiter Dolichenus, sustained martial spirit.

Professor Ramsay MacMullen's denial that a state religion ever really existed must be set against the considerable quantity of evidence relating to the deification of emperors and the dominating place of the greater gods of Rome, especially Jupiter, in town and fort. In a formal sense, he may well be right, for departures from established custom were tolerated to an extent impossible in later times. Provided one was loyal to 'the gods', no power attempted to impose orthodoxy; a fanatic ruler such as Elagabalus or later Constantine, who made moves in that direction, stands out.

The Roman tradition provided a framework for the veneration of the gods, whether they were ancient deities from the East or Celtic nature-spirits. All were 'Romanised', along with architecture and dress, even language. The cults of native Gaul and Britain were civilised by adopting a Roman guise; many deities were equated with state gods such as Jupiter or Mars or Apollo, and with goddesses – Venus, Minerva, Diana. They were also bound to Rome through the custom of including the Emperor's *numen* or a reference to the Imperial Family, the *Domus Divina*, in dedications. In lieu of an imposed faith, it was the civic ceremony or the local councillors or government official – presenting an altar or arch to a native shrine, giving a sacrifice or even being seen to be present – that made the religious citizens of the Empire conscious of the amity between the state and the gods.

At its very least, a religious ceremony on a fort parade-ground or in front of a

36 *Opposite* Sandstone relief showing Minerva and Hercules. From Corbridge, Northumberland. Height 89 cm. Site Museum

Capitolium would provide the sort of comfort that men and women of different backgrounds feel at the Cenotaph on Remembrance Sunday or at the Coronation of a monarch, with the added prospect of a feast, a party. Certainly the search for closer relationships with the gods and for a more intellectually challenging faith went beyond this, but we should not forget that there was no hard and fast division between formal religion and the practice of private devotion, whether that was merely a feeling of rapport with Silvanus and Diana, deities of hunting, or wholehearted devotion to one of the gods from the East – Cybele, Serapis, Jupiter Dolichenus, Mithras or the outlandish serpentine Glycon. The Oriental deities influenced some Westerners, but only because they themselves had been brought into the system, adding their own strengths to the health and preservation of Emperor and Empire. It is to these new gods from the East that we must now turn.

5 Mithraism and the other Eastern Religions

What caused men in both the Western and the Eastern halves of the Roman Empire to look beyond simple contracts with the gods and aspire to a deeper, more personal relationship with them? Sometimes, no doubt, it was a matter of sudden conversion, inspired by dreams and visions. Frequently, emotional tensions and the anxiety of daily life will have stimulated the search for a divine protector. The lead tablets from Bath, Uley and elsewhere throw a little light on this, for although the link between the dedicator and the deity is still contractual, sometimes appeals to morality and the justice of the gods break through. Another step and we are in the world of Apuleius, the devotee of Isis, or of Aelius Aristides, who wrote of his close relationship with Asklepios. Greek physicians, for instance at Chester, may have felt something of the same commitment to Asklepios, Hygeia and Panakeia, the mighty Saviour gods (37).[1] P. Mummius Sisenna Rutilianus, legate of the Sixth Legion in the Hadrianic period, became increasingly superstitious and allowed himself at the age of about sixty when proconsul of Asia to ally himself with the bogus oracle, Alexander of Abonuteichos – literally, for he married Alexander's daughter, whose mother was said to be the moon. Lucian, in his satire, portrays Rutilianus as the very type of the 'superstitious man' of Theophrastus and the New Comedy, but it should be noted that official inscriptions from Tibur near Rome show that he took the rites of conventional religion seriously as a member of the college of augurs.[2]

Alexander's new religion was a combination of theurgy (direct communication with the god), magic and traditional belief, and most of the cults which we shall discuss in this chapter shared in its emotional appeal, sense of theatre and also the idea that 'true' knowledge was secret knowledge (*Gnosis*). The mysteries of Eleusis in Greece and of the Orphics and Pythagoreans were very ancient and there is some reason to think that in the West, the Druids claimed access to secret doctrine. Now in the Middle Empire increasing numbers of people amongst the educated and literate classes wanted to escape the whims of blind fate, control their own destinies and secure salvation through initiation.

In some respects Judaism and above all Christianity belonged to this category of religious experience, offering rebirth and happiness both in this world and the next. The essential difference is that – in theory at least – the Christian convert had to make a clean break with the traditional religion of his past, while for the Isiac or the Mithraist there was no clash between old and new; He just added any recent revelation to his store of religious experience.

All the new cults originated in the East and were transmitted to the West. As far

as we know, there was no similar attempt to spread Druidic doctrine in Greek-speaking lands, probably because it was theologically rather naive and closely integrated with the political and social culture of the Celts. The influence of indigenous American religion in Western Europe today is likewise negligible, while Buddhism and Hinduism have made a mark on the religious thought of at least the intellectual classes. This relentless flow of 'the Orontes into the Tiber' was due to the higher state of culture in the Greek world, the greater flexibility of the Greek language in the expression of abstract thought, and population movements. Easterners came to Italy and the further West as slaves (who generally achieved their freedom and stayed), as artists or merchants in search of fortune and also as soldiers. They often prospered and were often better able to afford to commemorate their gods than their Western contemporaries.

A long chapter devoted to a few minority religious groups may appear excessive, but it is justified. First, our brief must be to record evidence on religious practices in Britain wherever it exists, and wealth and literacy (the ability to commission sculpture and inscription) means that our knowledge of some mystery cults, above all Mithraism, is relatively abundant. Second, the Oriental cults are interesting in themselves. Third, the mystery cults inspired genuine conversion, and in that respect were forces for change. Christianity was especially active here.

37 Opposite Altar of red sandstone from Chester with dedication in Greek to Asklepios, Hygeia and Panakeia. From the Valetudinarium (?) at Chester. Height 61 cm. *Grosvenor Museum, Chester*

Mithraism in Roman Britain

The comparative rarity of the Eastern cults in the Western provinces however, does mean that some religions are more fully represented in one province than in another. As Britain had a large frontier army, Mithraism is better documented here than in Gaul; there is more evidence for the Magna Mater across the Channel, and far more Isiac monuments have been found in Roman Germany than here.[3] While there may sometimes be reasons for such distribution patterns (an influx of foreigners, close trading connections, the presence of soldiers transferred from the Danube region etc.), chance of discovery inevitably plays a part as well. Since the excavation of an important Mithraeum and its sculptures at a site in the valley of the Walbrook, London, Mithras has been one of the most familiar deities worshipped in Roman Britain – indeed the strangeness and dramatic intensity of his worship had struck the imaginations of Kipling and John Cowper Powys long before the 1954 discovery.[4] Mithraea were always fairly small, and in Britain, with the exception of the London evidence, and sculptures from a Mithraeum at York, mainly confined to extra-mural settlements on the frontier.[5] For the majority of the inhabitants of Roman Britain, the cult of Mithras must have been as strange, secret and exotic as it is to us.

Like all ancient religions, Judaism and Christianity excepted, the Mithras cult was tolerant of other deities. Sculptures and inscriptions showing or naming Olympian and Romano-Celtic deities are sometimes found in very close proximity to Mithraea as at Carrawburgh and the Trier Altbachtal. The wide range of sacred objects from the area of the London Mithraeum suggests that the same situation applied there.[6] Mithraism nevertheless has a distinctive character which sets it apart from most of the other Eastern cults. Devotion to Mithras, who was often addressed as 'The God', required the total and lifelong commitment of the believer, a commitment analogous to service in the army. This comparison was often made by friend and foe alike. The third grade of initiation (see below) was that of *Miles*, the soldier.[7]

The special character of Mithraism arises from its origins in Middle Asia, specifically in India and Iran. Mithras is invoked both in the Hindu *Vedas* and in the Persian *Avesta* as the god of light. However, he arrived in the Roman world already partially hellenised from a sojourn in the North-Western fringes of the former Achaemenid Empire. At first he made little impact on the Romans, despite the fact that the Cilician pirates defeated by Pompey and sold into slavery may have been Mithraists. In the following century, Nero entertained King Tigranes of Armenia, a believer in the old Persian religion devoted to the sun; solar worship had an enormous appeal to that Emperor who liked to think of himself as the sun on earth. The passage of merchants and slaves, diplomacy and religious conversion within the army (especially of troops stationed on the Danubian frontiers in South-eastern Europe) no doubt all played a part in preparing the ground for a remarkable expansion of the cult of Mithras in the second century, a spread which may be seen as an aspect of a growing thirst for spritual values in the Antonine Age.

The second and third centuries AD, insofar as any period has a distinctive character, are described as an 'Age of Anxiety'[8] though it is more fitting to call them an Age of Enquiry. The writings of the Isiac convert Apuleius and the Stoic Emperor Marcus Aurelius are good examples of this religious quest. (Unfortunately we have no Mithraic source of the literary standard of either.) Two examples of this, affecting both Mithraism and the other Oriental cults, were an introspective care for the individual soul and a growing interest in the unchanging Cosmos. Walter Pater's novel *Marius the Epicurean* is a sensitive reconstruction of such a spiritual Odyssey. The interest in the heavens is apparent in the presence of the Zodiac in some portrayals of Mithras, as well as for instance in the great cosmological mosaic at Merida in Spain.[9] The increased yearning for personal salvation is perhaps suggested in the change of burial rite from cremation to inhumation, though there is some dispute here (see Chapter 8). Certainly, the use of large sarcophagi made it much easier to expound eschatological beliefs.

Mithraism was a religion of 'Enthusiasm' and of 'Religious Theatre'. It concerned itself with a spiritual journey from obscure darkness to the most brilliant light; from death to eternal life; from chaos to order. Its practice required effort and discipline, and, as in Christianity, art was seen as a way of presenting intellectual ideas in a striking manner. This is fortunate, for little of the Mithraic scripture or liturgy survive, only a few lines painted on walls or cut in stone, and the rather hostile presentation of Christian apologists who wished to blacken the reputation of a rival religion.[10] Although the chances of survival mean that not all aspects of Mithraic mythology and doctrine can be illustrated from British sources, the main features of the cult are surprisingly clear even from these – clearer certainly than would be the case of Christianity if we were entirely dependent on the record of British finds to elucidate its nature and doctrine.

Mithras, as a god of light, was associated with Sol (the Sun god), to whom a Greek slave or freedman called Herion dedicated an altar carved with a bust of Sol holding a whip in the Housesteads Mithraeum.[11] The tauroctony (bull-slaying scene) from York shows a compact between Sol and Mithras, but other evidence suggests that the two deities were conflated as Sol Invictus Mithras; the most striking example is an altar in the Carrawburgh Mithraeum depicting on the front

38 *Opposite* relief showing *Mithras Saecularis* (restored). from Housesteads, Northumberland. Height 127 cm. *Museum of Antiquities, Newcastle upon Tyne*

39 Altar to Mithras dedicated by
L Sentius Castus. Rudchester,
Northumberland. Height 127 cm.
*Museum of Antiquities, Newcastle upon
Tyne*

a male solar deity, his crown of rays pierced in order to transmit the light of a fire behind.[12] Whether separate from the Sun or identified with him, Mithras was subordinate to the creator god *Ormazd* or *Ahura Mazda*, whose name is included on the reverse of a silver Mithraic amulet from Verulamium (93),[13] but he is rather a shadowy figure compared to his obvious Greek and Roman equivalents, Zeus and Jupiter.

The Mithraic cult, as an offshoot from Zoroastrianism, was dualistic. Mithras supported *Ormazd* in his conflict with the evil principle, the god of this aeon, Ariman. It is at first disconcerting to find a statue at York inscribed 'Volusius Irenaeus dedicates this to Arimanes freely and willingly in discharge of his vow',[14] but this is not simply a case of Satanism. Ariman is a winged figure with a snake-belt holding keys. It has been remarked that 'the sceptre of (Ariman's) rule, the keys of heaven, the wings of the wind – and the snake course of the Sun's progress – are the powers of destiny which the initiate must be trained by ordeal to meet, and overcome'.[15] Ariman, Lord of this aeon, and Zervan, the Eternal aeon, are not always easy to distinguish, but the figures of youths encircled by serpents from Merida and Modena,[16] and in the case of the latter surrounded by the zodiac, put us in mind of the figure of Mithras born from the Cosmic Egg, also within the ellipse of the zodiac at the Housesteads Mithraeum (38). Mithras as *Saecularis* (Lord of Ages) belongs to the present age and also to the future age of Ormazd.[17]

The Orphic concept of the Cosmic Egg found in the Housesteads sculpture could only have been propounded by a 'dedicator with advanced religio-philosophical leanings'.[18] An altar dedicated by Litorius Pacatianus, a *beneficiarius consularis* (a legionary detached for civil duties on the governor's staff) to *Deo Soli Invicto Mytrae Saeculari* is cut on the same type of stone as the 'Egg-birth'; so is the great tauroctony of which fragments remain (see below) and a statue of Cautes. These all belong to the original furnishing of the temple.[19] As a sort of civil servant, Pacatianus was no doubt something of an intellectual, the very type of person who would want to improve on the normal theology. At Housesteads his 'reform' appears to have lasted; a centurion, Publius Proculinus, also made a dedication to Mithras Saecularis, in the middle of the third century.[20]

A more usual version of the legend of the Birth of Mithras is that the young god leapt fully formed from the rock – the primal matter of the world. This event is possibly shown on the top of Sentius Castus' altar from Rudchester, though the relief is badly damaged (39).[21] Much clearer is the face of the Verulamium silver amulet, an adapted *denarius* of Augustus showing Tarpeia being crushed by shields whose legend has been erased. In large-scale representations of the rock-birth of Mithras from continental Mithraea, the great powers of creation such as Saturn and Oceanus are present. This provides a possible context for the marble statuette of a marine deity, possibly Oceanus, from the London temple. The very fine bust of Zeus Sarapis from the same site might well have been interpreted as Saturn, and it should be noted that a stucco Sarapis head was recovered in the excavation of the Santa Prisca Mithraeum, Rome.[22]

The central mystery of Mithraism, represented in all Mithraea and thus in a sense comparable with the crucifixion in Christianity, was the episode of Mithras' sacrifice of the great bull which Ormazd had created at the beginning of time. Just as Christ's death was a sacrifice made once and for all the salvation of man, so did Mithras' act assume a unique significance for the believer. From the blood of the bull sprang all life, both animal and vegetable, and so an apparent act of destruction was transformed into one of creation. All the essential features of the tauroctony (bull-slaying) are preserved in ex-voto reliefs from London and York, though only a few small fragments of the major carvings which would have stood in the apses of Mithraea are preserved from any British site, the most notable being, perhaps, the fragments from Housesteads.

Mithras first had to master the bull as he does in a scene on the front of Castus' Rudchester altar. He ultimately drags it back to a cave and leaps on to the back of the great beast, bending his left leg in a half-kneeling posture which we can trace back in Graeco-Roman art to images of Victories sacrificing bulls. Mithras' cloak billows out behind him to symbolise his great panache and energy. He holds a dagger in his right hand which he plunges into the bull's side, while a dog and serpent, symbolising the teeming creatures on the earth, lap its life-giving blood. Ariman, however, sends a scorpion which seeks to expunge fertility at its source by attacking the bull's genitals. Mithras is flanked by two companions: on the right Cautes with his torch raised and on the left Cautopates with torch lowered. Like Mithras, both wear Persian dress, notably trousers and a Phrygian cap. They represent the opposing attributes, light and dark, day and night, life and death, and hint at a theological dichotomy not far removed from the Christian concept of Judgement, Salvation and Perdition. In the Housesteads tauroctony (very fragmentary, though the largest piece of it is nearly six feet in height) only Cautes, part of the bull, the hound and Mithras' shoulder and right hand survive. The London ex-voto set up by Ulpius Silvanus, a veteran of the Second Legion, is however complete (**40**). It is surrounded by the Zodiac which Mithras as Saecularis, Lord of Ages, controls.

The form of all Mithraea corresponded to the cave in which the bull-sacrifice took place. Some were literally constructed underground, though those so far excavated in Britain are at best only partially sunk.[24] Mithraic temples needed to be near water for purposes of purification and even in the more or less ground-level temples at London (**41**) and Carrawburgh (**42**) flooding was a problem. Superficially the ground plans of Mithraea resemble those of Christian basilican churches, but the virtual absence of windows ensured that the interior effect was very different. Firmicius Maternus wrote of the Mithraists that 'they celebrate the mysteries of the Sun-god they call Mithras in hidden caves so that plunged in the concealing squalor of darkness they avoid the brightness and clarity of light' (*De errore profanarum religionum* 5, 2).

Maternus is referring to daylight; there is evidence for the use of artificial light, not only in the candlesticks from Carrawburgh and London and lamps from Rudchester[25] but more remarkably in niches cut into the backs of altars. The Sentius Castus altar at Rudchester has two *aediculae* in its back face, probably for lamps which would throw a soft gleam back onto the Tauroctony reredos. M. Simplicius Simplex's dedication at Carrawburgh portrays the Sun god with radiate crown pierced to beam forward light on the congregation. The form of the Housesteads relief of Mithras Saecularis, where the space immediately around the god is largely open, suggests that the image 'may have been intended to be seen against a light'. The burning of incense (indicated by an incense-burner at Rudchester and pine cones and incense shovel from Carrawburgh) would also have heightened the senses. Archaeological evidence thus suggests a highly theatrical style which is confirmed by what we know of Mithraic ceremonies.[26]

The raised benches in the aisles of Mithraea were used by initiates to recline upon at their feasts. Food-bones, especially those of chickens, have been found in temples, scattered around or placed in ritual deposits (e.g. at Carrawburgh and London). Evidently participants sometimes wore masks appropriate to each of the grades of initiation through which the aspirant hoped to rise through knowledge and ordeal, from the humble servant grade of Raven, through those of Bride, Soldier, Lion, Persian and Courier of the Sun to that of Father. A relief from Konjic in Yugoslavia depicts a feast in which servants with raven masks and others wearing lion-heads serve a meal to the higher grades in the community.[27] The evidence of this relief is confirmed by a fourth-century Christian author who writes of Mithraic feasts at which 'some flap their wings like birds and imitate the crowing of a raven whilst others roar like lions' (Pseudo-Augustine, *Quest Vet. et novi. Test.* P.L.34 Col.2214).[28]

Ceremonies were dramatic and memorable. They included temporary burial alive – the initiate had to pass through death to a new life. A coffin-like ordeal pit at Carrawburgh is thought to have been employed for this purpose. It is possible that a fire was lighted above it to provide an additional terrifying trial through heat.[29] The same idea is suggested by scenes shown in relief upon the lid of a

40 Marble relief of *Tauroctony* dedicated by Ulpius Silvanus, from the London Mithraeum. Height 43 cm. *Museum of London*

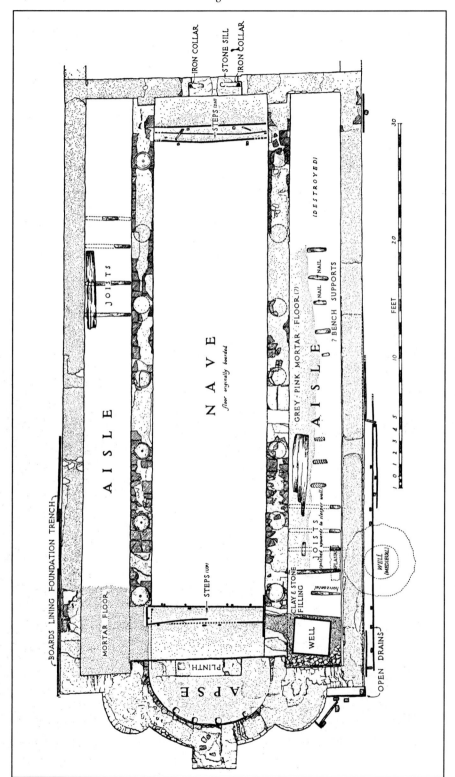

41 Plan of London Mithraeum. (Note that the apse is at the west end)

cylindrical silver casket from the London Mithraeum (**43**).[30] Apart from a wild beast fight (others are shown on the body of the box), we see a man emerging from a coffin-like chest. Two other chests are being assailed by winged griffins. Possibly in a literal sense they were decoys to capture these creatures which the Piazza Armerina mosaic – and for that matter the Barton Court and Woodchester pavements – show as winged felines as real as the lions and panthers which accompany them. Symbolically they are agents of death, and the man emerging from the 'coffin' has survived his ordeal and escaped from the danger of destruction. The same theme occurs (in a non-Mithraic context) on a fourth-century mosaic at Brading (Chapter 10).

The casket contained a strainer or infusor. Strainers of more normal form have been found in the fourth-century Christian treasure at Water Newton and in the late Roman pagan treasure at Thetford, and were probably used for straining the lees from wine, used sacramentally. This may have been the way in which the Walbrook strainer was used, but it is unusually deep. Ralph Merrifield has suggested to me that it could have been employed to infuse a concoction of herbs,

42 The Temple of Mithras at Carrawburgh, Northumberland

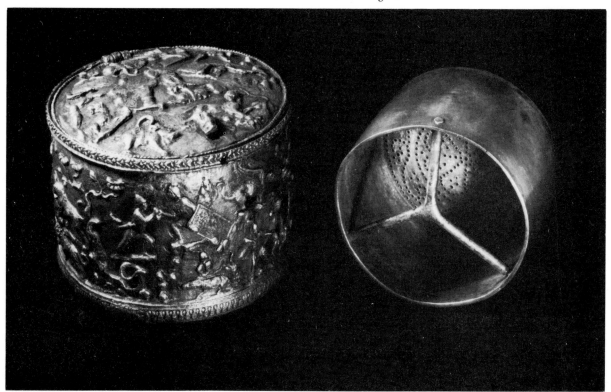

43(a) Silver-gilt canister and infusor
from the London Mithraeum.
Height 6.3 cm; diam. 8 cm. *Museum
of London*
43(b) *Right* Lid of canister

perhaps hallucinogenic in nature. However, spiced wine was very popular in the Roman world, and pottery infusors for making it are known. They include an example from Silchester, and another from a grave at Litlington near Cambridge, where it was employed in the funerary cult (Chapter 8). The trifurcate handle of the Walbrook strainer is paralleled on *modii* for corn, and certainly points to the measuring out of a fixed substance.[31] Zoroastrian ceremonies centred around the production and consumption of the *Haoma*, and this or its equivalent may have played a large part in Mithraism too.[32]

By their very nature, such consumable substances leave little or no trace. Honey, for instance, was used for ritual ablutions instead of water by the grade of Lions. Porphyry tells us that 'when those who are being initiated as Lions have honey instead of water poured over their hands to cleanse them, then are the hands kept pure of all evil, all crime and all contamination, as is right for an initiate' (*de antro nympharum* C, 15).[33]

Little of the liturgy itself survives. The Santa Prisca Mithraeum has interesting texts painted on its walls. One line, for instance, reads 'And you saved us after having shed the eternal blood' or 'the blood which grants eternity'.[34] This doctrine, as we have seen, is central, but it may be compared with the beliefs of other cults, Christianity obviously and, as we shall see, that of the Magna Mater: The inscription on the base of a marble group from the Walbrook Mithraeum is inscribed *Hominibus Bagis Bitam*, (**49**) possibly fourth century in date and certainly from a fourth-century context, refers to Liber-Bacchus who may have been worshipped here in place of Mithras after the Constantinian disruption and so is not necessarily relevant to Mithraism.[35] In its turn this may be compared to a 'magical' papyrus cited by John Ferguson which exclaims 'O Lord! I have been born again and pass away in exaltation. In exaltation I die. Birth that produces life brings me into being and frees me for death.'[36]

Another line mentioned by Tertullian is recalled by the simple dedication *Deo*, 'to the god', within a wreath, on Sentius Castus' altar. 'When the Soldier is being initiated in the cave '(i.e. the Mithraeum)', Tertullian writes, '. . . a wreath offered to him on the point of his sword and then placed on his head must be pushed off . . . with the words that Mithras alone is his wreath' (*De corona* 15).[37] It is interesting that Tertullian tells us that a soldier who is a Mithraist refused garlands and decorations such as the Roman army delighted to bestow[38] and says that 'it rests in his god'. This shows that complete conformity of religion was not demanded by the military authorities and that, as also in the case of Judaism, the sensibilities of a *religio licita* were respected.

Unlike Judaism, however, there was no ban on the worship of the Olympian and local gods. Thus L. Caecilius Optatus, tribune of *Cohors I Vardullorum* at High Rochester dedicated a Mithraeum to 'the unconquered god' and 'Comrade of the Sun', as well as inscribing an altar to 'Minerva and the Genius of the Guild' and being associated in a dedication to the local god Matunus.[39] Cocidius was welcomed into the Housesteads Mithraeum, a mother-goddess at Carrawburgh, while Minerva, Sarapis (perhaps identified with Ormazd) and Mercury (Protector of the first grade that of the Raven – he seems to be conflated with Cautes on the Housesteads tauroctony) as well as a Genius are amongst the marbles from the Walbrook Mithraeum. That temple incidentally provides the sole evidence from Britain of the Danubian Riders venerated in Dacia and Moesia. Presumably the marble roundel which depicts them was presented by an officer from this region.[40]

Mithraism was a sophisticated cult – its theology was probably as complex as that of Christianity and, had it survived, we might imagine there would have been controversies over the relation of Mithras to Ormazd and to the aeons as heated and obscure as the Trinitarian debates in Christianity. The weakness of the cult may be seen very clearly from the British remains. Mithraic cells were very small. The London Mithraeum, 18.3 metres long and 7.6 metres wide was exceptionally large for such a temple; the Carrawburgh Mithraeum at 7.9 metres by 5.5 metres was perhaps more typical.[41] The inscriptions suggest that they drew their congregations from a relatively narrow segment of society. Army officers from the rank of centurion (in a legion) upwards are most prominent.[42] They were the same people to whom the god and hero Hercules appealed (Chapter 4). Indeed one of the Labours of Hercules was the mastering of the Cretan Bull and the parallel may not have been lost on them.[43] As far as Mithraea outside forts are concerned, it is likely that they owed their foundation and continued support to particular officers. This does raise the problem of continuity as commands changed, but it is not unlikely that membership of a Mithraeum was keenly sought and any vacancies would soon be filled. Mithraism fulfilled a deep need for the soldier who needed the bosom comradeship of other men in his unit when exposed to the hardships and dangers of life on the frontier.

Even the London Mithraeum may have had a strong military element, drawn from the Governor's guard stationed in the Cripplegate fort, though here some of the fine marbles may have been brought from Italy by civilian merchants. As the large number of Mithraea at Ostia shows, Mithraism appealed to merchants as well as soldiers. For them the masonry element, with its stress on probity in financial transactions and the probability of finding a warm welcome from fellow believers in trading ports all over the empire would have been a great comfort.

The spread of Mithraism was only limited by the exclusion of women. This did not matter much at first in army circles where celibacy was encouraged, but as time went on unofficial unions, *de facto* marriages, meant that there were large numbers of women around the forts and Mithraism did nothing for their spiritual needs. Male exclusiveness put an even greater check on its spread in towns. London was an *emporium* with empire-wide links, but what of more ordinary towns? The Leicester 'Mithraeum' is doubtful (and may have been a *schola*, or the shrine of some other deity such as Bacchus). We have little other evidence – the Verulamium amulet is a portable object, and may have been dropped by a passing traveller.

While Christians were nowhere numerous enough in the age of Constantine to attack pagan religion as a whole, the very small number of the soldiers of the Persian god whose rites seemed Satanic parodies of Christian rituals (Justin., *Apolog.* i, 66) were easy targets. Archaeology can tell us something of its melancholy and apparently early end in Britain. The occasion, at least in London, might have been a visit to Britain by Constantine in AD 312 or 314. Here the great tauroctony was smashed, the marble head of Mithras being beheaded with a pole-axe; an axe-cut on the side of the neck is suggestive evidence.[44] It is true that the community was able to conceal the head and other sculptures as well as some of the temple plate (the canister and strainer, and a plate), but none of this was recovered when the crisis passed and although the temple was restored to paganism, it may well have been re-dedicated to Bacchus.

At Carrawburgh the principal sculptures were again destroyed or damaged beyond repair.[45] Little of the tauroctony remains, and figures of Cautes and Cautopates were deliberately broken. The altars remained, but even a Christian prefect might have been reluctant to destroy dedications made by his predecessors; it could be bad for discipline and against service *ésprit de corps*. We may recall that funerary effigies (the personal monuments of families) survived in English churches through Reformation and Commonwealth when religious statuary was torn down. It takes a revolutionary situation, such as that in France at the end of the eighteenth century, to attempt to blot out the memory of an *ancien régime* by rooting out family monuments as well as religious images. At Housesteads and Rudchester the story was the same; the religious statuary destroyed and the altars spared.

It is possible that evidence for Mithraism in the last century of Roman Britain will yet be found, for Mithras was favoured by the Emperor Julian (as were Atys and many other Saviour-gods) and remained popular in conservative circles in Rome down to the reign of Theodosius, but he is only attested here from the mid-second century to the early fourth century. It was a time when the Empire as a whole faced some dark days – inflation, usurpation, plague and invasion. The lot of the soldier and the merchants were not always pleasant. We may reflect that Britain's comparative security owed something at least to the inspiration given to her officers by this Persian god of light. In *Puck of Pook's Hill*, Kipling seems to have caught something of the idealism, mysticism and emotional piety of the cult of Mithras:

> Mithras, God of the Midnight, here where the great bull dies,
> Look on thy children in darkness. O take our sacrifice!
> Many roads Thou has fashioned: all of them lead to the Light,
> Mithras, also a soldier, teach us to die aright.

Cybele, Isis, Bacchus and Other deities

Amongst the other major Eastern cults, apart from Christianity, none had the same secret character. Cybele had been a Roman state deity from the end of the third century BC and her festivals (with those of her consort Atys) were noisy and public. Similarly, the cult of Isis entailed vast crowds, processions and high pomp. Like Mithras, however, these deities appealed to the emotions and offered salvation. So did the wine god, whether celebrated as Liber, Bacchus or Dionysos. He is generally regarded as a regular member of the Graeco-Roman pantheon, but this was not always the view in antiquity, when he was often believed to come from the East and specifically from India. His devotees indulged in extraordinary wild orgies and as early as 186 BC there was an attempt to suppress him in Rome and Italy, an attempt inevitably doomed to failure. As a saviour-god he will be considered here.

The presence of several other deities – Jupiter of Doliche, Jupiter of Heliopolis (Baalbek), Herakles of Tyre and Astarte – indicates no more than that gods travelled as well as men in the Roman Empire. Their worship has nothing much in common with the saviour-deities. Sol, the sun god, appears in many forms and we have already met him as an army deity (Chapter 4) and in association with the Mithraic cult, but he must also be considered as an indicator of the progress of Eastern Syncretism, especially in the third century. He prepared the way for Christianity. That religion itself has already been discussed by Professor Charles Thomas and the main question to which we shall address ourselves is how it compares with other Eastern cults, and where it differs from them in theology, practice and period of *floruit*.

The Great Mother of Pessinus in Asia Minor, otherwise known as Cybele, was brought to Rome in the third century, as we have seen (Chapter 2). In April, a great celebration was held in her honour. Ovid sets the scene: 'Eunuchs will march and thump their hollow drums, and cymbals clashed on cymbals will give out their tinkling notes; seated on the unmanly necks of her attendants, the goddess herself will be borne with howls through the streets in the city's midst' (*Fasti* IV, 183–7). The rites of Cybele spilled over from the city into the countryside and through the Roman provinces. A great mother goddess with fertility powers like Ceres and also a function of Mistress of Beasts equating her with Diana was quite acceptable to Roman tastes, as well as to Gaulish ones. It is under such a guise that we find the image of the Berecynthian Mother still being paraded through the fields near Autun as late as the sixth century AD (Gregory of Tours, *Liber in Gloria Confessorum* LXXVI).

The only document from Britain which expresses this depth of veneration is a poem set up and probably written by a tribune, Marcus Caecilius Donatianus at Carvoran. The poem (in iambic *senarii*) identifies her with the Empress Julia Domna, but it is no mere empty rhetoric. Religious enthusiasm and loyalty gush forth from the poem as well as loyalty to the regime. There is also a theogeny which shows that Cybele, like Isis, claimed universal sovereignty, '... she is the Mother of the Gods, Peace, Virtue, Ceres, the Syrian Goddess, weighing life and laws in her balance'.[46]

The dark side of her myth was less explicable to Roman taste, at least at first. Her paramour, Atys, driven to remorse and madness for infidelity towards her, castrated himself in her service, and the priesthood known as *Galli* were in their turn eunuchs. In one of his greatest poems, Catullus finally expresses his distaste and horror at this self-mutilation: 'Great Goddess, Goddess Cybele, Goddess who reigns on Didyme, keep far from my house your fury. Dare others to ecstasy, make others mad' (Catullus, *Carmen* LXIII). By the fourth century, the horror had given way to admiration amongst devoted pagans like the Emperor Julian, who wrote a hymn to the Mother of the Gods in which he spoke of the act of *eviratio* as 'a holy and inexpressible harvest' (Julian, *Oratio* V, 168 D).

The day on which the aspirant *Galli* castrated themselves was known as *Dies Sanguinis* and corresponded to 24 March. We are led to believe by Catullus and others that only the most primitive tools were used, a flint or a potsherd, but by the time of the Empire help may sometimes have been at hand to staunch the flow of blood, Farmers were adept at gelding their horses, and examples of clamps used by them for the purpose have been found at various places including Chichester in Britain; they are also depicted in a relief at Aix.[47]

An example in bronze was found in the Thames by London Bridge. It is elaborately ornamented with busts of Cybele and Atys as well as the busts of the deities of the week and the protomes of horses, bulls and lions (44).[48] Possibly it was

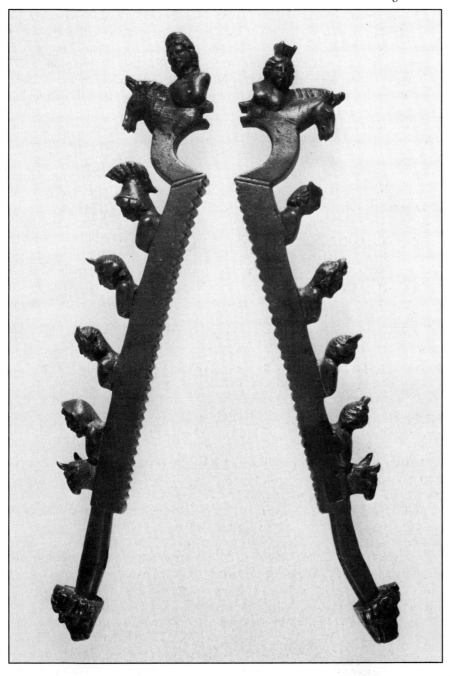

44 Bronze castration-clamp ornamented with busts of Cybele, Atys and other deities. From London. Height 29 cm. *British Museum*

used for removing the *vires* of bulls and rams, but it is equally likely that it was employed on men. The ornamentation suggests that it was a highly valued item of cult insignia, and the fact that it was found in the river indicates either that it was seized by angry Christians in the fourth century or that devotees of Cybele and Atys dropped it from the bridge to prevent its falling into Christian hands – more probably the former as the clamp appears to have suffered deliberate damage. A

45 Sculpture of Atys (?) in oolitic limestone, from Southwark. Height 73.5 cm

bronze figurine of Atys wearing short tunic and trousers, open at the front to reveal the *vires*, was found nearby.[49]

The site of the London temple is unknown. Three sculptures showing a youthful huntsman wearing a Phrygian cap have been found at different sites – at Bevis Marks in the East, by Goldsmiths' Hall in the West and at Southwark (45). It is probable, but not certain, that Atys is intended.[50] Service to Atys did not always take the drastic form described above. Guilds of 'tree-bearers', *dendrophori*, also played a part in his worship while at the same time acting as burial associations. The double role is logical, for after his mutilation Atys dies, is laid to rest and resurrected (on the *Hilaria*). A beaker from a cemetery at Dunstable was inscribed for the *dendrophori* of Verulamium, where it is possible that the so-called Triangular Temple was at Metroon associated with the cult, though evidence here is circumstantial. For instance cones of Italian pine recall the tree under which Atys died (See Chapter 6). At the festival of *Arbor Intrat* (the Entry of the Tree) on 22 March, a pine tree decked with purple ribbons symbolising blood was carried into the temple by the *dendrophori*. Part of a statuette, a hand holding a pine-branch, was found at the Hockwold (Sawbench) temple site. It probably depicted Atys and is suggestive of the god being venerated here in a 'native' shrine.[51]

A ceremony associated with the cult in the Imperial period was the *taurobolium* – bathing in the blood of a bull sacrificed on a slatted floor over a pit in which stood the worshipper who had paid for the sacrifice, eager to receive the blood, the principle of life all over his body. There is no evidence as yet for *taurobolia* in Britain (nor for the ram sacrifices or *criobolia* although they are well attested in Gaul, unless the ox-skull buried behind the altar in the court of the triangular temple at Verulamium was the remains of such a sacrifice (79).[52]

The cult of Isis originated in Egypt and retained much of its ancient Pharaonic character and mythology. Its central figure is a Mother Goddess, Isis, who suckles a baby son Harpokrates, who, like Mithras, is a heroic figure when he grows to manhood: He then avenges the death of his father Osiris (in the Graeco-Roman world Sarapis or Serapis) killed and dismembered by the evil god Seth and restored to life by Isis. The triad represented the supreme power of creation, ruling all and restoring life to the earth. Osiris who had died and been restored to life was regarded as an underworld god. The cult attracted devotees, effectively converts, amongst the highest ranks of society. They included Plutarch, author of a book on *Isis and Osiris*, and Apuleius who recorded his experiences in *The Golden Ass*. Another even more eminent Roman who was attracted to Isis was the Emperor Domitian, though in his case adherence to the Isiac cult was little more than gratitude; the priest of Isis had sheltered him in Rome during a dangerous riot which took place in AD 69 during the struggle with Vitellius. He eventually escaped disguised as a young devotee (Suetonius, *Domitian* 1; cf. Tacitus, *Hist.* III, 74). It does seem, however, that very many of the adherents of Isis were Egyptians or other Orientals, and the spread of the cult in late Julio-Claudian and Flavian times was due as much as anything to the large number of Easterners who came to the West at this time.[53]

The only certain Iseum yet recorded in Britain was in London, though the site is unknown. A jug, 'which would normally be dated before c AD 75', is said to have been found in Tooley Street, Southwark, though it probably comes from elsewhere in Southwark or London. It is inscribed with a graffito, *Londini ad Fanum Isidis*, which I see no reason to doubt.[54] The complete state of this vessel suggests careful concealment; if not derived from a burial it may have been placed in the *favissa* (repository for worn-out religious objects) because it was no longer suitable to contain holy water for aspersion in Isiac ritual. Purification by water (supposedly Nile water) played a significant part in the rites, and Isis is often figured with holy-water bucket (*situla*) and rattle (*sistrum*), for example upon a red jasper intaglio from Wroxeter long regarded as lost but recently rediscovered.[55] The other major find from London is an altar, re-used in the foundations of the late Roman riverside wall at Blackfriars, which records the restoration of a temple of Isis — perhaps the same temple — by a third-century governor of Upper Britain, Marcus Martiannius Pulcher.[56]

Other evidence for Isis in London is portable. It consists of a bronze figurine of the seated goddess, previously identified as Demeter, a bronze steelyard weight and a bust of Isis on the head of a bone hairpin. In each case the goddess is identified by her distinctive knot of hair. Two figurines of the child Harpokrates have also been found in London. One is of bronze, the other of silver and both show him with his right hand raised to his lips in a gesture commanding silence. Initiates must not reveal the mysteries. The bronze figure also shows him holding the *cornucopia* (horn of plenty) of Isis while the silver figurine reveals its owner's syncretistic manner of thought; the little god is winged, that is, conflated with Cupid, god of Love. In one myth Cupid is bound, and it is interesting that Harpokrates-Cupid is hung with gold chains. Does this indicate that the victory of God entails suffering? Animals (a dog, tortoise and bird) around him reveal that like Orpheus and Apollo he is Lord of created beings.[57] The figurine was worn as an amulet and we may note that Pliny (*NH* XXXIII, 41) tells us that images of Harpokrates were already employed as devices on the bezels of rings in his time.

Isis' consort Serapis, the Graeco-Roman equivalent of Osiris, was presumably venerated in the London Iseum. A splendid head of the god was of course found in the Walbrook Mithraeum. He certainly had a temple to himself at York, in the *colonia*, a building at Toft Green. It had an apse at one end, and perhaps a mosaic pavement, though it is imperfectly recorded and the details of the plan are uncertain. Luckily the foundation inscription was found, saying that the temple was built at the order of the Legate of the Sixth Legion, an oriental with the name Claudius Hieronymianus, who was in York in the second half of the second century (**46**). By the reign of Severus he was *praeses* of Cappadocia where he was a persecutor of Christians; so the York Serapeum cannot have been built in order to satisfy the enthusiasm that Emperor had for Serapis.[58] Outside London and York, great trading centres, where easterners were in evidence, there are few certain pointers to the cult. The best is a head of Serapis sculpted in Portland stone, found in Silchester and from the same workshop as the Tutela. It may have come from a temple of the Egyptian gods as yet unlocated, but Serapis was widely venerated in the Empire as a deity of merchants for he presided over the rich cornlands of Egypt. A third explanation is that it might be a civic compliment to Septimus Severus (if the head can really be so late). The fragment of an alabaster vessel from Silchester (*insula* VII), and another from Caerwent, have been identified as containers for Nile water. It is tempting to associate them with the Isis Cult although Nile water was also used by the Egyptians, at any rate, as a para-medical drug.[59] A tiny figurine, worn as an amulet, was excavated in the Chester amphitheatre; it shows Harpokrates and reminds us once again of Pliny's observation. The presence of easterners, notably Greek doctors, at Chester is certain, but a similar amulet-figurine from the Romano-Celtic temple at Woodeaton presumably shows a devotee of the Egyptian deities visiting a Romano-Celtic deity (a gold lamella inscribed *Adonaie* shows that another votary of an Eastern deity came to the temple at some time). This is the place to mention a little bronze head of Jupiter from the Romano-Celtic cache of regalia discovered near Felmingham Hall, Norfolk. It is provided with a crescent on his head and an aureole of solar rays and has been taken to represent Helio-Serapis, a conflation of the Sun god with Serapis. In the absence of the familiar corn-measure this is unlikely, but just as Serapis was a syncretistic creation of Ptolemaic times so now in the Imperial period similar complex religious ideas are to be seen at work in the West – at Felmingham Hall, perhaps in a shrine of the Celtic Jupiter Taranis. Oriental influences cannot be ruled out even in rural Britain. A bronze standard head depicting Serapis has been found at Flobecq in Belgium, and possibly the discovery of such an object may one day suggest the presence somewhere of a temple of Isis in the British countryside.[60]

For the most part, the cult of Isis and Serapis remained exotic in Britain, with a particular attraction to (Eastern?) women. A haematite Graeco-Egyptian amulet discovered in excavations near a Roman villa at Welwyn, Hertfordshire, can best be

46 Dedication of Serapeum at York. Length 91.4 cm. *Yorkshire Museum*

explained as the possession of an Eastern slave-girl. It figures Isis as a protective goddess against the evil forces which imperilled child-birth. The material of the gem, the type of amulet, and the Greek lettering of the spells all point to the East.[61]

Converts there may have been. Certainly Ammianus Marcellinus mentions an Alamannic chieftain called Serapio (Ammianus XVI, 12, 25) whose father had been a hostage in Gaul and had been taught certain Greek mysteries. Consequently he 'changed his son's original native name of Agenarichus to that of Serapio'. Evidence for the Egyptian cults is certainly stronger in Germany than in Britain, but for the passing stranger there was much to impress in an Egyptian sanctuary; first of all the distinctive plans of Egyptian temples, very lofty even in their Classical guise, their courtyards not infrequently containing figures of animal-headed deities and ornamented with nilotic paintings; artistically all very reminiscent of Chinoiserie in eighteenth-century England. Even more unusual were the chants of the priests. Their normal invocations to the gods might be interspersed with other euphonious sounds, like the intoning of the seven vowels (which are indeed engraved on the back of an amulet said to be from Colchester) and of course the rattle of *sistra*. The priests themselves, celibate and white-robed to indicate purity, carried in procession sacred regalia including jugs of Nile water for lustrations, – real (see above) or supposed – and posies of flowers. The gentle and mainly bloodless character of the ritual and the high moral tone of the faith impressed many of the best minds of the Roman world.

Quantitatively, the cult's significance can be over-stressed; qualitatively it deserves our interest and sympathy, as does Buddhism in the West today. It was the religion of prayer and praise, with a litany at least as rich as early Christianity, whose ceremonies employed incense and flowers, light and joyful celebration, for Isis controlled Fate and promised salvation.[62] Both Isis and Serapis were accorded unique status by their devotees. Isis herself, in the lovely Theogeny which Apuleius puts in her mouth, says, 'I am she that is the natural mother of all things, mistress and governess of all the elements ... At my will the planets of the sky, the wholesome winds of the seas, and the lamentable silences of hell be disposed; my name, my divinity is adored throughout all the world, in divers manners, invariable customs, and by many names' (*Metamorphoses* XI). Sarapis' acclamation: ΕΙS ΖΕΥC CΑΡΑπΙC – one Zeus Sarapis! an amazing claim to transcendance, which as a formula looks forward to Christianity, is to be found on a gem from Castlesteads (Chapter 7, (**87**)).[63]

Bacchus was much better known to Romans and to most Romanised Britons. He is the theme of many works of art, some of which certainly have a religious significance. For instance a standing Bacchus is carved in relief upon the altar of Sulis Minerva at Bath, together with Apollo, Hercules, Jupiter and other deities. A very large Corinthian capital from Cirencester is inhabited by Bacchic figures (**47**). There is a bust of the god himself, two representative members of his band of followers or *thiasos* (Silenus and a maenad) and an adversary defeated through his power, Lycurgus. (The maenad Ambrosia was victim of Lycurgus' importunate advances and prayed to Bacchus for deliverance. Bacchus metamorphosed her into a vine whose tendrils strangled her pursuer.) The Cirencester capital is thought to have been part of a Jupiter column, the commonest type of votive column in the North-West provinces. It does seem a little strange that Jupiter should have stood upon a column, the imagery of whose capital is so clearly connected with another deity but we may note that Bacchus was also shown on the shaft of a column at Wroxeter which displays the surface of scales characteristic of known Jupiter columns. The handle of a silver patera included with others from Capheaton, Northumberland (probably the silver plate of a temple) is ornamented in relief with a female bust (possibly Juno), Mercury seated within an aedicula, a river god, a water nymph and Bacchus with Ariadne (48). The other Capheaton paterae feature Hercules and Minerva (8), both saving powers, as well as Concordia(?) holding a military standard. It is thus evident that Bacchus-Dionysus had a secure place in the Graeco-Roman pantheon and his frequent presence as a companion of other Olympians need occasion no surprise.[64]

Bacchus was a saviour god who had indeed rescued Ariadne after her abandonment by Theseus on the Isle of Naxos (a scene shown on an altar from Bath) before making her his consort, and who had himself burst asunder the strongest chains when he was bound by his enemies. While we may identify him in some of his aspects with an old Italian god, Liber, he was viewed also as an Eastern Saviour who had come in triumph from India. Thus he rides a tiger or a panther and bears a staff, tipped by a pine cone and hung with ribbons (*thyrsus*) which was carried in procession as a mighty fertility – and self-evidently phallic – symbol. His

47 Capital from votive column (?) showing Bacchic figures. Cirencester. Height 106 cm. *Corinium Museum*

cantharus (wine chalice) designates both physical and spiritual refreshment. As we have seen, the Walbrook Mithraeum was probably taken over by his followers in the fourth century. The little statuary group showing Bacchus with a serpent, a Satyr, a Silenus, and a Maenad with its inscribed base acclaiming the god as the giver of (eternal) life to wandering men (**49**) has been dated as early as the third century AD, but its archaeological context at any rate is later and like the statuette of Bacchus from a grave at the Spoonley Wood villa (**84**), it will find a place in our discussion of late pagan spirituality (Chapter 10).

It is difficult to distinguish individual devotees because of the absence of inscriptions. Did the little silver openwork plaque from London showing Bacchus standing beside his panther (**50**), or the Leadenhall Street mosaic depicting Bacchus riding upon a panther indicate a prominent body of worshippers in the capital or merely acknowledge the fact that Bacchus was the deity of drinking parties and of emotional freedom? Even if the latter was the case, we may still count the cult of Bacchus as significant amongst the 'Eastern religions', for it was the means whereby many men were brought into contact with spiritual self-discovery and regeneration (just as the inhabitants of Roman Italy in the second century BC were confronted with it).[65]

The difficulty of fitting all the Eastern gods into a single category is demonstrated when we turn to Jupiter Dolichenus and his consort Juno Regina.

48 *Opposite* Silver patera handle showing Bacchus, Ariadne and other deities. From Capheaton, Northumberland. Length 14.3 cm. *British Museum*

49 Marble statuette showing Bacchus with his *thiasos*. Inscribed *Hominibus Bagis Bitam*. From the London Mithraeum. Height 34.25 cm. *Museum of London*

The ancient Hittite sky-god had an especial appeal to the officer class in the Roman army, especially amongst those from the North-east (Danubian) provinces, a region also prominent in the dissemination of Mithraism. Like Mithras, Dolichenus was a soldier-god – he even dressed like a Roman officer – but his cult was less complex. His worshippers seem to have made a particular virtue of associating him with other deities.[66] Part of a frieze from a *Dolicheneum* at Corbridge depicts the Sun-god, one of the Dioscuri and Apollo, while an inscription from the same site associates him with Caelestis Brigantia, the latter a Severan official creation (see Chapter 9).[67]

In this connection it is interesting to note the frequent connection of Jupiter Dolichenus with the health and safety of the Emperor and his family. Although not an official cult, the Dolichene religion certainly fostered loyalty and the very fact that the god was equated with I.O.M. – Jupiter Optimus Maximus – is highly significant. Not many worshippers would ponder on whether a sacrifice was a state rite as laid down in the military feriale or merely a private affair ordered by the commanding officer of the unit.[68]

From sculptural and epigraphic remains in Britain it seems that the worshippers of Dolichenus had a largely contractual relationship with their god and this is confirmed by the finds of silver leaves from Mauer an der Url (Noricum), analogous to those used by 'ordinary' religious cults in the Roman West, although as we shall see, there is one instance – at Water Newton in Britain – where silver-gilt 'leaves' were offered to Christ.[69]

The god, however, kept a tight rein on his worshippers, and the presence of such phrases as *iussu dei* on the Corbridge inscription, *ex iussu* at Piercebridge, *monitu* at Caerleon and perhaps *ex responsu* at Ribchester are typical of a cult which saw Jupiter Dolichenus as the divine reflection of the earthly Emperor.[70] Alas, the cult was too earthbound. It was too much associated with the Severan emperors to escape eclipse under the dour reaction of Maximinus Thrax, and the sack of the chief sanctuary of the cult at Doliché by the Persians in 253 or 256 was a mortal blow. A god who could not protect himself and his followers could hardly survive unscathed.[71]

50 Silver plaque in openwork (*opus interrasile*) showing Bacchus with his panther. Found in London. Height 3.6 cm. *Museum of London*

The Sun, Christianity and the Saviour-Cults

No such fate could affect the Sun, who rose each day, undiminished and unconquered – Invictus. As we have seen, the Mithraists made him their own but they could not monopolise such a universal source of light and life. The cult was given particular encouragement by third-century emperors (Chapter 9), and it has been suggested that the Sun-cult influenced the practice of orientation in burials – where the body of the deceased was laid East-West so that he could arise and face the rising sun on the day of resurrection. Certainly Christianity could not displace the birthday of the Sun – itself attached to the very ancient festival of the Winter Solstice – from the Roman Calendar, and it became Christ's natal day. Christmas, in the depth of Winter, answers to the hope of all men for the return of Spring.[72]

With regard to Christianity little need be added to Professor Thomas's account.[73] It is hard to view this religion except through the hindsight of history, but it is worth making the effort in order to imagine what sort of faith it would have seemed to be to a neutral observer in the time of Constantine. At the beginning of the fourth century it had found favour with the Emperor and the Roman state after years of desultory hostility and persecution, but it was very far from being the religion of the majority. In order to sense something of the spiritual environment of Christianity at this time, it would help to imagine ourselves transported to India, where a major polytheistic system (Hinduism) survives intact, and where churches containing images of Christ and the Virgin are in a tiny minority against the many temples of the gods and goddesses. Christianity remains an intrusive influence, even though it has been present in places almost as long as it has been in Britain.

Triumphant Christendom rewrote history; just as the Jews had been God's chosen instrument, so now had He given power and dominion to His Church. Even to non-Christians, a picture of the Middle Ages invokes thoughts of abbeys, friaries, cathedrals, scholasticism and (more sinister) the Crusades, ecclesiastical bigotry and religious persecution. It is salutary to remember that in India, sculptures of the twelfth, thirteenth and fourteenth centuries depict the traditional deities such as Vishnu and Shiva and the goddess Parvati, cousins of the Graeco-Roman gods which it is the task of this volume to study.[74] In one way Jesus of Nazareth was unlike Atys or Mithras. He had lived in the recent past as a Jewish teacher in Judea, and had been executed by crucifixion as a trouble-maker. In his human role he could be compared with certain pagan philosophers and magicians such as Apollonius of Tyana. However, according to his followers he was conceived in the union of his Virgin Mother and the Holy Ghost, rose from the dead and as Christ was manifest as an avatar of God.

The theme of death and resurrection was central to many cults, including the Eleusinian mysteries and the cult of Atys. It was natural for men to observe that after the 'death' of winter, life was renewed each spring. The Jewish Passover from which the Christian Easter originated, was a festival held at this time marking the end of bondage in Egypt and the renewal of God's Covenant with Israel. Like its parent religion, Christianity remained monotheistic and attached to scriptures which demonstrated that God manifested himself to his people through personal dialogue. In addition, Christians believed he had revealed himself in the person of Christ, 'His only begotten Son', and had given them a revised covenant.

The Church was of course, in origin, an offshoot from Judaism, and much of its early spread was amongst communities of the Diaspora. Although there is as yet no direct evidence for Judaism in Roman Britain, the name of one of the two martyrs at Caerleon named by Gildas (*De Excid. Brit.* 10) is Aaron, and that may be significant.[75] For all that the resurrection of Christ could be seen in entirely Jewish terms with Christ as the new Adam, it was inevitable that gentile converts would introduce the symbols of their own world. The death of Atys or Adonis must have readily come to mind, and with it the language of the mystery cults which so well fitted the Christian story. This may be demonstrated by looking again at a few of the themes mentioned above.

As God, Christ was ruler of the World – *Pantocrator* in Greek – and he is so shown in the centre of the Hinton St Mary mosaic, where the Chi-Rho behind his head has been compared to 'radiating sun rays'. He is indeed figured as the Sun god on the vault of a third-century tomb in the Vatican cemetery under St Peter's.[76] The sun was *invictus*, unconquered; this concept was part of the *lingua franca* of Roman religion and on altars from Britain both Hercules and Silvanus are described as *invictus*. It was especially associated with Mithras and the Sun. The word invoked power and demonstrated the fact that people needed the friendship of the All-Powerful Gods. If one was a soldier of *Deus Invictus Mithras*, how could one ever be defeated? The Emperor was a Comrade of the Unconquered Sun – Constantine perhaps never properly distinguished between Christ and the Sun god. Hercules had fought with Death and robbed Hades of its dead. The wreathed *Labarum*, the standard of Christ shown on wall-paintings in the Lullingstone house-chapel, is a suitable emblem of Christ's victory. It brings to mind Sentius Castus' altar to Mithras at Rudchester as well.[77]

At Hinton St Mary, Frampton and Lullingstone, mosaics show Bellerophon mounted on Pegasus slaying the Chimaera. Although it has been pointed out that the theme was not widely used in early Christian art, a late Medieval gloss on Ovid does draw the conclusion that the myth represents Christ victorious over Evil. The writer's use of allegory was evidently anticipated in Roman Britain.[78] In this connection we may note that the theme of a deity slaying the beast is found in Mithraism, but here the animal is certainly not evil. It is sacrificed that life may come out of death. This introduces us to a second, apparently contradictory feature of Christianity.

Although Christ was all-powerful, he allowed himself to be captured by his enemies and sacrificed. The power of God was released for the good of believers through sacrifice. The image of the Christian 'washing in the blood of the Lamb' brings to mind the actual *criobolium*, ram-sacrifice, of the Magna Mater, when votaries entered a pit and literally washed themselves in the blood of the animal slaughtered above. We also remember that Atys died underneath a pine tree for his goddess, and, like Christ, Atys was resurrected. The dying god theme is present in the myth of the death of Osiris, while both the resurrection of that god and the birth of his son Harpokrates show the ultimate triumph of good over evil. Bacchus bound by his enemies and bursting his bonds also provides a parallel of sorts.

The degradation of the god is emphasised by the suffering, mourning and abasement of his followers. The devotees of Atys lashed themselves and mutilated themselves. It is significant that one of the most learned of the Church fathers, Origen, made himself a eunuch for 'the Word's sake'. Christians were able to survive persecution by making even martyrdom a sacramental act, the seed of the Church. The pains of the Christian life are the subject of five panels of the Hinton St Mary mosaic, in which hounds chase deer. This interpretation, which seems preferable to the notion that they represent the animal paradise, has been given by Dr Katherine Dunbabin with regard to a similar mosaic in the basilica of St Cresconius at Djemila, but the allegory has been taken further by Roy Eriksen, who sees it both as a reflection of Scripture and a reminiscence of the myth of Actaeon.[79] The psalmist represents the soul's longing for God by the hind longing for running streams (*Psalm* 42, 1) and the Vulgate version of another Psalm (22, 16) reads *Circumdederunt me canes multi. Concilium malignantium obsedit me. Foderunt manus meas et pedes meos* – 'Many dogs surround me. The Council of the wicked laid siege to me. They pierced my hands and my feet'. The Actaeon myth (Ovid, *Metamorphoses* III, 138–252) was certainly known in Roman Britain and is depicted on a second-century mosaic at Cirencester.[80] If Roy Eriksen is right, Jewish and Graeco-Roman traditions are here bound together in the cause of Christian exegesis. It may further be noted that Actaeon was not the only huntsman slain in a legendary hunt. Meleager, Adonis and, in one version of the story, Atys were killed in hunting accidents (though admittedly not by hounds but by the boars they were pursuing). As we have seen, there are three representations of a huntsman, probably Atys, from London, and it is possible that this version of the story, told by Herodotus (I, 34–5), but best known to modern readers in a beautiful poem by A. E. Housman, was popular in Britain.

Alongside the image of death was that of birth. This was frequently miraculous, like that of Bacchus, born from the ashes of Semele. This story was shown on a mosaic from East Coker, Somerset.[81] Mithras leapt from the rock or from a Cosmic Egg; Christ was born of a Virgin. The theology of Christianity had no more place for a mother-goddess than had that of Judaism, but the human sympathy of the suckling mother gave the image of the Virgin enormous importance, comparable with that of Isis and the baby Harpokrates. It is virtually certain here that there were direct borrowings from the Isiac cult, not only in iconography but in hymnody. Both Isis and the Virgin are called 'Mistress of the World,' 'Star of the Sea' and other similar epithets.[82]

Finally, the god should be able to attract all creation. Bacchus was accompanied by wild beasts, especially felines, and they flank *canthari* (representing the Wine of Life) in art, for instance on several second and third century finger rings. Confronted stags, peacocks and small birds are so employed in Christian art. There has been much debate as to whether any or all of the Orpheus mosaics in Britain are Christian. We do not know, but the idea was certainly acceptable to Christians. Related to Orpheus is the shepherd – the Good Shepherd with sheep standing on each side appears on a paste intaglio from Barnsley Park, Gloucestershire.[83]

The Christian was not alone in having to adopt a moral code of behaviour. So did Mithraists and followers of the Egyptian gods. Christianity had a developed liturgy like other Eastern religions. Hymns and prayers were important, but the central mystery was a feast at which wine was drunk and bread eaten. The initiate believed that he was partaking of the essential essence of God. The cults of Bacchus and of Mithras were also centred around a sacred meal and there were early Christians, amongst them Tertullian, who believed that the Mithraic rite was a devilish parody of the Eucharist (*De praescr Haer.* 40). Sacred Meals seem to have been central to the cult of Atys too, as the following liturgical formula, preserved by the Christian writers Clemens Alexandrinus and Firmicus Maternus, attests: 'I have eaten from the *tympanum* (tambourine), I have drunk from the cymbal' (Clemens Alex., *Protr.* II, 15; Firm. Maternus XVIII, 8).[84]

The archaeological evidence for Christian feasts – the silver flagons, bowls, cups, spoons and wine strainers from Water Newton (**51**) and elsewhere – may be compared with vessels from secular or pagan religious contexts such as the Thetford Treasure of the fourth century (although that contained only spoons and strainers; if there was other plate it was buried elsewhere). All religions encourage giving. Not the least interesting thing about the Water Newton Treasure is that it demonstrates that a Church would depend on its wealthier members for whatever was needed for its ceremonies. Moreover, the treasure contained votive leaves or feathers with Chi-Rhos upon them and one of them also the legend *Iamcilla votum quod Promisit conplevit* – 'Iamcilla has fulfilled that vow that she promised'; the presentation of votive feathers to deities was a common custom, and the language of the inscribed example as Professor Thomas points out

51 Silver cup from Water Newton, Huntingdonshire, inscribed with a *chi-rho* and a dedication by Innocentia and Viventia. Height 12.4 cm. *British Museum*

is close to one from Lydney reading *Pectillus votum quod promissit deo Nudente M(arti) dedit* – 'Pectillus gave to the god Mars Nodens the offering which he had promised'. He has suggested that the Water Newton ex-votos might be explained by the fact that the community took over a temple where it was customary to dedicate such silver feathers to Mars, but he adds that if so, it was a 'sadly aberrant ecclesia'.[85]

No doubt in the fourth century there were many families split in their religious allegiance. Some men oscillated between accepting Christianity and remaining loyal to older ways; Julian cannot have been the only convert from Christianity to the ancient cults. Always classical culture remained a temptation. However, the exclusiveness of the Judaeo-Christian tradition inhibited the development of true syncretism in the sense that we find Isis claiming it in her appearance to Lucius or indeed Marcus Caecilius Donatianus on behalf of Cybele in the Carvoran poem.

Christianity was a problem to the Romans. They could accept that the Jews did not wish to conform, because, however anti-social their attitude might be, they were after all a nation entitled to have a national cult. Equally, the exclusiveness of Mithraea was tolerated and even encouraged; it was clearly no threat to army *ésprit de corps*, rather the contrary. Christianity claimed no nation and it did not appear to be patriotic; Rome was compared to Babylon and its end foretold. Christians claimed to belong to a City not of this world and actively sought proselytes. To the

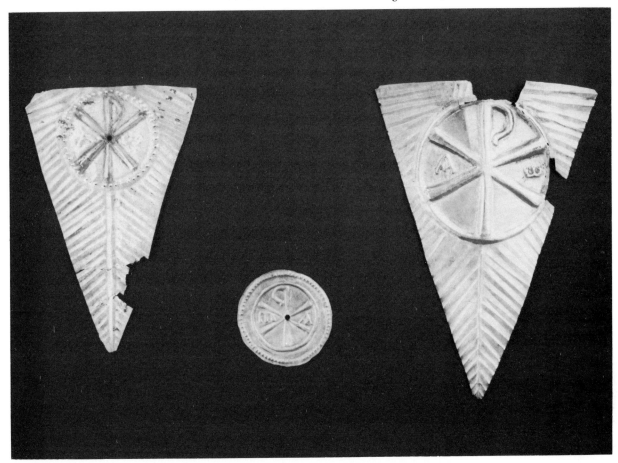

52 Silver plaques from Water Newton. Right with (central medallion gilded) height 15.7 cm; left 13.1 cm. In the centre a gold disc diam. 4.9 cm which may have been attached to this plaque. *British Museum*

Roman government, it appeared to be a secret and subversive society and had to be suppressed as a danger to the State; no doubt too Demetrius the Silversmith of Ephesus (*Acts* 19, 24ff) was not the only person engaged in producing temple ex-votos who feared the spread of what he regarded as atheism as a threat to his livelihood. In the event (as we have seen at Water Newton) he need not have worried so much, but popular resentment against Christians in the first three centuries of our era should not be under-estimated.

We know the names of three martyrs: Aaron (who is assumed to have a Jewish origin) and Julius at Caerleon, and St Alban at Verulamium, a city which in its Medieval and modern form bears his name. The date of Alban's death is disputed. It could have been as early as the reign of Septimius Severus as John Morris argues, or later, under Decius or Valerian as Professor Charles Thomas prefers, or even 'under Diocletian' (i.e. Constantius Chlorus) if Eusebius was merely trying to whitewash the reputation of the father of Constantine when he said no Christian was put to death.[86] It hardly matters; he was a Western, Latin-speaking convert, and he lived in a period earlier than any of the Christian remains from Roman Britain.

Here is another difference. Christianity was separated not only by spiritual distance but by chronology. It is true, as Ramsay MacMullen points out, that inscriptions become much rarer in the Late Empire, but that will scarcely account for the fact that none of the artefacts attributed to the other major mystery cults is as late as the fourth century.[87] Archaeology suggests that their place was taken by smaller, more local groups of worshippers at villas such as Littlecote or at temples of Romano-Celtic cults such as at Lydney Park and probably at Thetford. The London Mithraeum appears to have been replaced by a temple of Bacchus. Paganism became more traditional, but at the same time these *collegia* assumed many of the characteristics of the Eastern cults, emphasising communion with the divine in feasting, salvation and mystery. The new character of emotional paganism was dictated by the ascendancy of Christianity as we shall see in Chapter 10. The earliest Christian antiquities from Britain, the Water Newton treasure, show that at least one church had contacts with ordinary pagan cult-practice. It is by no means unlikely that a group of Christians might have taken over a Romano-Celtic building; this has long been suggested in the case of the Verulamium temple in front of the theatre.

Many of the Eastern Religions seem over-emotional and over-dramatic to us. It may not be to our taste to see tricks performed with hidden lights in Mithraea or to watch half-crazed votaries of Atys emasculating themselves. Euripides' play *The Bacchae*, written about one of the earliest of these orgiastic cults, that of Dionysos, still terrifies and repels. But to a well brought-up late Roman pagan aristocrat, Christianity itself may not have appeared to be entirely attractive. No-one was ever buried in a Mithraeum nor as a, general rule in a Classical or Romano-Celtic temple. The Christian found a new focus for his worship in the holy dead, only partially anticipated in the Egyptian veneration of tombs of Osiris and perhaps the rite of mummification, and in any case decidedly out of accord with normal Graeco-Roman practice. For the pagan it was a pious act to assemble at his family tombs at certain times of the year; However to build a shrine for daily use on the spot would entail pollution. At the site where St Alban was martyred and buried, a church was subsequently erected. Late Roman Britain provides other examples at St Bride's, London, St Pancras, Canterbury, and so it is claimed at Wells.[88] The Christian cemetery at Poundbury, Dorchester (Dorset) which included notable painted mausolea may mark a stage in the process. Even for a pagan there were limits to tolerance; a Mithraist could make an offering to Minerva or to Serapis in his temple, but to venerate the bones of a corpse would have appeared to be singularly horrible. Many an early Christian convert with a taste for Classical culture and Classical manners must have shared his sensibilities, and have been aware of an intense aesthetic conflict within himself. Nevertheless, the Holy Dead have their uses; they are present – literally tangible – and can even, as in the early Dark Ages, be divided up and used as relics. Other ancient religions did not have this advantage. Further, the Christian Church had always been centralised and organised. We know the names of Christian bishops from Britain who attended the Council of Arles in 314.[89] There was no central organisation in the case of the other cults, even that of Isis with its learned priesthood and (perhaps) continuing links with Egypt.

The reason why the Church succeeded where other cults failed will be further considered in Chapter 10, but the brief answer would seem to be that it combined many of the most attractive features of the mystery cults with certain practical advantages, such as central organisation, the will to suppress heterodoxy within its ranks and opposition from other religions outside, and the provision of new foci of worship. Above all, it had a greater success in making its message – its gospel – popular. Archaeologically this is evidenced by the fact that Christian remains, at least in late Roman times, are often found in the countryside where they replace not Mithraea or Isea but Romano-Celtic temples. The conversion of a moneyed or intellectual elite was not enough for the moving spirits of the Church.

6 Religion in Britain: Cult and Social Function

'On the side of the hill are many pretty springs; at one of them we drank a bottle of wine, to the memory of the founders, then poured some of the red juice into the fountain-head, to the Nymph of the place.'[1]

When he visited the Roman fort at Papcastle, William Stukeley indulged in a nostalgic and romantic evocation of ancient ritual. He poured a libation into a spring, an act which has left us no tangible remains. This emphasises the fact that the archaeologist is always hampered in his study of the past by the fact that he can only find objects, not ideas. Animal bones and smashed pottery can be the material remnants of ritual – or just rubbish. Objects can be items of daily use or – by virtue of their abandonment or means of deposition – *may* have been dedicated to the gods.

Of course, it is always tempting to use the term 'cult object' as an explanation for anything whose use we do not understand. Some caution is necessary here: many finds, even from temples, have secular uses and in many other instances the relationship of an artefact to a ritual can only be surmised with the greatest hesitation. However, the place of religion in ancient life is so marked that we are often justified in suggesting a religious function first for such problem pieces as bronze twelve-sided *dodecahedra*, one of which was discovered at Lydney, or the little enamelled stands which have frequently been found on temple sites (53). Both may have been used as supports for little candles or tapers used in cult ceremonies.[2]

Written evidence, consisting for the most part of inscriptions on altars and ex-votos, is supplemented by descriptions of ceremonial in literary sources. We need also to keep an eye on works of art which show processions and religious ceremonies with priests in their regalia, and worshippers dedicating offerings. Archaeological discoveries, while they are not conclusive proof of the ways in which people thought, can provide an indication of the level of Romanisation achieved by the natives of Britain. They reveal the externals of faith and sometimes (in the case of inscribed 'curse-tablets' and ex-votos) even the forms of prayers and supplications.

Altars and Sacrifices

As we have seen, one of the major methods of approaching the gods was through sacrifice, upon an altar. Large altars in front of major temples, like those at

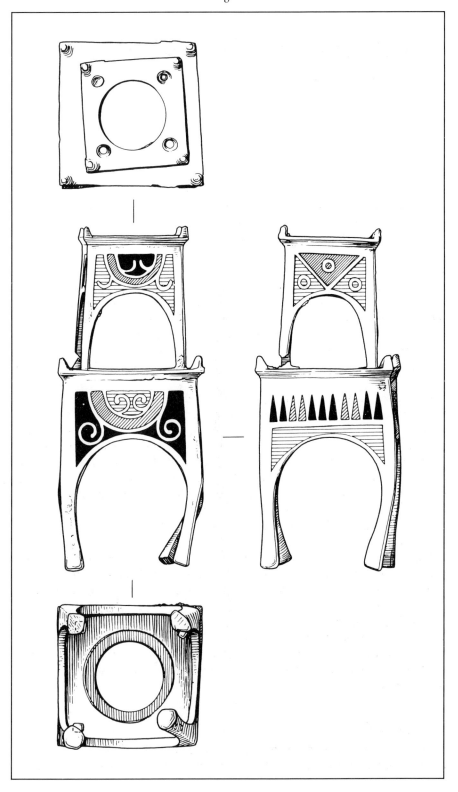

53 Miniature enamelled stands from Water Newton, Huntingdonshire. Large stand height 4.5 cm; smaller stand, height 3 cm

54 Corner block from Great Altar at Bath showing a water-goddess pouring from a vessel. Height 127 cm. *Roman Baths Museum*

Colchester and Bath, were elaborate. At the former there was a screen wall (as at the altar of the *Tres Galliae* at Lyon or at the *Ara Pacis*) to exclude sights of ill-omen. More remains of the Bath altar. It was made of dressed blocks and at the corners were carved reliefs portraying a number of deities, including Bacchus, Hercules, Jupiter and Apollo and a water-goddess or nymph (**54**).[3] Altars dedicated as votive gifts by individuals were usually much smaller and cut from a single block of stone. They would bear a written dedication, relief carvings or in many instances both an inscription and figural work.

The altar allowed selected parts of sacrificed animals as well as corn and wine to be offered to the gods; for this purpose a little fire could be made on the flat or bowl-shaped top (*focus*). The animal was generally stunned with a pole-axe and then stabbed with a sacrificial knife. Both axes and knives are depicted on altar reliefs. The knife is sometimes associated with the bull's head (*bucranium*).[4] However it is not easy to recognise these objects archaeologically, because they are the same implements generally used in butchery and also (in the case of knives) food-preparation. A bronze cleaver from the temple at Muntham Court is almost certainly sacrificial; not only is the findspot suggestive, but the use of bronze for a cutting implement instead of the more serviceable metal, iron, is an archaism which probably had a ritual significance. Nevertheless, iron knives were no doubt often used, and a large knife from the Nettleton temple may also have had a sacrificial use.[5] A bronze axe, found near Canterbury, partially modelled in the form of a bull, was either employed as priestly insignia or dedicated as a votive offering; smaller model axes are extremely common as ex-voto finds from temples (see below).[6]

Blood sacrifice is attested by animal bones, frequently buried in pits in temple enclosures. We have already seen (Chapter 3) the probable nature of a festive occasion, combining veneration of the gods with an opportunity to indulge in meat-eating, giving the site the rather unpleasing hint of the abattoir. The excavator on a temple site after a day of clearing out pits full of bones with the occasional potsherd may feel disappointed that more obviously interesting cult objects have eluded him, but a moment's thought will lead him back to the realisation that a high proportion of Roman ritual practice was concerned with animal sacrifice. The bone expert should be able to tell us even more – for instance at Uley the majority of the bones were of goat with a significant percentage of bones of domestic fowl, both cult animals of Mercury, to whom the temple was dedicated. The circular temple on Hayling Island also provided a significant quantity of goat or sheep, but pigs were here far more important. Presumably these mark the remains of sacrifices and of subsequent feasts, while their burial within *temene* suggests that even as rubbish they remain sacred, consecrated to the gods. In the temple at Hockwold (Sawbench) deposits of fowl bones were found in pits together with third and fourth century coins.[7]

Flagons and shallow bowls (*paterae*) were essential equipment, both for ritual ablutions before sacrifice and by themselves for pouring libations of wine and other liquids to the gods. Libations were far cheaper than animal sacrifices and must have been the usual means by which men established contact with the divine world. Certainly flagons and *paterae* were commonly carved on the sides of altars.[8] Examples are relatively plentiful – indeed they have been found more frequently than sacrificial knives and exist in a range of materials, including pottery, pewter,

bronze and silver. Occasionally dedications were inscribed on them; a pewter *patera*.
dedicated to Mars by Livius Modestus was found in a sacred shaft at Bossens in the
parish of St Erith, Cornwall; silver and pewter *paterae* excavated at the spring at
Bath were inscribed for the goddess Sulis Minerva (**55**). It has been suggested that
the simple workmanship of the pewter examples indicates specially made ex-votos,
while one of the silver *paterae* which had been used, broken and repaired before
deposition may have seen long service at the sanctuary. A splendid silver *patera*
from the Backworth cache is inscribed in gold letters on the handle *Matr(ibus)
Fab(ius) Dubit(atus)* 'Fabius Dubitatus [dedicated this] to the Mother Goddesses' and a
bronze *patera* from the fort of South Shields was dedicated to Apollo, the great
protector (*Anextiomarus*) by Marcus Antonius Sabinus (**56**).[9]

In most instances, save those of the cheapest pewter, there was probably an
intention to make regular use of the vessels. Rituals of purification outlasted
paganism and blood sacrifice, and the presence of a silver flagon, probably a gift of
household silver, in the ecclesiastical Water Newton treasure should occasion no
surprise.[10] This would have served as a container for water or wine in the Eucharist.
The temple treasure of Berthouville in Gaul contained domestic silver re-
dedicated to Mercury.[11] Flagons with specifically religious associations include a
bronze example found at Carlisle ornamented with a relief scene showing the
sacrifice of a pig. (**57**) A bronze jug inlaid with *niello* from Hockwold with a mask of
Atys at the base of the handle, and a pottery jug from Southwark inscribed *Londini
ad Fanum Isidis*, whose complete state supposes ritual deposition (in a
Favissa), are in one case possibly and the other certainly to be connected with
Eastern Cults.[12]

Other items of temple plate hint at more complex rituals. Strainers in the pagan
Thetford treasure and in the Christian Water Newton treasure were probably used

55 Three paterae, one of silver and
two of pewter from the spring at
Bath. Note dedication to Sulis on
the handle of the foremost. *Roman
Baths Museum*

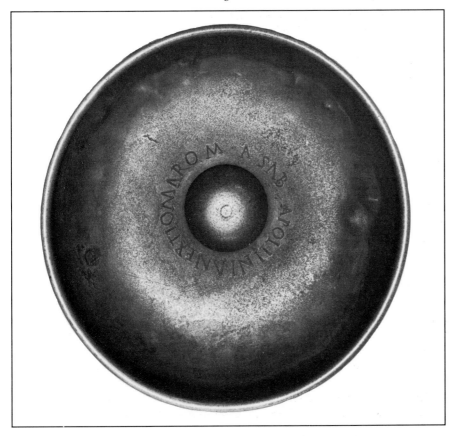

56 Bronze patera with dedication to Apollo Anextiomarus. South Shields, Co. Durham. Diameter 15.5 cm. *Museum of Antiquities, Newcastle upon Tyne*

to purify wine from unwanted lees.[13] The much deeper strainer in its special box from the Mithraeum beside the Walbrook in London could have served the same purpose (43), but it raises the possibility that infusors were employed to lace wine or other drinks with drugs. Zoroastrian ritual centres round the *Haoma*, prepared in a special way and offered in the *Yasna* rite.[14] We need not go so far as to see a direct transfer of this oriental ritual to the West, but the ecstatic nature of Mithraism would lend itself to drug-induced states in which enlightenment consisted in a separation from what we should call normality.

The spoons found at Thetford and dedicated to Faunus (107), as indeed knives and spoons from temple sites in general (for instance Nettleton and Lydney) were presumably used in ceremonial feasting. Great platters were necessary for many of these meals, and the Berthouville plates dedicated to Mercury would have been used then. Is it just possible that some of the Mildenhall vessels, especially the great Neptune dish, had been designed for use in sacred meals (albeit not in a public context)? We see the preparations for such a meal on the Trier Kornmarkt Mosaic.[15] The settings for such sacred feasts range from *temene* of temples to private cult rooms, especially in late antiquity; for instance what is to all intents and purposes a *triclinium* at Littlecote, though, as is suggested below (Chapter 10), the excavator, Bryn Walters, is almost certainly right in ascribing a religious function to it. While many temples must have owned a sufficient quantity of silver plate for regular use, we must remember that sacred vessels could also be made from clay.

The Isis jug from London (Southwark) has been mentioned, but other flagons must have been employed. Shallow cups ('tazzas') such as Wheeler found in the 'triangular temple' at Verulamium, and which are certainly associated with burials at Colchester for example, were probably used as *paterae*.[16]

Priests and other temple officials

In order to maintain a temple, a varied staff would have been needed, just as in cathedrals and lesser churches today. The priests, *sacerdotes*, were at the top of the hierarchy. Some were recruited from the curial (i.e. magistrate) class and served only part-time; others were permanent paid officials.[17] The tombstone of a *sacerdos* of Sulis Minerva has been found at Bath; he was called Gaius Calpurnius Receptus, the *tria nomina*, of course, proclaiming that he was a citizen. Bath was an important sanctuary with a specialist group of priests, *haruspices*, to examine the entrails of sacrificed animals. This form of prognostication came from Etruria and perhaps the *haruspex*, Lucius Marcius Memor, also a citizen, who dedicated a statue base in front of the main altar at Bath, was a North Italian.[18] To be a priest at a large shrine was a matter of some social prestige; at least, Ausonius' friend Attius Patera was proud of his priestly connections (Chapter 3). Such men were important in securing patronage for shrines, from their fellows amongst the gentry,

A man who was probably a priest of Ausonius' time, with the by then old-fashioned *tria nomina* Titus Flavius Senilis, dedicated a mosaic floor at the temple of Nodens, Lydney Park (**58**). He is described by the abbreviation *Pr. rel.* which has been read as *praefectus reliquiationis* or 'prefect in charge of the naval repair yard'. However, Mark Hassall's suggestion that the letters be expanded to *praepositus religionum*, 'superintendent of religious rites' is preferable, especially as Senilis seems to have had charge of the temple offering-box. The mosaic was paid for *ex stipibus*, 'out of offerings'. Another title with a similar meaning is recorded on an altar to Brigantia, from Greetland, Yorkshire, dated AD 208. *Mag(ister) s(acrorum)*; 'master of sacred rites' implies that T. Aurelius Aurelianus, of whom nothing else is known, was a specialist in religious lore. It is logical to see him as a priest of *Dea Brigantia* whom we will find (Chapter 9) to be in large part a Severan political creation. If so, he may well have been an official Severan appointment.[19] Another *sacerdos* made a dedication to Nemesis at Housesteads; his name was simply Apollonius, a religious name implying devotion to Apollo, and he was presumably not a citizen.[20] The only evidence from Britain which indicates the marital status of priests is Receptus' tombstone set up by his wife. Even the *Flamen Dialis* in Rome, whose life was highly circumscribed by ritual and taboo, was married.

Priestesses were seldom equivalent to priests in the ancient world, at least in this respect, for virginity, the withholding of sexuality in the service of the divine, was an important function of their vocations. The Vestal Virgins, in charge of the sacred hearth of Rome, are in fact examples of such priestesses. The guardians of the circular temple on the Loire Island mentioned by Strabo (IV, 4, 6) sound like such a college of virgin priestesses in a pre-Roman setting. The only priestess mentioned in a British inscription, however, was a devotee of an oriental rite. Diodora dedicated an altar to Herakles of Tyre at Corbridge. She describes herself, in Greek, as an *Archiereia*.[21]

Temple servants would have a wide range of functions; acolytes for processions

57 *Opposite* Sacrificial scene shown upon handle of a bronze flagon from Carlisle. Height of handle 19 cm. *British Museum*

58 The Cella Mosaic; Lydney Park Temple, Gloucestershire (now lost)

and ceremonies, guides to look after visitors, gate-keepers to secure the site, clerks and interpreters. Slaves and menials brought coal to burn on the altar of Sulis at Bath (Solinus 22, 10), cleaned the *temenos* or acted as servitors at cult-meals. While there is much archaeological evidence for such activities, only Victorinus, the *interpres* from Lydney, who oversaw the laying of Senilis' floor is mentioned in an inscription. Here it is suggested that he was a specialist in interpreting dreams and oracles (shrines frequently had such experts), though he may have been adept in the Latin and Celtic tongues.[22] As an overseer, he seems to have been below Senilis' priestly rank, but we cannot be sure.

Religious paraphernalia

It is not surprising that no textile remains from priestly vestments actually survive from Britain. No doubt the *toga* was often worn, drawn up over the head at the time of sacrifice. The officiating officer on the Bridgeness distance slab wears a toga, as do the figurines of *Genii* from the shrine of the Nymphs at Carrawburgh and the temple at Lamyatt Beacon.[23] Such conventional dress must often have been modified to accord with local traditions.

We do have some remains of metal crowns or diadems worn by priests which must stand to give us the flavour of priestly dress as a whole. They suggest that, on festal occasions, priests appeared in the same majestic splendour that we expect of the clergy today. Certainly surviving head gear may be compared with crowns worn by priests portrayed on sculpture and reliefs from elsewhere in the ancient world.[24]

A crown from a cache of regalia found on Cavenham Heath, Suffolk, was once richly adorned with silver plaques and gems or glass pastes. Similar diadems have been found at Hockwold-cum-Wilton, Norfolk, without any surround for gems but with silver plaques still in place. Another crown from Hockwold is in the form of a head-band which supports two arched strips at right angles to one another. At the point where they intersect is a disc and spike, very probably adapted from the traditional *apex* of the Roman Flamen (**59**) although priests of Cybele are known to have worn elaborate crowns, and as we have seen, a flagon adorned on the base of the handle with a head of Atys, was found nearby. A similar priestly crown forms part of the Felmingham Hall cache. Here the meeting-pieces on the sides are ornamented with human masks, and the '*apex*' originally supported a figure of a bird (although only a foot of the creature remains). The strapwork would have been of leather. The human masks, mounted on discs from the Hockwold (Sawbench) temple – which produced amongst other objects a hand holding a pine-branch, perhaps part of a figure of Atys – may also come from a priestly crown.[25] Other head-dresses are simpler: they consist of medallions linked together by chains. One was found with the Cavenham Heath crowns and two others with silver ex-votos in a temple cache from Stony Stratford. The ex-votos (and an accompanying statuette) showed that they belonged to a priest of Mars.[26]

In religious processions, the priests and their acolytes carried sacred objects. These included show-plate for use in lustrations and sacrificial implements. Incense burners like the Bacchic *balsamaria* from Carlisle, Corbridge and York,[27] garlands and bunches of flowers would have ensured that sweet smells and vivid colours met the eyes of the deity. Sometimes special bouquets might be required; in *The Golden Ass*, the priest of Isis carries a bunch of roses. Musical instruments, rattles, tambourines, cymbals, and pipes were carried and played. Some such as the double pipes (*tibiae*) were required at most sacrifices, but others had more

59 Priest's crown from Hockwold-cum-Wilton, Norfolk. Bronze. Height 15.9 cm. *British Museum*

specialised use. The cymbals and the tambourine (*tympanum*) seem to have been associated in particular with wild orgiastic rites such as those of Bacchus and of Cybele and Atys. Isis had a special rattle (*sistrum*) but other sorts of rattles may have been used in other cults as a way of attracting the attention of the deity and of driving off demons. One has recently been recognised by George Boon amongst other objects from Felmingham Hall.[28]

The singing of hymns was probably very important. It has left no direct trace in Roman Britain, but the use of verse forms in a number of dedications may be a significant pointer to the fact that one should approach the gods with more 'elevated' language than mere prose. Even apparently nonsensical chanting, for example of vowels, practised by some Egyptian priests as we have seen (Demetrius, *De Elocutione* 71), might be efficacious. Certainly in late Roman times the chanting of Christian priests would have been familiar to St Patrick and Gildas. We may suppose that something of the insular bardic traditions may have survived through the Roman period (when it would have imparted a distinctive sound to temple services) into the world of the Early Church.

The most distinctively religious items in the procession were the standards and sceptres. Nothing as elaborate as the ensign from Flobecq in Belgium, ornamented with openwork, appliqué masks of lions, panthers and a figure of the god Serapis has been found in Britain, although Serapis standards are shown flanking an inscription from York and a head of the god on an intaglio found at Beckford, Gloucestershire.[29]. However, there are a number of simpler sceptres and their heads. Two sceptres surmounted by busts of Mars were found in a grave near Brough on Humber (Petuaria). The shanks were of iron, bound with bronze bands, and the busts were also of bronze. It seems that they were being treated as the personal property of the deceased, rather in the way that medieval bishops carried their croziers with them to the grave. A sceptre-head from Stonea, Cambridgeshire is in the form of a bust of Minerva; indication of a shrine of Minerva in the vicinity is provided by a gold ex-voto plaque inscribed: *Dea(e) Mi(ner)va(e) D(onum)* – 'a gift' for the goddess Minerva'.[30] Two bearded heads wearing laurel wreaths, probably the god Jupiter, have been found at a site near Amersham, Bucks (**60**) and are either sceptres or more probably tripod mounts.[31]

Other heads appear to be those of emperors; when carried in procession they would have emphasised the close connection between deity and the *Numina Augustorum* (Chapter 4). As we have seen, they include heads of Hadrian from Worlington, Cambridgeshire (**61**) and Antoninus Pius at Willingham Fen (**25**). Not all such sceptre-heads were necessarily of metal. A female head with the coiffure of Crispina, wife of Commodus or Plautilla, wife of Caracalla, was found at Llanio in Wales. It is made of yew wood, tough and durable, and if it was painted and set on a staff it must have been an impressive sight.[32]

The Roman nature of these objects should now allow us to ignore the Iron Age precedents for human-headed sceptres. One has been found in the Hayling Island temple, and a similar mask-like head from Chalton, also in Hampshire, is also probably pre-Roman.[33] Many other masks and heads of Iron Age date are known in both Gaul and Britain, as we have seen. A coin of Verica shows a head on a sceptre or stand (see Chapter 1). Although it might be a severed head, it is more probably a graven image, analogous to the Roman bust: Classical influence is apparent here as well as in the appearance of the priest alongside it. This evidence reveals that the

60 Front and side view of bronze head depicting Jupiter. Found near Amersham, Buckinghamshire. Height 3.2 cm.

61 Bronze head of Hadrian (?) from Worlington, Cambridgeshire. Height 11.4 cm. *Museum of Archaeology and Anthropology, Cambridge*

62 Bronze maces or sceptres from Willingham Fen, Cambridgeshire. Owl at top right is 5.5 cm in height. *Museum of Archaeology and Anthropology, Cambridge*

human-headed sceptre was used in the Roman period as an emblem of power, as indeed it continued to be in Saxon times: witness the famous Sutton Hoo sceptre.[34] Animals and birds also epitomised the strength of the divine, and it is not hard to imagine the existence of boar-standards (like those that the pre-Roman Celts carried into battle); none has yet been found, unless the little boar head from Willingham Fen is to be classed as a mace-head. A bronze wolf, once mounted on a staff, comes from Caister by Yarmouth. The tradition of such zoomorphic sceptres continues with the stag on the Sutton Hoo Sceptre. An owl-like bird on a tubular pedestal from Willingham (**62**), and various other birds including one standing in a globe and supported on an iron shaft from Felmingham Hall, are presumably from maces or sceptres which are in themselves reminiscent of the eagle-headed Imperial maces shown on Roman coins.[35] Birds seem to have been especially important to the cult here, for as we have seen, a similar bird-figure embellished the priest's crown.

An interesting sceptre was found in a large circular building within the hillfort at Dinorben in Wales, which was possibly a temple although interpreted by the excavator as a native hut. It has a head shaped as a pine-cone, suggestive of the Bacchic *thyrsus*. Another form of sceptre, in the form of a spear, with point pierced for the suspension of rings, perhaps for the attachment of ribbons or else to produce a rattling sound, would be especially appropriate in the cult of Mars. Examples include one over 40 cm. in length from the River Nene near Milton Ferry, others from the temple (of Mars?) at Brigstock.[36] The head of a ceremonial spear in silver has been found at Caerleon. It is very likely that it was carried on military parades as an emblem of authority. There is no real distinction between religious standards and the *signa* kept in the *aedes* of a unit and regarded as sacred (Chapter 4). Incidentally, *vexilla* (banners) of the Second Legion appear on the sacrificial scene of the Bridgeness distance slab, the best portrayal of a religious ceremony in the art of Roman Britain.[37]

The Furnishings of the Temple

The shrine itself and all its furnishings were strictly speaking themselves votive gifts to the gods. Temples with their cult images and altars, arches, screens and columns were built or given by officials, merchants and gentry, to enhance their prestige in the community. Examples of all these are known from Britain either from archaeological remains or inscriptions. As examples, we may point to gifts of temples to Neptune and Minerva by the Guild of *Fabri* (? Shipwrights) of Chichester and to Sarapis at York by a legionary legate, while at Castlesteads, a centurion restored a temple to the Mother Goddesses. Virtually all altars were ex-voto dedications, whether they stood in *temene* or elsewhere, and this surely would have included the Great Altar at Bath. There was a screen at Bath, part of whose dedication remains. Another great temple screen is known from London, as well as an arch, while inscriptions from York and the vicinity of Lincoln record the gifts of an arch and shrine by a merchant from Rouen to the *genius loci* and perhaps Jupiter Dolichenus; and by a citizen of Lincoln, 'an arch at his own cost' to Mars Rigonemetos. The base of a Jupiter column which stood in or near the forum at Chichester (perhaps in front of the *Capitolium*) and an inscription recording the restoration of one at Cirencester in the fourth century by a *praeses* of Britannia

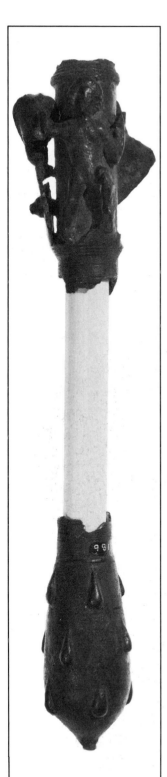

Prima, can be laid alongside actual remains of column shafts and capitals at Springhead, Wroxeter, Catterick, Ringstead (Northamptonshire) and Cirencester. Most are Jupiter columns of a type known in Germany, but not all need be. An image of Diana is shown on a column on a mosaic from Lillebonne, and a Mercury column appears on a plate at Berthouville. They adapt a Graeco-Roman form which clearly accords with local custom, to thrust the image of the deity high above the heads of mortal men. Mosaics like those in the temple at Lydney (**58**) and in Temple I at Springhead (**5**) were also given by devotees, and this is stated in the case of the Lydney temple.[38] The distinction between such large-scale works and smaller objects is not absolute. The bronze club from Willingham Fen, Cambridgeshire is portable (**63**) but similar *betels* shown on samian pottery and on a silver vessel from Wardt-Lüttingen in Germany appear to be much larger.[39] The hollow-cast head of Jupiter from Felmingham Hall (see Chapter 3) is rather larger than similar heads believed to have been attached to sceptres – and it almost certainly belongs to a votive image from the shrine (**64**).[40]

The gods would, of course, help the pious and so, as in the Christian Middle Ages, a great deal of wealth was expended on religion. Frequently gifts were made as a result of a bargain with the gods; this is clearly so in the case of many altars, but also other objects which carry the *solutio* formula V S (L) M which implies that the dedicator paid his vow with a light heart, freely and willingly (see Chapter 2). The *solutio*, the formal payment on presentation to the gods at their temples for favours received as a result of a bargain with them, was sometimes merely a libation or a sacrifice and has left no trace; fortunately for the archaeologist, on other occasions it consisted of a stone altar or a metal plaque carefully inscribed with the name of god and donor. It was preceded by the *nuncupatio*, an announcement of intention, provided that the gods gave what was asked of them. A splendid example of such a document is inscribed on a slab set up at Bowness-on-Solway by the merchant Antonianus. This records the dedication of a shrine to the Matres, and promises them in tetrameter verses that if they aid his venture he will gild the letters of the inscription.[41] The best examples of *nuncupationes* from Britain are to be found in the so-called 'curse-tablets'. This term is a misnomer in many instances. Only where magic arts are involved and the powers are summoned involuntarily, at the behest of a sorcerer, should it be used. Such maledictions will be considered at the end of this chapter in considering magic. Many of the tablets are simply requests to the gods to recover stolen property and punish wrong-doers in exchange for a reward, either a proportion of the lost property or a separate gift like a gold ring. We can see in the recovered and transcribed texts on such lead tablets the part that religion played in regulating society, backing up legal sanctions with religious ones.

Vows, Requests and Prayers

Roman Britain is now one of the best provinces in which to study these messages to the gods. Apart from a number of separate finds, often from known temple sites such as Lydney Park and Harlow, there are two considerable archives. One of them comes from a room attached to the temple of Mercury at Uley and comprises requests to that god, sometimes equated with Silvanus or Mars. The other has been extracted from the spring of Sulis at Bath, and consists of tablets addressing that goddess. Although one of the shrines was a major one and the other merely local, the character of the two sets of documents appears to be similar. If there is a difference it lies in what was done with the tablets at Uley; it is clear they were kept by the priests, while at Bath they were removed from any possibility of further consultation by mortals by being thrown into the sacred spring (**65**). The examination of these tablets is proceeding year by year and the reader is referred to the inscriptions section of the journal *Britannia* for the full texts.

Apart from these major groups we may note requests to Jupiter Optimus Maximus, the chief god of the Roman state, at Ratcliffe-on-Soar, Nottinghamshire; to Mercury at Kelvedon; Neptune at Caistor St Edmund; Nemesis, goddess of vengeance in the Caerleon amphitheatre and the Celtic Nodens at Lydney. In each of these cases too, if we regard the tablet as a *nuncupatio*, it was vital to specify the name of the god and also to be absolutely clear as to what was required. If one did not know, for example, who had stolen one's goods, it was best to use a formula to cover all eventualities; one did not assume that a man was a thief, because if a woman has done so or a slave (a chattel), the god cannot be expected to respond. Write *Si vir si femina si servus si liber* 'Whether man or woman, slave or free', or some variant such as *Si mulier si mascel* 'Whether woman or man', or (as on a late Roman

63 *Opposite* Bronze club from Willingham Fen. Height of cylinder at top *c.* 9.5 cm; base end also *c.* 9.5 cm. *Museum of Archaeology and Anthropology, Cambridge*

64 Bronze heads of Minerva and of Jupiter Taranis from Felmingham Hall, Norfolk. Height: Minerva head 11.4 cm; Jupiter head 15.5 cm. *British Museum*

example) *seu gentilis seu Christianus* 'Whether pagan or Christian'.[43] Where there were specific suspects these had to be listed, just as they would be in a legal indictment. The language is a curious melange of the court formulary and local rustic Latin. We can compare it to the sort of English used in an Indian village, and as in India we may often suspect the hand of the professional scribe played a part in writing down the requests of the illiterate and barely literate. Was this one of the functions of Victorinus, the *interpres* at the Lydney temple? A few examples give the flavour of the requests. Most are concerned with theft, and the deity is asked to recover stolen goods. The malefactors who stole Docilianus' *caracalla* (the name of a type of cloak from which an early third-century Emperor took his nickname), Saturnina's linen cloth and Silvianus' ring are to return the property to the temples at Bath, Uley and Lydney at the respective behests of Sulis, Mercury and Nodens.[44]

The gods enforce moral behaviour, and this is explicitly stated on a Uley document inscribed with Cenacus' complaint to Mercury about Vitalinus and Natalinus his son who had stolen the draught animal. Cenacus begs the god that neither of them may have health *unless* they repay the stolen animal and give the god 'the devotion which he himself has demanded of them'.[45] Piety also lies behind a request to Mercury at Kelvedon, Essex: 'Whoever has stolen the property of Varenus, whether woman or man, in his own blood and from the money which he has consumed let him pay gifts to Mercury and sacred offerings to Virtue'.[46]

Other tablets lay stress on punishment, for example the Ratcliffe-on-Soar tablet

65 Docilianus' request to Sulis scratched on both sides of a leaden tablet from Bath. Height 10 cm. *Roman Baths Museum*

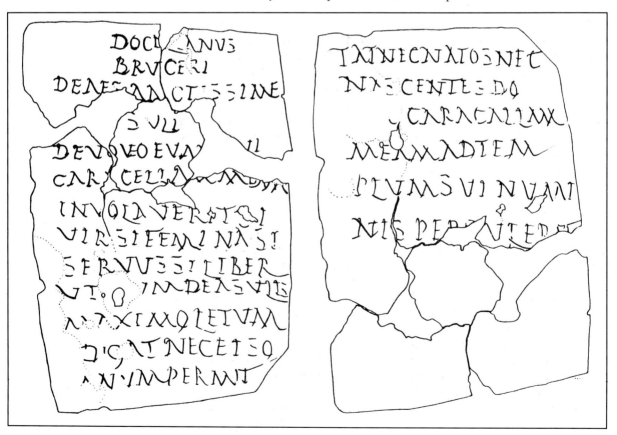

addressed to Jupiter 'that he may hound ... through his mind, through his memory ... his intestines, his heart, his marrow, his veins ... whoever it was who stole away the *denarii* of Canius Dignus'.[47] The god is here offered a tenth part of the sum of money and generally the writer of one of these requests would make it worth the deity's while by giving money, a proportion of the value of the loss or a gift such as a ring, or even a pair of leggings. An amusing tablet from Caistor St Edmund lists an extensive theft: fifteen *denarii*, a wreath, bracelets, a suit of clothes, a mirror and ten pewter vessel. 'If you (Neptune) want the pair of leggings' it says, 'they shall become yours at the price of his (i.e. the thief's) blood.'[48] It is hard to imagine the great god of the sea in trousers, but no doubt stranger objects were frequently left in shrines.

Sometimes tablets concern conduct rather than property. A tablet from Old Harlow is written by a distressed lover entrusting to Mercury his affair with Eterna: 'and may Timotheus feel no jealousy of me at the risk of his life-blood'. Timotheus has been warned; if he does not desist in his pursuit of Eterna, he will risk the anger of the god for his presumption.[49]

The tablets should help us to unify our view of religion in Britain. Latin names, Celtic names and even Greek names jostle together in the lists of suspects who had stolen Annianus' six silver pieces one morning: Postumianus, Peregrinus, Latinus and Victor are all Roman enough, but Aessicunia and Gunsula, for instance, are natives while Euticius (i.e. Eutychus) and Calliopis are of Greek origin, and some of the suspects may even have been Christians.[50]

Thus the temples of Britain helped to resolve conflicts, to punish transgressions which would sometimes be hard to bring to court without risking a breakdown in social order, and to remove intolerable tensions. In this way they played a part in maintaining the *Pax Romana* down to the time of the Christian Empire and beyond. It may incidentally be noted that there was a strong similarity between requests to the gods and those sometimes sent to officials, such as to a minor army commander in Egypt, Flavius Abinnaeus: 'Heron, son of Sakaon ... like a robber, contrary to justice, attacked my sheep and carried off ... eighty-two. Wherefore I request and beg of your philanthropy to apprehend this man and compel him to restore to me what he has wickedly seized.'[51]

Votive Offerings

The *solutio*, as we have seen, took varied forms. One of the most fascinating is the plaque, often feather-shaped or gabled, carrying an inscription or relief appropriate to the deity.[52] Examples are known in gold, silver and bronze and they are dedicated to every sort of god — Oriental, Celtic and Roman. In Britain, recipients include the Christian God at Water Newton (52), Minerva at Stonea and Maiden Castle, Mercury at Uley, Mars at Stony Stratford, Barkway (4) and Woodeaton, Vulcan at Stony Stratford and Barkway, Abandinus at Godmanchester, Nodens at Lydney and Cocidius at Bewcastle, the Matres at London and Apollo at Nettleton. A special example from Great Chesterford, Essex, is in the form of a small bearded mask (66) which invites comparison with the great mask of Neptune(?) on the Bath pediment.[53]

Although the circumstances of dedication are not often recorded, we may note a silver plaque from Stony Stratford on which a certain Vassinus promised six

66 Silver plaque in the form of a mask of Neptune from Great Chesterford, Essex. Length 10.5 cm. *Museum of Archaeology and Anthropology, Cambridge*

denarii to Jupiter and Vulcan to bring him home; as a result of the successful fulfillment of this *nuncupatio*, the money was paid presumably into the temple treasury. As the plaque can in no way be worth six *denarii*, presumably it is either representative of part of this sum or more probably an extra gift to ensure the future favour of the gods.[54] It was never wise to be too parsimonious to the divine powers.

These plaques seem in some degree equivalent to the silver shrines of Artemis sold in Ephesus by Demetrius the silversmith and his companions (*Acts* 19, 23–39). Although they were so thin and flimsy, they had a considerable surface area and would have looked very fine when displayed on a ledge near the cult image. Such ex-votos were tempting merchandise for visitors to a shrine, and gave the stalls outside the temenos a reasonable profit. The presence of *aedicula*-shaped scars on the front of one of the Cavenham crowns, and the surviving silver plaques on a head-dress from Hockwold suggest that the same workshops were involved in the manufacture of regalia. Most of the votive leaves, which were doubtless intended to resemble palms of Victory, probably date from the second and third centuries, with the Christian Water Newton examples coming later, in the fourth century. It is of some interest that similar objects are shown in manuscripts of this time, the *Virgilius Romanus*, illuminated in all probability in the North-Western provinces, and the *Notitia Dignitatum*.[55] Other plaques, rather thicker and with *ansae* as handles, were attached to figurines or to other gifts. There are numerous examples, for instance, one dedicated to Mars Medocius and two to Silvanus Callirius (these last actually from a temple) at Colchester, another to Mars Nodons from Lydney, and one to Mars Toutatis at Barkway.[56]

Their place might be taken by inscribed bases to figurines. Generally, the inscription is very short, for example that on the base from Martlesham, Suffolk, which announces that Simplicia gave it to Mars Corotiacus. However, the pedestal of the statuette of Mars from the Foss Dike, Lincolnshire (15), carries an informative explanation of how one particular *solutio* was accomplished. Two brothers (?), the Colasuni, called Bruccius and Caratius, dedicated the statuette to Mars and the Emperor's *numen* at the cost of one hundred sesterces (which is twenty-five denarii). This covered the cost of labour alone for the coppersmith. Celatus, who made the figure, gave the bronze at a cost of three *denarii*, thus joining them in their dedication.[57]

We must remember that many votive offerings were made of organic materials which have not survived. A little wooden statuette of a goddess has only been preserved at Winchester because it lay in a waterlogged deposit. On a larger scale, the tin mask from the culvert leading out of the spring at Bath has been recognised as the facial covering of a wooden idol (67). However, no trace at all remains of Neptune's leggings, if they were ever presented to the deity, at his shrine by the River Tas (see above). Equally, with regard to written testimonials and records of gifts, such as we might find today in a Catholic healing shrine, we must remember that many inscriptions were on non-permanent material. We shall never know how much was recorded alongside figurines and other ex-votos on wood or papyrus.[58] We do know that visitors to shrines could purchase bronze or gilt-bronze letters and nail up their own inscriptions on a wooden board. There are a number of such letters from Woodeaton (68), Lydney, Harlow (Holbrooks), Hockwold (Sawbench) and elsewhere but none has ever been recovered in

67 Tin mask from Bath. Height
33 cm. *Roman Baths Museum*

sequence and no inscription has been reconstructed.[59] Presumably the dedications
were usually very short and formal, merely recording the names of god and donor
who had paid his vow – vs(l)lm. As we have seen (Chapter 3), figurines of deities
were appropriate offerings to temples; sometimes they seem to have been closely
related to a specific cult: the horsemen (?Mars) from Brigstock, Mercury figurines
at Uley, the hounds of Nodens found at Lydney and the eagles from Woodeaton.
But other bronzes are found at these sites, at Woodeaton a relatively large number,
and the lack of exclusiveness amongst pagan deities is revealed most decidedly by
the size and variety of the votive cache from Southbroom near Devizes, and also by
the range of deities from the Lamyatt Beacon temple. The ancient gods were truly
one great family.[60]

    Model implements and tools are also found (see Chapter 1 for pre-Roman
examples); they could have been made with far less labour, by the same
metalworkers. They can reveal something of the nature of a deity. The *caducei* from

68 Bronze letters from Woodeaton, Oxfordshire. M. height 6.2 cm; T. and I (*ligatured*) height 7.5 cm; N. height 6.2 cm. *Ashmolean Museum*

Uley in silver (69), bronze and iron show that Mercury was endowed with his classic attribute. However, miniature spears from the same temple are suggestive of a warrior and huntsman, and this explains why he is sometimes confused or conflated with Silvanus and Mars on the 'curse tablets'. Miniature spears from what may have been a temple of Mars at Woodeaton, Oxfordshire have been deliberately bent (70). The bending of weapons and the smashing of pots in ritual and funerary contexts is one way of presenting a gift to the world of the gods. It is explained by the distinguished French anthropologists Henri Hubert and Marcel Mauss as a form of sacrifice. They write, 'We must designate as sacrifice any oblation ... whenever the offering or part of it is destroyed, although usage seems to limit the word sacrifice to designate only sacrifices where blood is shed. To restrict the meaning of the name in this way is arbitrary.'[61] A miniature ballista must have been dedicated at Bath by a Roman soldier, who threw it into the sacred spring. Miniature axes presumably represent the chief implements of sacrifice and are very common on sacred sites. They frequently carry X-shaped or other markings on the blades which perhaps have a votive purpose signifying dedication (70). Six axes given to a temple in Switzerland actually carry the names of deities.[62] Almost as characteristic as axes are little enamelled stands which are designed to stack one above the other (53). In appearance, they are not unlike miniature altars, but it has been suggested that a taper might have been inserted down the central hole and as it burnt down, the sections removed one by one; thus as with a rosary one would have been able to time one's devotions. Brooches were also enamelled, and one particular type in the form of horse and rider is so characteristic of temple sites that it is tempting to see the form either as an ex-voto or as a souvenir to be carried away by visitors, like pilgrim badges in the Middle Ages (71).[63] Other objects purchased at temple shops for dedication at shrines were made of pottery. They include figurines imported from Gaul in white pipe-clay, lamp-covers, little lamps, tiny votive pots (72) and the incense burners made by Saturninus Gabinius and dedicated by him to Coventina at Carrawburgh (73).[64]

Gifts of precious metal – apart from plaques – would no doubt reflect more than a passing impulse to buy from the temple shop. It was, after all, a most splendid and public-spirited gesture to hand over personal wealth to the temples and the gentry around Berthouville. Q. Domitius Tutus, Julia Sibylla and the rest knew what they were doing when they handed over antique jugs, cups and bowls

69 Silver caduceus from Temple at Uley, Gloucestershire as found (prior to conservation). Length 6.2 cm. *British Museum*

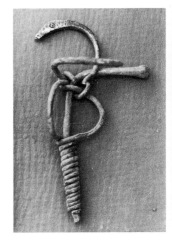

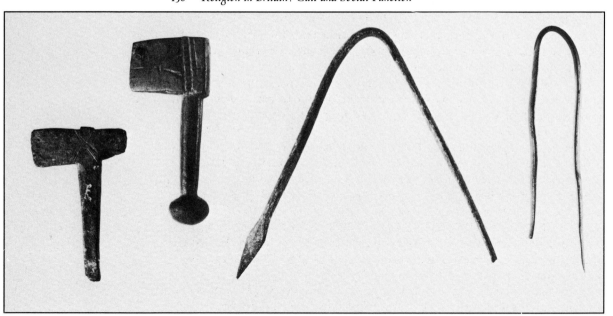

70 Bronze miniature spears (both bent) and axes from Woodeaton, Oxfordshire. Spears lengths 14.2 cm and 12 cm (broken); axes 3.9 cm and 4.8 cm. *Ashmolean Museum*

71 Bronze enamelled brooches, two showing horses with riders, one with a horse alone. Lengths 2.6 cm; 3 cm and 2.5 cm. From Hayling Island, Hampshire

to the shrine. We can only guess that Fabius Dubitatus and his family were responsible for the gift of more than the one inscribed *patera* from the Backworth treasure, but that alone may have been enough to ensure that Fabius Dubitatus was known as a man of piety and munificence in his community.[65]

Rings of gold, silver and bronze were also appropriate offerings. A gold ring (and also bracelets) are mentioned in this connection on the lead tablets as suitable gifts for deities. One of the Backworth rings was dedicated to the Matres; other inscribed rings are known – two from York carry the names of Sucelus and Teutates; some rings with almost illiterate inscriptions from Owslebury and the Henley Wood temple have been tentatively identified as ex-votos. It is clear that the ostentatious gift of precious objects provided that element of theatre which was never entirely absent from any sacrifice but was here augmented by the fact that the donor was divesting him- or herself of what everyone recognised was real wealth. Such customs outlasted paganism, and in St Patrick's *confessio* (49), a pious woman presented unsolicited gifts to the saint and cast some of her jewellery on to the altar. Similar ostentatious giving to churches continues to this day throughout most of Christendom.[66]

Curse-tablets reveal that some people came to a shrine and left gifts because the god had restored property or punished an enemy. Vassinus' dedication and Antonianus' slab at Bowness-on-Solway show that others were given because of travels safely completed or after successful trading ventures. Perhaps the commonest reason for visiting a temple was simply health. The evidence consists not only of inscriptions on altars, but of finds of medical ex-votos, represented at Bath by breasts carved on a piece of ivory (74). Eye complaints were common, to

72 Miniature pots as found in the courtyard of the triangular Temple at Verulamium. *Verulamium Museum*

73 Incense burner from
Coventina's Well, Carrawburgh,
Northumberland with dedication
by Saturninus Gabinius. Height
21.6 cm. *Chesters Museum*

judge from finds of stamps used by oculists to stamp their salves. A pair of gold eyes
from Wroxeter (**75**) and over thirty-five other representations of eyes cut out of
pieces of wall-plaster found in the same place are surely votive gifts to a deity who
cured such complaints. Limbs include bronze arms from Lydney Park and
Springhead (**76**) and legs from Muntham Court and Uley. The dedication of model
parts of the body was a widespread phenomenon throughout the ancient world,
for instance in the *Asklepeia* of Epidaurus and Corinth and in Gaul at the Forêt de la
Halatte shrine.[67] So far the quantity of medical ex-votos from Britain remains
modest, but that is presumably just a matter of chance.

Friends of God, Oracles and Dreams

Even so, the religion of Roman Britain may not be reduced merely to matters of
contract, the Oriental cults excluded. It is important to remember that some
people came to temples in order to find mystical experiences. Actual evidence is, of
course, sparse, but it can be filled out with the testimonies of such men as
Rutilianus or Arnobius (before his conversion to Christianity) who fell on their
knees before any idol or sacred stone. The gods intruded into their lives just as
Christ and the saints were intimate companions of the devout in the Middle Ages.
Such 'friends of the gods' were not alone in dreaming, nor were they alone in
believing strongly in oracles and portents. Indeed to picture Roman religion in
terms of Classical tranquillity, even to the extent of thinking it meant very little
apart from maintaining man's obligations to the gods, is wide of the mark. For
what a throbbing emotional reality it was: on the one hand sacrifice, contract and
gift, on the other the stupendous possibility of a meeting with the divine. Nobody
in antiquity (apart from one or two dispeptic intellectuals) thought that the gods
were make-believe, toy gods, any more than a child today thinks he will remain

74 Ivory breasts from the spring of Sulis Minerva at Bath. Diameter of plaque 7 cm. *Roman Baths Museum*

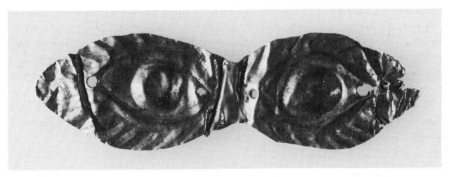

75 Gold Eyes from Wroxeter. Length 6 cm. *British Museum*

unharmed if he clutches at the live wires of an electricity pylon.

Ancient man approached the gods in two ways. One of them, the superstitious or magical way, saw the divine as 'power' which could be manipulated by man. Sorcery is never to be confused with religion, but we will examine it briefly at the end of this chapter. The visitor to a temple, however humble and ill-educated, would have adopted the second 'rational' view of nature. His presence at the shrine of a god inevitably proclaimed that events have their causes in the will of the gods who preside over the seasons and the lives of men. Religious responses to natural phenomena are found in inscriptions from sanctuaries. A prodigy like lightning was caused by an appropriate deity, probably Jupiter the Thunderer. The place he struck was *sacer* and belonged to him alone. It was enclosed as a *Bidental*. Such a designated plot of land seems to have existed near Halton Chesters, where a stone inscribed *Fulgur Divom*, 'The Thunder of the gods', warned men to keep out.[68] Although astrological phenomena would have been taken into account by a *haruspex* such as Marcius Memor, who knew that different parts of the liver of a beast corresponded to different parts of the sky, he worked in the context of temple-sacrifices and he knew that his job was to interpret the omens sent by the divine.

Professional oracles were more a feature of Greek than of Roman culture, but they continued to be much frequented in the Roman period and attracted the patronage of Romans as well as Greeks. The oracle of Apollo at Claros in Asia Minor assumed a special importance.[69] Here, enquirers could pose questions to the god and were answered in verse by a *thespiodes*, who interpreted the prose responses of the god's prophet. Both *thespiodes* and prophet were male. The oracle is mentioned in an inscription from Housesteads set up by *Cohors I Tungrorum*, probably as one of a number of units who had responded to an offical directive to seek divine aid when Caracalla fell ill in AD 213. It does not, therefore, prove the existence of private requests to oracles from men living in Britain.[70] Nor does the adherence of Rutilianus (the ex-legate of *Legio VI*) to the bogus oracle of Alexander of Abonuteichos cast much light on British conditions. However, something like an oracle may have existed at many shrines where there was an Interpreter of Dreams, for dreams which came so mysteriously in the night came from a god. As we have seen, Victorinus may have interpreted dreams to visitors at Lydney. At both Lydney and Nettleton, long stoa-like buildings were erected which, it may be suggested, were used for incubation. Here people slept overnight and awaited a divine visitation. In the morning they would go to the dream-interpreter for an explanation of their dreams, and they could depart refreshed in the knowledge that Nodens or Apollo cared for them.

Interpreters, intermediaries between man and the gods, were not always necessary. At least, they are not mentioned in inscriptions said to have been put up *ex visu* as a result of a vision, or *monitu*, as the result of divine warning. Priestly intervention of any kind is least likely when the inscription does not come from a temple site, as in the verse inscribed on the altar set up beside a stream near Risingham (Chapter 4). An even more ambitious poem was set up by M. Caecilius Donatianus at Carvoran.[71] Although it is hard to see the complex syncretistic thought within it as entirely arising from a dream-state, it shows how simple ideas coming to the mind could be interpreted by the individual. In a sense Donatianus was his own oracle: *ita intellexit numine inductus*, 'thus he has understood, led by the *numen*'. First the goddess Virgo Caelestis is equated with the Magna Mater, Ceres and the Dea Syria, and then with the empress Julia Domna, wife of the Emperor Septimius Severus: 'Syria has sent the constellation seen in the heavens to Libya to be worshipped.' The comment by the editors of *RIB* that 'this dedication to Virgo Caelestis is really in honour of Julia Domna' misses the point. It assumes that the Imperial cult was entirely political and contrived rather than an expression of religious faith, but as we saw in Chapter 4, the State Religion was much less empty of emotion than might have been though, emperors had *numina* and they and the divine house as a whole stood close to deity. In some respects they were saviour-gods, in the tradition of the Hellenistic kings called *Soter* or *Epiphanes*, divine names for 'Saviour' and 'God made manifest'. The tone of Donatianus' poem is distinctly reminiscent of the epiphany of Isis, appearing to Lucius in Apuleius' *Golden Ass*.[72] Isis tells Lucius that she is equated with numerous goddesses throughout the world and he at last comes to understand her greatness. There is no need to doubt Donatianus' enthusiasm for the manifestation of deity in Julia Domna. Indeed, an altar from the same site was dedicated to *Fortuna Augusta* by T. Flavius Secundus,

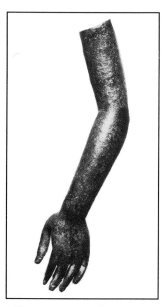

76 Bronze votive arm from Temple Ditch site, Springhead, Kent. Length 4.7 cm

prefect of the First Cohort of Hamian Archers, for the health of Lucius Aelius Caesar, *ex visu*, and that was in the traditionally less extreme Antonine age.[73]

The circumstances of dreams must for the most part be surmised from brief references on inscriptions. Thus an inscription from the baths in the south-west of Roman Bath, the Hot Bath, reading '... son of Novantius set this up for himself and his family as the result of a vision', suggests that Sulis Minerva promised full healing from a complaint such as rheumatism, provided the sufferer published his cure.[74] The god Mars Condates, venerated at Piercebridge by the surveyor, Attonius Quintianus, was presumably also a god of sacred waters, for *condate* is a watersmeet. As healing shrines were often connected with water, we may imagine the shrine of a god rather like Nodens, and perhaps a sleep-house as at Lydney.[75] Visions were very often associated with the god Jupiter Dolichenus (from Asia Minor) who was prone to admonish his votaries or bring them visions and dreams. The reason for his particular activity in the area of dreams is uncertain.[76] The dedication to Nemesis from the Nemeseum in the Chester amphitheatre (77) shows that Sextius Marcianus the centurion believed that Fate would discomfit his enemies if only he gave her something, for she had appeared to him in a vision. The man who made his *nuncupatio* desiring the return of stolen property on a lead tablet found in the Caerleon amphitheatre did not have that certainty; he could only hope.[77]

The quantity of evidence from Roman Britain is minute when compared with the impressive documentation which exists for the operation of healing shrines in medieval England.[78] Striking similarities existed between them. In both societies, visions certainly played a part; some of the medieval ones are exceedingly odd. Was the dream of William Rufus, that he ate of an angel 'lying naked above the altar' on two occasions, a fitting one for an English king? On the second 'the angelic expression of his countenance changed into one of such intolerable disgust, such inexpressible hate, that from the frowning of such a brow it was possible to presage the fall not of one man only but of the whole world. He spoke to me, saying, "Thou shalt not eat of me henceforth".'[79] This dream, of course, foretold his death. It would not have surprised Artemidorus, author of the *Oneirocriticon*, and one suspects that the *interpres* at many a Roman shrine would have had to interpret cannibalistic yearnings.

Similarly, vows were made in medieval shrines; sometimes coins were bent, consecrated in the same way that miniature weapons and tools were folded over or snapped in two, so as to devote them to the powers of the otherworld.[80] Also, the practice of dedicating models of parts of the body previously diseased and now healed continues – until this day. What strikes us as one major difference between the habits of mind of pagan antiquity and of the Christian Middle Ages is that medieval cults grew up around the graves of the dead, and specifically around the tombs of saints or holy men, what Peter Brown has designated 'the very special dead'.[81] In antiquity, pagan deities stood detached from mortals. Burials are seldom recorded on religious sites, where corpses might bring pollution. We recall Artemis' sad farewell to Hippolytos at the moment of the latter's death and that strange and mournful music in the air as Herakles and the other gods forsook Mark Antony. Following this, it may be suggested that there was a difference in terms of respectability. Whereas the healing cults of the Middle Ages belonged to the murky borderland between Orthodox Christian belief and magical, super-

stitious practices, the Roman shrines were in the mainstream of ancient cult practice. The gods were present as self-evident, visible powers of nature, while the saint remained a human *patronus* between man and a more distant God.[82]

The priests knew what was expected of visitors who were bidden to conform to local regulations affecting conduct. Magic existed in this ancient world, but less here, where experts recast the human anxieties brought to them in the spirit of Roman justice and law.[83] Everyone who came knew that the gods could both bless and punish; they could give health and strike malefactors with disease.

The Different types of Shrine

Religious men and women had almost unlimited choice in cults to patronise. We do not know in the case of most votive altars what attracted the donor to the shrine. Sometimes (not often?) it may have been a casual whim, a passer-by entering a sanctuary which lay beside his road. More often advertisement and reputation spread by word of mouth, and the written word will have gone before, just like Gython's oracle at Abonuteichos or Ephesian Artemis or, to judge by the explicit *ex-votos* from her shrine, Maionian Artemis.[84] The temple of Sulis Minerva was certainly known abroad for its miraculous altar-fire where coal was burnt instead of wood. Nodens at Lydney, Apollo at Nettleton and the rest presumably acquired similar reputations, for only thus could their temples have been so richly sustained. In addition, there were devotees of particular deities who would seek out the local sanctuaries of their favourites. The mighty Saviour gods, Asklepios and Hygeia, were particular favourites of the Greek physicians in the employ of the army – note the dedications from the *Valetudinarium* at Chester (37), and in the case of Asklepios, of Aelius Aristides, whose personal dialogue with the deity is a landmark of both Roman religious history and of Roman hypochondria.[85] All temples – or almost all, excluding little personal ex-voto shrines set up by individuals by the roadside or deep in the moors[86] – would have been the settings for festivals, processions, sacred dramas, sacrifices and, at a more personal level, possibilities for achieving personal communion or advice from the god in the form of prayers and petitions, backed in most instances by gifts; but that is not to say that all temples had the same function.

The divisions between temples have often been made on the basis of architecture: 'Classical temples' (rare in Britain) offer a local version of the religion of Rome; 'Romano-Celtic temples' (the majority) preserve the age-old customs of the indigenous people; the temples of the Oriental cults and Christianity, often basilical in plan, provide a new form of spiritual experience. Clearly this model has elements of truth in it, but it relies far too much on external factors. Nowadays, if we were to group churches in this manner we might conclude that the little village church and the city cathedral belonged to separate concepts of religion – they do not, but they nevertheless serve separate functions.

In like manner, we may divide temple types into large urban (the equivalent in some respects of cathedrals), small rural (like parish churches), temples of pilgrimage and the centres of private or restricted cults. There may be a tendency for cult practices of a Romano-Celtic temple to be less highly developed and 'Roman' than those of a regular Graeco-Roman temple, but such an assumption must be a generalisation at best; in many instance it is clearly untrue.

77 Opposite Altar in red sandstone dedicated to Nemesis. From Nemeseum in the Chester Amphitheatre. Height 47 cm. *Grosvenor Museum, Chester*

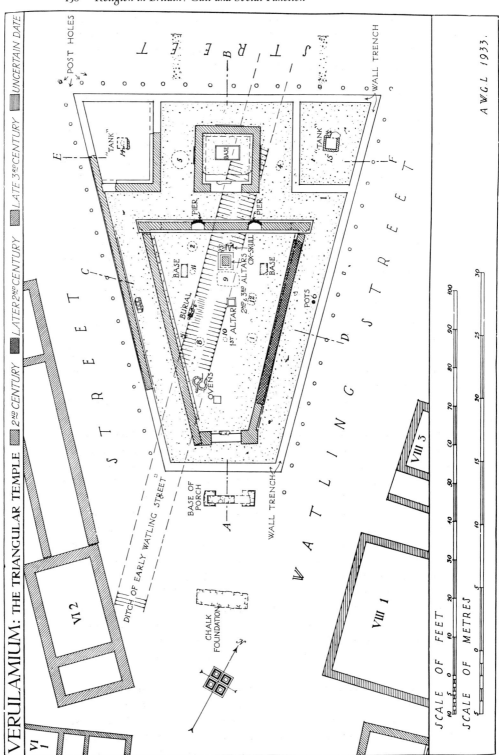

78 The Triangular Temple at Verulamium (plan)

The temples to which Tacitus refers in *Agricola* 21 were probably mainly urban. Unfortunately few have been excavated with much care. Large city shrines such as the Verulamium forum temples (one of which must have been the *Capitolium*), the Temple of Neptune and Minerva at Chichester and the Temple of *Divus Claudius* at Colchester acted as venues for civic and provincial ceremonies. No doubt they were sometimes given offerings, but they have yielded little in comparison with rural, pilgrimage shrines. In the fourth century, of course, it could be argued that the measures taken by the Christian government against pagans were effective in cities and ineffective in the countryside, but that will not explain why there is a dearth of non-valuable ex-votos from such shrines, or why early temples like the one situated near the original forum of London should be empty of finds. The most convincing reason is that many urban temples were poor and little frequented: their main altars and cult-images their most distinctive possessions. Some were associated with guilds or confraternities, even built by them (for example the Chichester temple and the temple in *insula* xxxv at Silchester), but in Britain at any rate they would appear to have lacked the wealth of their Medieval equivalents, the parish churches.

An exception may be made for the 'Triangular Temple' on the south-east side of Verulamium (insula vii) sited at an important road intersection (78). The temple itself was tripartite with a central *cella* for the cult image and flanking rooms for water tanks. In front was a large courtyard with an altar, the base of which was still in place. The plan with the *aedes* lying well back in its court does not accord with the majority of temples in Britain, and the ready availability of water for purification is suggestive of an Eastern cult.

Finds from the courtyard demonstrated that the temple was much visited. Many pits contained animal bones. Of special significance was the ox-skull buried behind the altar as a foundation-deposit (79). The presence of carbonised pine-cones might point to the cult of Cybele and Atys, for the latter died under a pine. A considerable number of little pots were found in the courtyard as votive-offerings (72). None was inscribed but they bring to mind the pot excavated near Dunstable dedicated by the *dendrophori* (tree-bearers of Atys) from Verulamium.

The best find from the temple was a lamp-cover of terracotta, evidently used to give shaded illumination, so necessary in the temples of Eastern deities where a mystic and emotional atmosphere prevailed (80). However it must be pointed out that lamp-covers have also been found in the normal Romano-Celtic temples at Chelmsford and Godmanchester.[87] The Walbrook Valley lies west of the political administrative and commercial nucleus of Roman London. With the exception of the Mithraeum, evidence for religious activity consists of a large number of small finds including votive pots, white clay Venus-figurines, a leaf-shaped plaque showing the three Matres, theatre-masks, bronze letters and *defixiones*. It is reasonable to see the area as a special religious complex like the Altbachtal near Trier.

Springhead too was less a town than a religious centre. Its shrines expected to welcome pilgrims, and it is not surprising that numerous ex-votos have been found in the course of excavating them.[88] The same is even more true of Bath which, like such richly appointed sanctuaries as Fontaines-Salées in Gaul was first and foremost a religious site. Later it was defended by a wall and assumed some of the attributes of a town. As such it managed to survive into the dark ages, and

79 Triangular temple. Ox skull buried behind altar

80 Terracotta Lamp Chimney from Triangular Temple. Height 49 cm. *Verulamium Museum*

ultimately re-emerged as a town and a Christian religious site. The temple at Bath is architecturally comparable with that at Colchester; it functioned differently, however. Far from being an *arx aeternae dominationis* it was thronged by Romanised natives, by Celts from the Gallic provinces, by Roman soldiers and by their Greek freedmen. It attracted tourists who came to marvel at its hot springs and also at the curious stones which were burnt on Minerva's altar, coal from the Forest of Dean – though coal seems to have been used quite widely in Roman Britain for heating purposes. Furthermore it was a pleasant social centre which provided an urban focus for the rich villa-estates in the surrounding countryside. Apart from agricultural produce, some of these estates manufactured pewterware. Moulds have been discovered at Landsdown, while appropriately pewter vessels have been found as offerings in the spring. Over 16,000 coins in all denominations were recovered recently in a partial clearance of the spring. They include four of gold and a few coins struck in the Greek East, the gifts respectively of the very wealthy and of the occasional oriental traveller. Some coins had possibly been cut and defaced, in other words 'killed' in the same way as the miniature weapons and pots from other temple sites discussed above.[89]

The Bath temple is not the only pilgrimage centre to have been examined in the area. The temple of Mercury at Uley was probably more restricted and local in its clientele, but offerings were numerous. Auxiliary buildings such as an inn and baths were provided for visitors and there was a priest's house (the pagan equivalent of a vicarage) for the officials of the cult. Certainly people came from throughout the surrounding countryside in order to consult the god.[90] The magnificent octagonal temple at Nettleton Shrub, Wiltshire, was dedicated to Apollo. Here the settlement seems to have been more extensive than the sacred area itself, but the shrine was extremely impressive in what was otherwise simply a ragged village, and included a beautiful riverside pavilion perhaps where the god, whose powers of healing are well-known, could visit those struck with disease, although its excavator suggests it was a *schola*, where a 'brotherhood' associated with the cult met.[91] The temple of Nodens at Lydney Park was probably dedicated to a healing cult as well. Unlike Nettleton, it stands on a hill and is not on a major road; nevertheless it became wealthy and the temple was embellished with mosaics. As we have seen, it too had a healing pavilion (*abaton*) and an inn, as well as a suite of baths. All these bring to mind the great Greek pilgrimage sites such as Epidauros (and indeed those of the Christian Middle Ages).[92]

Special sanctity might also explain the temple at Woodeaton near Oxford. Certainly it is not near any major urban centre, but it may have lain at a conveniently central point in a prosperous countryside to be a market and a fairground, at which the gods would preside, or on the tribal boundary between the Dobunni and the Catuvellauni.[93] A little Harpokrates pendant and a gold magical 'gnostic' charm show that even practitioners of the Oriental cults were not inhibited from coming here. This is also true of a temple at Hockwold, where finds relate to Atys, and which in general also looks like a market centre of some sort (see Chapter 5).

For most of the year visitors to Woodeaton must have been few but at times, perhaps just before the harvest when extra labour was needed or after harvest when the produce was marketed, there were great and colourful celebrations. So far, no theatre has been found as at nearby Frilford, where an 'amphitheatre' has recently been recognised. This shows that crowds were expected on festival days at least. Large numbers of coins recovered from the temple also suggest a successful local shrine, which in this case is known to go back to Iron Age times. As at Nettleton there were other buildings which either directly or indirectly must be connected with the existence of the temple, as a centre of pilgrimage and of trade.[94]

Temples must often have owed a great deal to commerce, not only because they provided convenient venues for fairs or facilities for travellers like inns and baths, though that was important, and is part of the explanation for the development of the town of Bath Spa, *Aquae Sulis*. The merchant's life in the ancient world was dangerous and uncertain. He was often the stranger, alone in a strange land, in especial need of divine favour. He also had the money to buy an offering or even to embellish a shrine.

Our best evidence for merchant dedications connected with Britain comes from two temples of *Nehalennia* in Holland (Chapter 3). We may imagine the great barges laden with Rhenish pottery waiting in harbour while their owners made vows to the goddess which they joyfully discharged a month or so later on their return from trading across the sea, by the dedication of an inscribed and sculpted altar in the temple courtyard. An interesting analogy is to be found at the great prehistoric mound at Newgrange, Co. Meath in Ireland, where a number of coins, many of them of gold and silver as well as jewellery, were deposited. It is most likely that these were dedicated to the gods by Irish freebooters. However here, outside the Imperial frontiers, we have no idea what deity or deities were involved.[95]

Temples also existed at British ports. There are two temples at Richborough which are worthy of investigation in this respect and there were surely others elsewhere. Dover is a very likely spot and so is London, though the evidence here for a wealthy trading community patronising religion is largely Mithraic, thanks to the discovery of the Walbrook Mithraeum which, like the Mithraea at the port of Ostia, probably had a largely mercantile membership.

Small rural shrines serving a far more local population also existed. There can be no firm dividing line between these and the pilgrimage centres. However small the sanctuary, it will have had some outside visitors and even a stall for trinkets. The temples at Lancing Down in Sussex and Brean Down, Somerset are perhaps typical examples, though unfortunately absence of finds deprives us of knowledge of dedication and ritual.[96] However, in the Gloucestershire Cotswolds, where limestone is abundant and easy to carve, we may see many examples of modest 'village' sculpture from minor local sanctuaries such as the figures of Mars from King's Stanley near Stroud, and of mother-goddesses and the local Genius at Daglingworth and of Mars Lenus at Chedworth – the last a temple very near the villa.[97] Temple 6 outside Colchester was dedicated to Silvanus as two inscriptions on bronze tablets and a little ex-voto figurine of a stag proclaim. It was surely patronised by citizens of Colchester who liked hunting in the woods and fields around. A similar purpose was served by the larger of the two shrines of Vinotonus Silvanus on Scargill Moor near Bowes in Yorkshire (Chapter 3). There were at least six other dedications here, as well as the primary one (and a quantity of coins and pottery), so the shrine was visited no doubt by hunting parties from time to time. A smaller shrine with an altar dedicated by a centurion, Julius Secundus, seems to have been less frequented; it was simply a personal act of piety comparable with the embellishment of a guild chapel or house-shrine. It is unlikely that either shrine was properly inaugurated, especially the smaller one, or had regular priests serving at its altars.[98] Nemesea were visited by soldiers, gladiators and others in especial need of the services of the goddess of retribution and fate. She had shrines in the military amphitheatres of Chester and Caerleon (**81**), and probably also in the civil amphitheatre at Silchester.[99]

Mithraea outside forts may be regarded as intermediate between private chapels on the one hand, and public temples on the other. A mithraeum was hardly private in the sense that the man in the street could miss it; at the Trier Altbachtal, at Carrawburgh and in the Walbrook valley, London, the mithraeum was cheek by jowl with other temples. Yet not everyone could enter into a mithraeum.

In some ways analogous were *Collegia*, dedicated to one of the regular Graeco-Roman gods, where one had to belong to a particular status grouping; for instance to be a foreigner (*peregrinus*) at Silchester or to belong to a particular trade such as that of the smiths (*fabri*) at Chichester.

Evidence of organisation is sparse. The *Collegium Peregrinorum* erected statues of an offical character in a temple in insula xxxv, but it will normally have met in its own *schola* behind closed doors. It is very likely that this 'Society of Foreigners' consisted of wealthy merchants with considerable influence in the town. A possible meeting place is the *schola* in insula xxi. The Silchester 'church' is thought by some to belong

81 A probable *Nemeseum* in the Caerleon Amphitheatre

to a pagan cult and perhaps it could have served as guild chapel, though it is probably too late for the Peregrini[100] (Chapter 10). At Lincoln there were guilds of Mercury and Apollo. From one of these or from another guild was the *curator*, perhaps the treasurer of such a society, who dedicated an altar to the Fates. Another title for such a treasurer was *arkarius*, and an *arkarius* at Chichester set up a dedication to the mother-goddesses, the Matres Domesticae. This cult was probably Rhenish in origin and the members of the cult perhaps came from this region. To judge from the central position of the Temple of Neptune and Minerva, the Guild of Smiths (*Collegium Fabrorum*) was an influential body in the town from an early date. The combination of the goddess of artificers (Minerva) with the god of the sea (Neptune) would have been appropriate for a guild of ship-wrights, though the actual choice of deities may have owed more to the position of Chichester or even to the agents of Romanisation, having Athens and its cults in mind (Chapter 3), than to the whims of the *Fabri*.

Hunting and forestry would have been under the patronage of Silvanus. A bronze finger ring found at Wendens Ambo in Essex is inscribed *Col(legium) Dei Sil(vani)*. It is not a signet, but it may have been a pass to allow members to enter meetings.[101] In the 'military zone' of Britain, we may note a guild of Mercury established at Birrens. Here two statues of the god were dedicated, presumably in the guild-chapel. *Scholae* have been recognised in the eastern compound at Corbridge, and the well-known temple of Antenociticus at Benwell looks more like such a *schola* for a group of friends who had undertaken to honour the god than a normal local cult-site. It is to be noted that the men who dedicated altars are all military officers, and the building is more suitable for meetings (as would be held in a mithraeum or church) than for normal public temple-activities.[102]

There is sufficient evidence to show that guilds were widely disseminated. Apart from burial clubs (in the army, and the *dendrophori* of Atys), and members of licensed Oriental cults, these religious and quasi-religious confraternities were the only societies sanctioned by the Roman government. Like the medieval guilds (such as the Guild of the Holy Cross at Stratford-upon-Avon) their influence on religious, social and economic life must have been very considerable.

Sorcery

If guilds were allowed, sorcery was certainly illegal: for calling on the 'powers' was not like calling on the gods. Witches and Sorcerers were deemed to have entire control of these forces for good or ill. Religion was linked to morality; magic could be used to disturb society. It was often destructive and could not in any case be overcome by normal means. Ancient literature is full of its dangers (for instance the 'werewolf' story in the *Satyricon* and the necromantic beginning of the *Golden Ass*) and Roman history reflects the anxieties of the rulers that sorcery could be used by opponents of the regime (e.g. Tiberius' expulsion of 'soothsayers' in the first century and the great sorcery-treason trial in the reign of Valens in the fourth century). This widespread belief in sorcery is shown by the vast number of amulets which survive as protection against it.

Magic is the antithesis of religion and, strictly speaking, belief in the gods should have cast out superstition – but it did not, and uneasily the two lived side by side; magic practices even intruded into the Roman religious calendar, for instance on the *Lemuria* (see Chapter 2). The holy shrines, as we have suggested, like beacons of light held magic at bay. Priest-power, based on learning and tradition, must here surely be seen as a force of enlightenment casting out secret and strange terrors.

We may note the use or rather misuse of lead tablets as *defixiones*, to 'fix' enemies with a curse, often by the practice of transfixing the tablet with a nail.[103] Such practices go back to early Classical times, and continue to at least the sixth century AD. There is a famous account in Tacitus' *Annals* of the resort to Black Arts by Germanicus' enemies in AD 19, which effectively secured his death: 'It is a fact that explorations in the floor and walls brought to light the remains of human bodies, spells, curses, leaden tablets engraved with the name "Germanicus", charred and blood-smeared ashes and others of the implements of witchcraft by which it is believed the living soul can be devoted to the powers of the grave' (Tacitus, *Ann.* II, 69). Lead tablets from the Athenian Kerameikos were thrown down a well, probably in order to reach the infernal deities.[104] Rivers and springs are sometimes used in Roman Britain for the same reason. A *defixio* found in the London Walbrook curses Titus Egnatius Tyrannus and Publius Cicereius Felix, and of course a great number of tablets have been found in Minerva's spring at Bath. Strictly speaking, the only magical ones are those where the goddess is not invoked, like the first to be discovered, where a man and a woman who had abducted a girl called Vilbia are pronounced accurst with a list of horrible effects that will happen to their bodies. The *defixio* from a burial at Clothall, Hertfordshire, curses one Tacita. She might be the woman buried there, and the tablet thrown in by an enemy, but this seems unlikely. Another possible explanation is that this Tacita is the Mother of the Lares, and that the curse is aimed at her as a malevolent spirit who might torment the deceased. Ovid describes a witchcraft ceremony aimed at propitiating Tacita. An old hag binds threads together with lead, and then after placing seven black beans in her mouth, mumbles a spell. She roasts the head of a small fish which she sews up and pierces with a bronze needle. Upon it she drops wine and concludes by saying. 'We have bound fast hostile tongues and unfriendly mouths' (Ovid, *Fasti* II, 565ff).[105]

Cursing belongs to an ancient strand of anthropological experience which continued to thrive. Laurence Sterne reproduces a supposedly Christian form of excommunication with a list of the parts of the body to be cursed, because it seemed so ludicrous to him in the Age of Reason, and a grave fault in Catholic Christendom at the time. Regardless of their religion, some of his less educated contemporaries were sticking pins into felt hearts and placing them with urine, nail-clippings and other things into bottles; the witch-bottle was (and maybe still is) a response to the same fears that gripped men in antiquity.[106]

To guard against 'the powers' often envisaged as the Evil Eye, then as now men had recourse to amulets (Chapter 7). Some amulets show a phallus balanced by a representation of the *mano fica* gesture, a thumb clasped by the fingers. This gesture was aimed against hostile powers, and in discussing the bronze amulets incorporating the *fica*, Dr Graham Webster writes that it must have appeared 'all the more necessary in the army, pitted against barbarian foes with their own powerful gods'. However, it was by no means confined to soldiers. On the *Lemuria* each year, the head of the household made this gesture in a primitive ritual which involved splitting black beans from his mouth with averted head and saying, 'with these beans I redeem me and mine' (Ovid, *Fasti* V, 421ff).[107]

The fertility virtue of the phallus was emphasised on the *Liberalia* (17 March) when a giant phallus was pulled around the countryside on a cart; at Lavinium a virtuous matron wreathed such an image. Eloquent testimony to the power of the phallus may be seen by any visitor to the bridge abutment at Chesters fort, where a large phallus is depicted in relief upon one of the lower blocks of stone. Phalli are depicted, as well, in humorous compositions; at Wroxeter a winged phallus combined with a hand making a *fica* gesture pulls a cart and from Long Bennington in Lincolnshire, a man rides upon a phallus with two legs. Presumably these were attached to the walls of houses, where the ribald humour of the owner and his need for security from evil powers were equally obvious to the passer-by, who probably shared both.[108]

The import of this chapter may be summarised by saying that if people brought their problems to the gods, the gods (often through the agency of priests) could solve them. For many men the comforts of faith were less sure after they had left the reassurance of the temple precinct, and there was frequent resort to superstition. Soldiers engaged on building or repairing the Wall had many gods, and Jupiter and Mars could have been invoked (and probably were) when the Chesters bridge abutment was constructed. As a divine power, the phallus makes little sense except as an attribute of the procreative deity, Priapus, but that is to ignore the irrationality of man, then and now. Even the great and almighty gods have their limitations in practice. Amulets could always provide protection, even when the wearer was devoted to religion. Only the most rigorous of Christians or philosophical pagans would refuse to adopt so pragmatic and circumstantial an approach to the uncertainties of the universe.

7 Religion and Superstition in the Home and in Daily Life

Religious practices played an important part in Roman daily life. They bound members of families together and regulated the relationship of the individual to the state. On the one hand the bystander at a state sacrifice felt personally involved in something important; on the other, even a prominent politician would appreciate the sanctity attached to groves and streams and boundary posts or, indeed, his own household shrine. The world of the gods was very near when every fountain had its nymph, every valley its *genius loci*.

Spirits of the Place

Genii loci are widespread in the ancient world, even in Roman Britain. They were no less important for being unnamed. Roman Britain was largely a land of quiet countryside, of pleasant farmland, dark woods and rugged moors. The mood of the traveller riding along the roads might vary from elation when passing through well-cultivated fields to fear and trepidation as he went into a dark valley or a forest, but the whole land was full of little gods whom it was a good idea to propitiate.[1]

For Romans everywhere, the most important god of the place was the spirit who presided over the household, the *Lar familiaris*. One such *Lar* is a central character in the play *Querolus*, written for an aristocratic and probably pagan household in fourth-century Aquitaine.[2] His first words express his importance: *Ego sum custos et cultor domus*, 'I am the guardian and caretaker of the house'. In this play, indeed, the *lar* successfully guards a young man's inheritance – a pot of gold – from the machinations of an evil servant. In origin the *lares* were probably gods of the fields and beneficent spirits of dead ancestors. They were worshipped in particular at the *Compitalia*, held in early January, shortly after the Saturnalia, at crossroads and in the home. It was a happy festival in which slaves participated alongside free men. There is an iron axe from Newstead on which is a punched-out inscription, *C(enturia) Barri Compitalici* – the Century of Barrus Compitalicus. The cognomen of this centurion, as Mark Hassall has pointed out to me, suggests that he was born on the *Compitalia*, but this event took place no doubt in Gaul or Italy.[3] The *Lar familiaris*, who can be seen as the *lar* of the *familia*, the servants, belonged especially to the home. His place was in the house-shrine, the *Lararium*, of which examples from Pompeii and Herculaneum survive in good condition. In Britain slight traces of *Lararia*, the bases of platforms, have been found in houses at Silchester and Verulamium, and an apsidal *aedicula* in the middle of the wall of a room at Dorchester, Dorset, also probably held a *lararium*. We have to reconstruct the contents of these and others from evidence abroad. Certainly there would have been the Lares themselves, probably in the form of youths wearing short tunics and holding wine vessels (*rhyta* and *paterae*) and frequently dancing. This Hellenistic conception of what a young servant should be like was probably invented in Augustan times. Figures of *lares* have been found at Silchester, London and Cirencester, amongst other places. An image of the *Genius Patris-familias*, who presided over the head of the household, also stood in the *Lararium*. He is shown wearing a *toga* with head covered and holding a scroll and *patera*. There are numerous examples from Roman Britain including one from Silchester pierced by two nail holes so that it could be permanently attached within a shrine. Others have been found at Richborough and in the shrine of the Nymphs and the *genius loci* at Carrawburgh where we may suspect that the figure was interpreted as the Genius of the Place. That may also be the explanation of the *genii* in the caches of figurines from Lamyatt Beacon, Somerset, and Southbroom near Devizes, Wiltshire. Similarly, the *Lar* in the Felmingham Hall hoard, Norfolk, was perhaps a country spirit, as indeed the *Lares Compitales* were intended to be.[5] Foundation deposits under the floors were probably intended for the *lares*. For instance, in the natural sand at one corner of a room in the villa at Moor Park, Hertfordshire, 'was buried a small 'poppy-head' beaker of good form and fine, thin ware. Beside this was a handful of bird bones, perhaps from a domestic fowl.'[6]

The probable association of *lares* with ancestral spirits makes them relatives of the *manes*, however much this might seem to be belied by their gay, Hellenistic guise. The *manes* were principally invoked on grave monuments, dedicated *Dis Manibus*, 'to the divine Shades', but for many Romans the individual personalities of the ancestors were kept alive in the busts (*imagines*) displayed in the house. Busts are regarded as so much part of the general repertory of Roman art that we do not stop to question their significance. For the Romans, the seat of life resided in the head, an idea which they shared with the Celts. If they could retain a likeness of the head, surely the spirit which had once inhabited the man would reside there.[7]

The notion is a primitive one, but it retained its force even in one of the most sophisticated houses yet excavated in Roman Britain, the Lullingstone villa. It is thought that the second-century owner may have been involved in the administration of the province. His two portrait busts (of immediate forebears?) were sculpted from Greek Pentelic marble, probably by Greek artists (**82**). We do not know whether the owner's family was also Greek. It is most interesting to find that a century later, at the end of the third century, when the house had a new owner, the busts were again venerated, as powerful house-spirits no doubt. Two vessels, one of them containing the rib-bone of a sheep, were set up before the portraits. The excavator, Lieut.-Col. G W Meates believes that the new family was Romano-British and if so, the rites show that the cult of the ancestors had made an impression on the upper reaches of provincial society. Indeed, it is at this time that the temple-tomb, or mausoleum, was erected (see Chapter 8) for the veneration of deceased members of this later family.[8]

The 'palace' at Fishbourne is clearly a special case; a 'Campanian' country house transposed to Britain. It is likely that the hall at the eastern end of the north wing held statuary. Some at least may have been family portraits, which may have included a child whose head, in Italian marble, was found in the excavations. At

Caerwent, a remarkable find was made in house VII. A sandstone head stood on a low platform. It was not a polished example of Roman art, but reflects local Romano-British tradition. A similar head has been found at Llandysul. It could be regarded as a translation into local stone of the Etrusco-Roman *imago*.[9] *Imagines* were not necessarily beautiful marble portrait busts like those from Lullingstone, and the chapel in *exedra* 25 of the House of the Menander at Pompeii contains some remarkably primitive 'idols'.[10]

It may be noted that this aspect of commemoration using portraits could be transferred to actual tombs; that at Weyden near Cologne was fitted up as a house and contained busts. In Roman Britain, as we shall see (Chapter 8), busts appear on tombstones. The *Genius* was incidentally shown as a serpent in paintings on the walls of household shrines, and although this is not attested for Britain, it is possible that serpent-bracelets and serpents shown on pottery were often thought of as representing genii. A complete example of such a pot containing the ashes of the deceased, with serpent handles, was found at Verulamium in the eighteenth century.[11] (But see Chapter 10 below, for an alternative explanation of serpent-vessels, connecting them with the Thraco-Phrygian deity Sabazios – who had Bacchic associations.) The link between house-shrine and tomb may be found in the February festival of the *Parentalia* as well as on the anniversaries of birth and death of parents and loved ones. On such occasions the family would troop out to the tomb to feast and celebrate (Chapter 8).

Apart from the regular items of household gods and *imagines* (not necessarily kept in the *Lararium* as such), other deities might be represented in a house-shrine. Trimalchio's held a marble statuette of Venus, as well as a box containing clippings from his first beard, an entirely inappropriate sign of vanity. A beautiful bronze Venus-figurine was found in the cellar of a house at Verulamium (building XIV, 5). It may have been discarded in late Roman times because the owner had become a Christian, although it is doubtful whether many Romano-British Christians of the curial class would have been so puritanical that fine works of art would have been scrapped. It is better to see the latter day owner as a scrap merchant lacking in taste. Unfortunately, although many bronzes no doubt come from domestic contexts, few have been published as definitely from houses. A suggestive group from the centurion's quarters at the end of a barrack block at Chester consists of a miniature altar, for private devotions, a silver spear (perhaps from an image of Mars) and a bronze tortoise (one of Mercury's familiars).[12]

The difficulty when it comes to better quality works of art is to distinguish between statues kept for their aesthetic value (and the houses and gardens of Pompeii, Herculaneum and Ostia were full of such pieces), and figures kept for their religious value. We may suspect that the marble cockerel from the Bancroft (Bradwell) villa comes from a Mercury group, and we know that Mercury was widely worshipped; The Diana-Luna and Cupid and Psyche from Woodchester are far more likely to be mainly decorative. A large marble statuette of Bacchus from the villa at Spoonley Wood, Winchcombe (**84**), would very possibly have been regarded as a *triclinium* ornament if found in the house itself, but it was buried (with the owner of the villa?) and it is clear that it was then taken extremely seriously as an image of the Saviour of the Dead.[13]

82 Marble bust from Lullingstone
Roman Villa, Kent. Height 71cm.
Property of Kent County Council

Fortuna, Bonus Eventus, Ceres and other nature gods

There are a fair number of stone figures and reliefs of Fortuna from houses, confirming that she was as popular amongst civilians as in the army, and as protector of the state and Emperor. There are at least six sculptural representations from villas and one from a town house in Cirencester (**83**). Several of them come from bath-suites as Fortuna was particularly needed by naked, defenceless men, and the baths themselves were the major fire risk of the house. An attractive figurine from Chilgrove, Sussex, shows her seated with wheel and globe; at Llantwit Major, Glamorganshire, she stands with globe, rudder and wheel, and at Rudston, Yorkshire, she is also figured with a wheel. At Kingscote, Gloucestershire, she stands holding a cornucopia and *patera*, and at Stonesfield, Oxfordshire, her attributes are the same, but a *Genius* (to be equated with *Bonus Eventus*) stands beside her. The veiled head from Bignor, Sussex, now lost, is probably Fortuna conflated with Ceres.[14] Ideas associated with Fortuna extend from the world ruler, a goddess equivalent to Nemesis, to Ceres, companion to *Bonus Eventus*. An especially graphic illustration of the importance of Fortuna comes not from a house but from a ship. A vessel excavated in the Thames mud at Blackfriars was launched

83 Statuette of Fortuna from a house in the Beeches Site, Cirencester. Height 54 cm. *Corinium Museum*

with a foundation deposit in her mast-step consisting of a worn coin of Domitian. It had been selected because its reverse depicted the goddess Fortuna. The ship ran aground while carrying a cargo of rag-stone; on that occasion Fortuna let it down![15]

We must remember that most villa owners were engaged in agriculture, and thus the corn-goddess *Ceres* was important to them. Ceres is a very popular deity on signet rings, and people were far more attentive to her than epigraphic evidence and other finds suggest. A fragmentary clay stand with depressions around its sides, originally eight in number, found in a corn-drying kiln at Crookhorn, Purbrook, Hampshire, is probably an offering-table or *Cernus* for first fruits.[16] A deep concern with nature may be seen in a house-shrine at Lullingstone (the Deep-Room), a tiny cult chamber dedicated to the nymphs, to judge from the painting in the niche on the south side. It portrays 'a triad of Water Nymphs, perhaps regarded as the deities of the River Darent, which flows north just to the east of the villa'. In front of the painting was a ledge 'upon which may have stood some votive object'.[17]

This was not the only *nymphaeum* in a villa. If a country house had a convenient water supply, it was as well to be friendly with the controlling deities. The *nymphaeum* at Chedworth was actually the reservoir of the villa. An altar (uninscribed) was found buried in the north-east corner, discarded no doubt when the owners of the mansion became Christian. Even then, a distinctive pagan aura may have lingered around the 'sacred spring' leading to Chi-Rho symbols being deliberately scored on the facing stones around the rim – unless, as Professor Charles Thomas suggests, that was to turn it into a baptistry.[18]

The *nymphaeum* theme could be treated with the utmost seriousness as here, but it was always open to playful conceits. Did the owners themselves know where one attitude ended and the other began? The Chedworth example, though close enough to be regarded as part of the house, had something of the character of a garden pavilion, the sort of structure that the Romans themselves loved as much as their spiritual descendants at Stowe, Stourhead or Rousham in the Neo-Classical age. Furthermore, the great *atrium* at Woodchester with its major mosaic portraying Orpheus and the beasts appears to have had a central basin, a device which the nymphs at the corners of the mosaic take up. At Brantingham in Yorkshire too, nymphs surround the image of a City-Tyche (perhaps equated with Brigantia) in the reception room of a villa.[19]

As we shall see in the final chapter, there is reason to think that some of the highly decorated rooms in late Roman houses were used for religious cults, pagan in the case of Littlecote and Brading, Christian at Lullingstone and Hinton St Mary. Frampton offers a mixture of elements which point to to use in private cult, and certainly demonstrate seriousness and preoccupation with otherworldly concerns.

There was nothing to limit the diversity of one's private religious life. Even in the *triclinium*, the fire on the hearth was *Vesta* to whom the *Paterfamilias* would offer a morsel of food, just as the head of a Christian household says grace.[20] Especial devotion leads to house-shrines being expanded, and at Lullingstone and Verulamium (building XXVIII, 1) cellars were constructed for this purpose. The Verulamium shrine was never finished; its fine apse, 'suitable for a cult statue almost life-size', offered no clue as to the character of the cult.[21] The late Roman cult rooms are a natural development considering the increasingly spiritual nature of late antique thought.

Countryside preoccupations had always meant that Romans worshipped and sacrificed in their own fields, orchards and forests. The festival of the *Compitalia* in early January has already been mentioned in connection with the *Lares*, but there were very many other rural rites. For instance, there was the *Terminalia*, dedicated to Terminus, the god of boundaries, on 23 February. Boundary stones were set up around the property with elaborate foundation sacrifices and each February farmers garlanded the stone and performed a sacrifice. An example of such a boundary stone from Caerleon was inscribed *Termin(us)*.[22] Excavators of villas are now paying much more attention to estates and should be on the look out for such markers. The bound-beating ceremony of the *Ambarvalia* in May resembles later Rogationtide custom.[23] Such rites themselves suggest a measure of continuity, better demonstrated in Gaul where, if we follow Gregory of Tours, Gallo-Roman paganism was still alive in the sixth century.

Amongst the spirits on the land who needed propitiation was Silvanus. He was a god of gardens and orchards and also of hunting. One of the very few inscriptions recovered from a villa in Britain is a mid second-century altar dedicated to Silvanus by a Roman citizen Gaius Indutius Felix (Keynsham, Somerset). Silvanus was also venerated at Chedworth, where the evidence is a relief. The dedication to Unconquerable (*Invictus*) Silvanus by Gaius Tetius Veturius Micianus on Bollihope Common near Durham shows that personal veneration extended far from the dedicator's home (see Chapter 3). The two Vinotonus shrines near Bowes discussed in the last chapter also belonged in the first instance to Roman officers learning how to cope with the wild.[24]

Every tree, spring, cross-roads, the weather, birds and animals provided contact with the divine or demonic. St Clement of Alexandria mentions a cave in Britain (probably Wookey Hole in Somerset if the account is taken as factual) at which the wind produces a sound like the clashing of cymbals (Clemens Alex, *Stromata* vi, 3); this wonder was the subject of religious – or superstitious – awe amongst the pagans, although the Christian bishop adopts a strictly rational approach.

Arnobius gives us a graphic picture of how the superstitious pagan might behave in his daily life: 'Recently, o blindness, I worshipped images drawn from furnaces, gods fashioned on anvils and with hammers, elephants' bones (ivory figures?), paintings, ribbons on trees, hoary with age. Whenever my gaze fell upon an anointed stone, daubed with olive oil, I would, as if there were some power in it, show great respect to it; I would speak to it, and ask blessings of it though it was a block without feeling' (*Adversus Nationes* i, 39).[25] It differs little from the advice given by Cato in telling the farmer how to farm. Clearly prayer and ceremony were as important as the quality of the soil, farm stock and tools.

Not much of Arnobius' list would have survived to confront the archaeologist. For the ribbons on trees and stones, apparently sacred, we have to turn to sacro-idyllic painting, but for the anointing, the bowing down in front of natural features, the actual behaviour of the Roman Britons, we are almost at the mercy of imagination. Almost – but not quite.

The evidence of mosaics and paintings

Provided we are prepared to accept that the wall-paintings and mosaics in houses meant something to their owners, and that there was some reason why particular themes were chosen for jewellery and especially the bezels of signet-rings, we may get a little nearer to the spiritual attitudes of individuals. Such material may suggest ideas not found in temple dedications. For instance, an obsession with death is attested on jewellery and mosaic from Britain, an observation which is to some degree confirmed by Petronius' satirical reference to Trimalchio's morbidity.[26] We see, especially in mosaic, the employment of mythological themes to illustrate moral points, piety or the victory of Good over Evil, the power of fate; a use of art resembling that of the Christian employment of Bible stories. Another new dimension in religious life is the appearance of certain deities – Bacchus and Ceres for instance – who are hardly represented in inscriptions.[27]

Mosaics are especially informative, because they were expensive and were only laid after much thought. Moreover, since they adorned floors, many of them survive. The British material has been well studied by Dr David Smith, in a number of important papers. He concludes that while most of the figured pavements 'appear at first glance to consist of conventional representations of gods, goddesses, and mythological heroes, or of personified phenomena, or of favourite episodes in mythology', others are harder to dismiss in this way and even 'raise far-reaching questions'.[28]

The theme of the *memento mori* is presented quite explicitly on some mosaics in Italy as a skeleton, and a floor from Verulamium showing a ravening lion carrying a stag's head in its jaws comes into the same category. It is possible that a roundel on the Dyer Street pavement at Cirencester showing Actaeon torn to pieces by his hounds, a theme found on many Etruscan ash-chests and Roman sarcophagi, also has this meaning; other roundels here depict Bacchus himself, Silenus and the Seasons, so it could be interpreted in the words of a tombstone from Wroxeter as proclaiming that 'the gods prohibit you from the wine-grape and water when you enter Tartarus'.[29]

However, the pessimism is vitiated in both instances by the fact that Bacchus was known preeminently as a saviour-god. The *canthari* on the Verulamium floor represent the spiritual refreshment Bacchus offers his devotees, while the Cirencester mosaic is more justly interpreted as saying that the life given by Bacchus and his *thiasos* is greater than death. Bacchus appears in his own guise not only in Cirencester but at a town house in London, as well as at several fourth-century villas, including those at Stonesfield, Oxfordshire, and Thruxton, Hampshire. Although Bacchus was the god of wine, we have already seen him invoked as a saviour-god in the marble figure from the Spoonley Wood grave (**84**), and should not reject the explanation that he was present as a preserver from death on mosaics – even though he was also, naturally, Lord of the feasts (held in the *triclinia* where these were laid) – inebriate diners would no doubt have considered that he was banquetting there in person.[30]

Certainly the themes of the marine *thiasos* (i.e. Neptune and his followers), and of dolphins and other marine creatures, probably represent the voyage of the soul over the sea to the Blessed Isles. Dolphins are shown flanking a wine jar in a Verulamium mosaic, and one carries Cupid on his back on a floor at Fishbourne. Dolphins flank masks of Neptune or Oceanus in a third-century mosaic at Dorchester and on the fourth-century Frampton pavement.[31] Here, a Latin verse inscription refers to 'the head of Neptune . . . his deep blue brow encircled by a pair

84 Marble statuette of Bacchus from a grave near the Spoonley Wood Villa, Gloucestershire. Height 39.9 cm. *British Museum*

of dolphins'. This might be a literary conceit like the elegiac couplet about Europa and the Bull at Lullingstone, but there is some reason to believe it has an esoteric meaning. The mosaic also includes a Chi-Rho, which suggests either considerable Christian use of pagan themes, or that the floor was laid with Christians and pagans in the same household in mind.[32] In a subsidiary chamber, one of the devices has been recognised as showing Aeneas cutting the Golden Bough from a sacred oak prior to descending into the underworld (Virgil, *Aeneid* VI, 210–11). As Anthony Barrett writes, 'the mosaic lends great support to those who see in these pavements a deep spiritual significance . . . no other mosaic scene provides better evidence for preoccupation with the mysteries of the afterlife'.[33]

It may further be noted apropos the dolphins on the Frampton and other pavements, that they and other sea creatures were figured in the *cella*-mosaic at the Lydney Park temple, where they refer to Nodens in his capacity as a healing and saving deity with otherworldly functions. If the mosaic has a real meaning in a temple, we are entitled to believe that it also had significance in a villa.

The representation of the birth of Venus from the foam of the sea carried with it the idea of generation and regeneration – there is a splendid wall-painting in Pompeii showing Venus carried to land on a sea-shell and this is echoed by a mosaic with the same theme from Hemsworth, Dorset. It must have been a common subject in Roman art.[34] Venus is shown in the centre of a floor at Rudston, Yorkshire, accompanied by a triton and a bust of her appears on the Kingscote pavement where a separate panel shows fish.[35]

The amorous aspect was not excluded, but it is not necessarily a light-hearted genre theme. At Kingscote, the wall decoration of the room shows Cupid approaching a figure seated on the ground with a shield beside him or her. The published explanation is that it shows Achilles in disguise amongst the daughters of King Lycomedes, implying that Love must perforce yield to the mission of the hero, but I am inclined to see here the same mighty earth-goddess, 'source of life and power', who appears on the great Boscoreale fresco, again with a shield beside her, mourning the dead Adonis.[36] Whatever the explanation at Kingscote, there can be no doubt that on the Virgilian pavement at Low Ham, Somerset, Venus is the controlling power over human life and passion.[37] She stands flanked by cupids, one with torch raised (life) and the other with torch lowered (death), while around her we see the story of the ill-fated amours of Dido and Aeneas. The patrons of both Kingscote and Low Ham knew what they wanted to be portrayed, and what was shown was essentially religious in its connotations.

Legends about the gods were part of the background to religion, and they certainly occur in art from houses rather than in temples. On mosaic, apart from Aeneas plucking the Golden Bough, and Dido and Aeneas, we find the *Lupa Romana* (Aldborough, Yorkshire), Hercules lifting the giant Antaeus with Minerva helping Hercules (Bramdean, Hampshire), Apollo and Marsyas (Lenthay Green, Dorset), Jupiter as an eagle abducting Ganymede (Bignor, Sussex (**85**)) and as a bull carrying off Europa (Keynsham, Somerset, and Lullingstone, Kent). A number of mosaics show Orpheus charming the beasts (for instance, at Woodchester and Barton Farm in Gloucestershire), and Bellerophon on Pegasus, slaying the Chimaera, is to be seen on three floors (Hinton St Mary, Frampton and Lullingstone).[38] The myths can be interpreted in a number of ways. The rapes of Ganymede and of Europa for instance might signify the rapid transition from this life to one of greater

85 Ganymede and the Eagle on a polychrome mosaic at Bignor, Sussex, *in situ*. Diameter of roundel 213.4 cm

splendour in the heavens. They could be used as funerary images, and the Ganymede theme, adapted to that of Imperial apotheosis, is shown on the soffit of the Arch of Titus. At Lullingstone, the journey of the Europa Bull over the sea accompanies Bellerophon's similar flight. However, there is nothing heavy-handed here. The dining guests read a witty couplet about Jupiter's infidelity and enjoyed the Europa myth as a good story.[39]

The Marsyas myth is a warning against pride; Marsyas challenged the god Apollo to a musical composition and lost, so humans beware! Far better to trust in a deity like Minerva for help, as Hercules did. Orpheus floors may sometimes be associated with villa chapels, for instance at Littlecote, Wiltshire (where Orpheus-Apollo presides over the seasons), but not necessarily in every case. However, even in the great *nymphaeum*/reception room at Woodchester we remember the immortal singer who went down to the underworld for love and who charmed the beasts. As we have seen (Chapter 5), the Bellerophon theme could have a Christian explanation, though it must be emphasised that the legend had been used widely in the Roman Empire, and indeed earlier on Greek mosaics.

Virtually all the pavements mentioned date from the fourth century, when literary culture was at its peak, manifesting itself in renewed interest in mythology, and a renewal of obscure cults. In the final chapter we must return to the theme to assess the significance of those mosaic schemes where – as at Frampton – the religious impact is so strong that we may speculate that we are dealing with cult chapels. Here we may conclude by noting one element to be seen on several floors including Fishbourne, Cirencester (Dyer Street), Brading and Bignor; the head of the Gorgon Medusa. The terrifying mask, which turns all who look on it to stone, was transformed into the head of a sad and beautiful woman in its classical version, but it never lost its power in attracting and holding the powers of Evil, turning them away from the individual. It was a life-giving image, and an Ostian mosaic appropriately carries the legend *Gorgoni Bita*; 'Life to the Gorgon'. This is a charm found as clay *antefixa* upon buildings, and in pediments, including that of the Temple of Sulis Minerva at Bath, where the type is conflated with a water-god, probably Neptune. It also occurs on tombstones and coffins and again, as we shall see, on amulets. Its ubiquity demonstrates the shadowy co-existence of super-stition and religion to which we have already referred.[40]

Signet-rings and other portable objects

In his companion volume, Professor Thomas gives portable objects such as jewellery a low 'weighting' as evidence.[41] Our aim here is rather different; not to establish where there were communities of worshippers of the Roman gods (an impossible and pointless task given the fact that few if any Roman sites fail to give us any evidence on the matter), but rather the range of individual expression. Every aspect of daily life may be included. For instance, while modern working tools are essentially utilitarian, a Roman blacksmith might own a *butteris* ornamented with a bust of Minerva to give 'further protection from the goddess of craft'. Steelyard weights were sometimes cast in the form of divine figures, for instance, Isis at London, Bacchus at Silchester and Silenus at Richborough.[42] One from Kingscote in the form of the bust of an Empress (Faustina II or Fausta) invokes the Imperial cult for the same reason. It warns the owner not to invoke the gods or the *Domus Divina* in vain, as he would in effect be doing by giving short measure.[43]

At feasts, images of Bacchus, satyrs and maenads ornamented the tripods used to hold mixing bowls; in the baths men – especially soldiers – might like to be reminded of Hercules. A strigil from Reculver has a handle in the form of a Hercules club (1), while, even more splendid, the handle of one from Caerleon has the Labours of Hercules rendered in inlay. Hercules too appears on an ivory knife handle from Eccles in Kent.[44]

Women sometimes wore hair pins in the form of *thyrsi* or with a *cantharus* at the head, invoking Bacchus, or else the bust of a deity; Isis perhaps, or Minerva. The sun and the moon are shown on necklaces and bracelets in the Backworth treasure (piece, of jewellery closely matched at Pompeii, so not Celtic in origin) – a reference to the *aeternitas* of the heavens.[45]

Signet rings are especially sensitive indicators of individual preoccupations, religious and otherwise, because we know that they were chosen with care. Our ancient authorities tell us of the pride and deliberation with which the great men of antiquity adopted particular devices. Even more interesting is St Clement of Alexandria's advice to his congregation, respecting the choice of devices to be employed in seal-rings (Clemens Alex, *Paedagogus* III, 12, 1) and especially his worry that some of his flock might be so lax as to wear signets portraying idols.[46] Many ringstones were probably selected for religious reasons in that the owner wished to keep the image of a particular god ever near him; others were chosen for more superstitious reasons – the device would drive away the force of the Evil Eye. The dividing line between these is not always easy to determine. Even today, the relative religious and amuletic significance of a crucifix or of a St Christopher is difficult to determine and will vary from individual to individual.

Something of the range of religious preoccupations may be appreciated by citing a selection of the intaglio devices recorded from Roman Britain. Religious ceremonies are sometimes shown, usually with men and women bringing offerings to altars. Although the female votaries shown on gems from South Shields and Mumrills could be bringing offerings to any deity, on other intaglios the scene is more complex and there is sufficient evidence to reveal that it belongs to the sacro-idyllic tradition, wherein Bacchus or Priapus are the predominant deities. A very fine red jasper intaglio from Corbridge shows a man bringing an offering to a circular shrine which matches one on a gem from Vindolanda, where it seems to contain an image of Priapus. On the Vindolanda gem, the worshipper was the fertility-god Pan, and other members of the *thiasos* are sometimes shown as votaries, especially Cupid who makes offerings at altars on gems from Bath and Strageath.[47] Many gems show Bacchus and his *thiasos*, and this suggests that the god was more important than the almost total absence of inscriptions on stone and the relatively modest quantity of surviving sculpture suggests. One very fine red jasper intaglio found in Carlisle and almost certainly engraved in the region shows a satyr holding the infant Bacchus. The young god, born from the ashes of *Semele* grew into a potent power of nature. A memorable portrait of Bacchus as an adult is to be seen on another red jasper intaglio from Cambridge. A gem found near Rodborough, Gloucestershire, shows Bacchus or a satyr with a panther. It is cut on an amethyst which, as its name implies, was a specific against inebriation; the *bon viveur* might well think that Bacchus on an amethyst would be a valuable specific against drunkenness (see *Anth. Pal.* IX, 748). For the same reason, images of inebriation (*Methe*), figured as a woman holding a wine cup to her lips, appeared on gems.[48]

As the Bacchic *thiasos* was associated with prosperity, so were *Bonus Eventus* (equated with the Greek demigod Triptolemos) and the goddess Ceres. Fortuna too is very frequently shown on gemstones, sometimes holding the fruits of the earth, which equate her with Ceres. A cornelian intaglio found in recent excavations at Carlisle shows Fortune enthroned. A small figure kneels before her – he is probably to be taken as the owner of the sealstone, her votary, who thus commits himself into the hands of Fortuna just as his medieval equivalent would be shown, in a Book of Hours or a Triptych, in homage before the Virgin Mary.[49]

Other major deities of the Roman State often portrayed include Jupiter, Juno, Minerva, Apollo, Mars, Venus, Diana, Mercury and Victory. Mars and Victory are figured especially frequently on gems from military sites, as we might expect. Mercury's ubiquity matches that of figurines and dedications around Britain. *Dea Roma* is shown on gems from York, Cirencester (**28**), Silchester and Colchester, which are all large cities, and we may wonder whether her appeal was not mainly to city councillors (*curiales*) and to the freedmen priests of the provincial cult

(*Augustales*). The Colchester gem was set in a gold ring (the prerogative of men of high rank and specifically of the Equestrian order); could it have been the seal of a member of the Provincial Council?[50] A complicated symbolic language allowed deities to be invoked simply by the use of symbol. For instance, a gem from Silchester shows raven, lyre, tripod and laurel, and must refer to Apollo, while a glass intaglio from Waddon Hill has a palm of Victory, the club of Hercules, the steering oar of Fortuna and the corn-ear of Ceres.[51]

The ready recourse to symbol can help us to understand larger-scale religious sculpture. The figure of Roma or Britannia upon the Hutcheson Hill distance slab is depicted handing a wreath to an eagle. It may be compared with a gem from Caerleon showing Mars crowning a trophy, or others from Newstead and Newcastle-under-Lyme, where Victory does the same thing. The pantheistic Brigantia from Birrens is to all intents and purposes the *Dea Panthea* on gems from London and York, who like her wear the helmet of Minerva and display the great wings of Victory (**103**). The veneration of the standards implied in inscriptions is brought home to us as individual piety when we find the eagle and standards theme on gems. These gems were actually worn by legionaries, who were in desperate need of divine succour, so they wore the image of the protecting powers of their units almost as an invocation to the gods of Rome. In the light of these gems, it is surely mistaken to see such inscriptions as those to the standards of a cohort at High Rochester as purely formal.[52]

Gems were worn by members of the literate upper reaches of society, and they do demonstrate very clearly one of the major findings of this study: that for the Romanised provincial, the gods were envisaged in fully Roman guise. A huntsman shown in a fine gem from South Shields, probably cut in the same studio that produced the Carlisle satyr, in northern Britain has been plausibly identified as Cocidius (**86**). Otherwise the Celtic element is *entirely* lacking here, and this lack of evidence cannot be without significance when we decide how people approached the gods.[53] The rarer Eastern cults, however, are represented amongst gems from Britain by a number of interesting intaglios. Each of them was in all probability owned by a devotee of the cult, and so these finds augment our knowledge of the presence of oriental religion within the province. One gem implies that someone thought it worth invoking Zeus Heliopolitanus even as far from Baalbek as Corbridge. This deity is only otherwise attested in Britain by two inscriptions from Carvoran, garrisoned by the *Cohors I Hamiorum*. The Corbridge gem may have been owned by a member of the local oriental community which included Diodora, the priestess, who set up an altar to Herakles of Tyre (Melkaart) and Pulcher, whose dedication was to Astarte. Barathes of Palmyra came from a city situated even further east.[54]

A cornelian intaglio from the fort at Castlesteads is now only known from a drawing. It depicted a bust of Serapis between two other busts which were probably those of Isis and Harpokrates, the divine triad being accompanied by the acclamation 'one Zeus Serapis' (**87**) (Chapter 5). Also from the Wall region is an intaglio found at Chesterholm (*Vindolanda*). Here, a youthful bust of the Sun god is shown with the corn-measure of Serapis on his head. He also wears the horn of Zeus Ammon. This conflation of two or more deities became common in the Middle Empire (**88**).[55]

Oriental gems from the Wall region probably belonged to traders or to military personnel. This is certainly true of the intaglio set in a ring, found in the strong room at the fort of Great Chesters (Aesica), where it may have been put for safe keeping. One of the brooches in the hoard is distinctively Pannonian, and the owner of the treasure, including the seal-ring, may have served in the Danube region. The subject is here the great cosmic deity *Iao*, a version of the Jewish god. He is a curious figure with the head of a cockerel, the body of a Roman officer and snaky feet – perhaps symbols in turn of the upper air, the earth and the underworld. Iao was identified with Hades, Zeus and Helios, according to an oracle of the Clarian Apollo (Macrobius *Sat.* 1, 18, 18–20), and amulets showing him often carry the name Abrasax (or Abraxas), the letters in Greek adding up to the days of the solar year and also Sabaoth, which means 'Lord of Hosts'; or 'Ruler of All'.[56]

In the towns of southern and midland Britain, small settled communities of orientals probably existed for much of the period. At Wroxeter, gems showing Isis and Serapis have been found, while at Silchester, an intaglio cut with the image of Iao and another showing a sun god mounted on a horse also surely came from the East. Most remarkable of all is a beautiful green plasma gem on which the Genius of the Roman People wears the corn-measure of Serapis (31). The victory of Roman arms is made dependent on an Eastern god. It is likely that this gem was intended to refer in addition to Caracalla, who was very attached to Serapis. Imperial

86 *Left* Silvanus-Cocidius (?) on a red jasper intaglio from South Shields, Co. Durham. 2 × 1.5 cm. *Museum of Antiquities, Newcastle upon Tyne*

87 *Above* Isis, Serapis and Harpokrates on a cornelian intaglio from Castlesteads, Cumberland. Drawing: original gem is lost. 2 × 1.6 cm

encouragement of Eastern deities is well attested especially in the case of the Unconquered Sun, and one of the sides of an official seal of an Imperial estate from Kingscote shows a head of *Invictus Sol*.[57]

Christianity is represented by a glass gem from the Barnsley Park villa, depicting the Good Shepherd. This was a widely accepted allegory of Christ. Bellerophon slaying the Chimaera seems to have a Christian meaning on the three Romano-British mosaics of Hinton St Mary, Frampton and Lullingstone, and it is largely for this reason that the glass intaglio also showing the episode, set in a fourth-century gold ring from Havering-atte-Bower, Essex, may be regarded as Christian. No doubt attaches to the engraved bezels of bronze, silver and gold rings listed by Charles Thomas, which figure the Chi-Rho. They are certainly Christian.[58]

The great interest in cosmology with the pseudo-science of astrology was largely Eastern in origin, but men and women who wore the device of Moon and Stars (ringstones from Silchester, York and Caerleon) may have been doing no more than taking up a well-known symbol for *aeternitas* which had even occurred on the coinage. Nevertheless, the eternity of the Heavens had neo-Platonic ramifications, and implied belief in the Afterlife.[59] An Orphic gem from Piercebridge figures the strung lyre (of Orpheus) with arms composed of dolphins (a reference to the voyage to the Blessed Isles?), and a sleeping hound (hounds

88 Helioserapis on a red jasper intaglio from Vindolanda, Northumberland. 1.6 × 1.15 cm. *Vindolanda Museum*

89 Iron ring from Piercebridge, Co. Durham containg a red jasper intaglio portraying an Orphic lyre. Diameter of ring 2.4 cm; gem measures 1.2 × 1 cm

were often associated with the otherworld) (**89**). It hints at the earlier presence of this optimistic philosophy a century and more before the great fourth-century series of Orpheus mosaics was laid in Britain.[60]

The Use of Amulets

The high philosophical ideals of a Christian – or a neo-Platonist – contrast with the superstition of the many. Not surprisingly, it is at the personal level of amulets that we find most evidence of superstition. This is a very large question, and we should begin with a few general remarks. The use of the term 'magical amulet' has often been restricted to double-sided Eastern gems like those portraying Iao cited above, and the Welwyn childbirth amulet which invokes Isis against the malignant power Typhon, who is responsible for contractions in childbirth, and to gold lamellae (like those from Caernarvon, York and Woodeaton, with secret formulae engraved on them). These are very interesting, but they are very rare in Britain. No more than nine are known to me. Others are recorded from Germany, and there are rather more from Italy, but Dr. Sena Chiesa, who has made a study of glyptic material from Aquileia and Luni is firmly of the opinion that they are imports. We are probably in almost all instances looking at the possessions of a small Eastern immigrant community.[61]

Something further may be said of them, but first we must look at gems and related objects which Westerners would have worn. Immensely popular throughout the Empire were combinations of human and animal heads and parts. There is a hint in Plutarch that these grotesques attracted to themselves, and away from the wearer, the force of the Evil Eye. However, the almost universal inclusion of a Silenus head and the appearance of such Bacchic attributes as elephant heads demonstrate a Bacchic connection. Appropriately religion is conjoined to superstition here.[62] Examples have been found on both military and civil sites, including Corbridge, Castlesteads, Silchester, Wroxeter (**90**), London and Kirmington (Lincolnshire). The most intriguing is a gem from Caistor St Edmund showing three heads joined as a triskele, with an elephant head apparently reinterpreted as a bald pate with a long lock of hair, and the palm in the trunk as a corn-ear. An inscription around the head seems to read *CEN*; if so, perhaps an abbreviation for the Iceni.[63]

90 Combination of four heads upon a red jasper intaglio from Wroxeter, Shropshire. 1.6 × 1.3 cm

This combination of Celtic and Roman themes in an amulet may now be compared with a bone rectangle from the villa at Bradford Down, Pamphill, Dorset. It is carved in relief with the head of a cat joined to a human head. The amulet was probably attached to the wrist with a leather strap. Similarly shaped objects but in bronze and ornamented with abstract designs were made in the pre-Roman Iron Age, and it is possible that here the main Roman element lies in the relative naturalism of the double mask.[64]

Gorgoneia, masks of Medusa, were frequently worn in jewellery, often as cameos cut out of onyx and set in finger-rings or worn as pendants. Many pendants were made of jet, a black fossil wood mined near Whitby and probably carved in or near York. The black colour and electrostatic properties of jet were important reasons for choosing it for amulets designed to combat dark, underworld forces. Presumably it would attract, mesmerize and destroy the evil powers. Some jet pendants, including *gorgoneia*, have been found in graves, where they were re-used to protect the dead (**91**), and a fine example from Chelmsford was included in what seems to be a votive cache of jet objects.[65] Some enigmatic jet pendants (examples from Richborough, Wroxeter and Milton Keynes) are approximately axe-shaped.[66] Pliny writes that the Magi (Sorcerers anywhere?) are said to use jet on what they called 'divination' by the use of axes (in ea quam vocant axinomantiam – *NH* XXVI, 142) and it is tempting to see these pendants as connected with the practice. Ultimately, they are probably reflections either of sacrificial axes or prehistoric implements (Neolithic and Bronze Age axes), discussed below.

The phallus was a universal charm in all sections of society. Small gold rings

91 Jet pendant from Strood (near Rochester), Kent showing mask of Medusa. 4.9 × 4.3 cm. *Ashmolean Museum*

with phalli in relief on their bezels, such as have been found in London (**92**) and at Faversham in Kent, clearly belonged to the children of wealthy men, probably of Equestrian rank. Infants seem to have been regarded as especially vulnerable to the baleful stare of the Evil Eye (*fascinatio*) and required the protection of the spirit of the phallus, *Fascinus* (Pliny, *NH* XXVIII, 39). Other phalli were made of bronze, like those excavated in London after the Great Fire, and once in Elias Ashmole's collection which interested John Aubrey and other early antiquaries. Soldiers and their horses used bronze phallus charms; one from the Lunt is combined with a hand making the *mano fica* gesture against the evil powers. Two from sites in Kent (Boughton Aluph and Margate) combine human heads with phalli, thus allying the apotropaic power of the genitals with the *genius* inherent in the most obvious and important part of the body. The bases of antlers were also used, probably because of a sympathy between a powerful male animal and human virility. We have seen in Chapter 1 that a stag's antlers gave potency to the Celtic god Cernunnos. The antler base alone might be enough even without the phallus, like one from the legionary base at Longthorpe near Peterborough, also a soldier's charm, perhaps rivetted onto his belt.[67]

No example has yet been found in Britain of the gold *bulla* (an oval, box-like amulet) which well-to-do Romans, following Etruscan precedents, hung around their babies' necks, but we do have specimens of other distinctive Roman charms, like the wheels and crescents, representing the sun and the moon, clubs of Hercules and cylindrical amulet cases either for a written prayer on gold leaf or for some magical substance such as sulphur. A clay bust from London represents the infant Bacchus wearing a *lunula*, and it shows that these amulets, like *bullae*, were suitable for children, but the Backworth necklaces figuring both the sun and the crescent moon were owned by adults. It is tempting to see the wheel-like solar emblems here, and from Dolaucothi, as connected with the local manifestation of Jupiter, the wheel-god Taranis, in view of the wheel which appears between the horns of the Cernunnos on the Petersfield coin, and in the copious evidence for

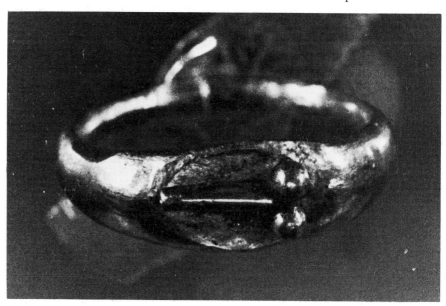

92 A child's gold ring with phallus in relief on bezel. From London. Diameter of ring 1.5 cm; length of phallus 0.7 cm. *Museum of London*

wheels in the religious art of Roman Britain, including the Felmingham Hall wheel, and also a mace-head from Willingham Fen. A complicating factor in so simple an explanation is that the sun and moon are universal symbols and the specific items of gold jewellery mentioned have Italian and even Near Eastern prototypes.[68]

The Hercules club, represented by examples from London, Birdoswald, and the Thetford treasure is certainly fully Classical in inspiration. Like the Reculver strigil, it invokes the hero who could do everything, and it was clearly lucky. The larger examples, like that at Thetford, were probably hung from the neck as charms, but the smaller ones were ear-rings and we can only speculate that they were regarded as amuletic by their owners.[69]

There is no such doubt about the amulet cases; similar objects are still employed by Orthodox Jews who bind *tefillin* (or in Greek *phylacteries* which means 'to guard against evil') to themselves containing sacred texts from the books of *Exodus* and *Deuteronomy* including the Great Prayer the *shema*, 'Hear O Israel, the Lord our God, the Lord is One'. In addition *mezuzoth* are fastened to the doorposts of their houses, again including the *Shema* text. The word *Shaddai*, 'Almighty' is visible through an opening and this, a Name of great power, should be touched when entering or leaving the house. We are reminded of the invocation *Adona(i)e* on the gold amulet from Wood Eaton. Jewish practice in preparing the texts preserves much of the attitude of sanctity and awe towards the sacred which was general throughout the ancient (pagan) world. For instance, before beginning to write one of these invocations, the scribe should say 'I am writing this for the sake of the holiness of *tefillin*' and when he comes to one of the names of God he says 'I am writing this for the sake of the holiness of the Name'. If even one letter is missed out the whole text is worthless (see Chapter 2). Amulet boxes made of gold have been found in Britain at York (contents still unknown) and at Thetford where it contained sulphur, regarded as a magical substance, instead of a text. Apart from the Woodeaton leaf mentioned above, there are examples from Caernarvon (containing a Hebraic element in its phrasing) and another from York. Their formulae are closely comparable to those on magical papyri which have not survived in the damp climate of the Roman West. There may be some sort of link between the use of gold here, and the employment of silver – and sometimes gold – for ex-votos to deities. Noble metals, especially incorruptible gold, suit the high purposes of personal protection, while base lead is the metal for retribution and cursing.[70] This reminds us that particular materials may have had amuletic importance to their wearers. Jet, as we have seen, was one; amber (which also has electrostatic properties) was another. Artemidorus tells us that to dream of amber rings was of benefit to women (*Oneirocriticon* 2, 5). A ring figuring the head of Minerva in relief has been found at Carlisle and may have been owned by a woman who wished to invoke the saving power of the goddess.[71]

It may be observed that gemstones depicting Jupiter are frequently cut on milky chalcedony; those showing Sol are often on heliotrope which was thought to reflect the sun's rays; of Mars on red jasper or cornelian, the colour of blood; of Demeter on green jasper which has a sympathy with vegetation and of Bacchus on amethyst which was believed to be wine coloured hand to prevent drunkenness. Such systems of correspondences, differing in detail no doubt, form a continuous tradition linking the Hellenistic age to the very end of the Middle Ages. During all that time lapidaries, stone books, were consulted. No doubt they were in Roman Britain.[72]

The Graeco-Egyptian amulets combine elements from Egyptian, Greek, Jewish and other sources.[73] They are much more complicated in their symbolism than the phalli, the Hercules clubs or even the fabulous combinations on intagli which were fully at home in the West, but their purpose was similar: to grant protection to the wearer and to overcome hostile powers. They generally contain an element in Greek letters which consists of spells and names, often 'forward and backward anagrammatised', thus providing a link with some of the lead tablets. In both instances this is presumably because the demons can read better when invoked in looking-glass language and because mirror-writing requires knowledge (*gnosis*) to be interpreted. They are inscribed on gold like the amuletic *lamellae* mentioned above, or engraved on gemstones, in which case iconographic devices are generally engraved on at least one side of the stone. When mounted in a ring or pendant, one side remains hidden as a secret word of power, a *vox magica* or unspoken name for the divine like 'Abrasax Sabaoth' on a gem depicting Iao in the Thetford treasure.[74]

Religion or Superstition?

The borders between religion and superstition are very imprecise and shadowy. Iao has been considered in this work as a deity despite the fact that all the stones which show him are double-sided 'amulets'. The haematite birth-charm from Welwyn used against Typhon depicts the goddess Isis, legitimately the protector of women: Could this not have been employed as a prayer on stone addressed to Isis? The silver Mithraic charm from Verulamium shows on one side the birth of Mithras from the rock and on the other, the names of *Ormazd* and *Mithras*, as well as the Egyptian sun god *P'Re* (**93**). Is this an example of a Mithraist imbued with Middle Empire syncretism, wishing to be reminded of the beneficent powers in the world, or is Egyptian magic involved as well?[75]

Superstitious objects do not of necessity deny the religious attitude entirely. We can understand the complexity of the situation if we think of Christian experience. On Christian rings, the Chi-Rho may have the same magic significance as a representation of the cock-headed god Iao. Indeed the Chi-Rho had appeared in the sky to Constantine, so both can be regarded as emblems of the power of the divine in the heavens. What did the invocation *Vivas* or *Vivas in Deo* mean to a Christian? It was surely much more an amuletic catch-phrase than a spur to faith. The question of religious motifs in jewellery has remained unresolved through history. Are they aids to faith or superstitious charms? The problem increases in the case of those too unromanised or too impoverished to express themselves through their possessions. The Irish sacred site at Newgrange has been mentioned in the last chapter. Similarly, the beads and broken pieces of glass and natural pebbles tell us nothing of what the Caledonian owner of a cache of objects from Cairnpiple, Aberdeenshire thought of the world around him. The very fine glass intaglio depicting a satyr from the deposit helps to date it to Roman times, but it is scarcely credible that its meaning was understood. A Late Bronze Age palstave which had been embellished with silver studs was found in the immediately pre-Conquest Lexden tumulus, and a small Neolithic stone axe was found unstratified

93 Silver Mithraic amulet, from Verulamium. Diameter 1.8 cm. *Verulamium Museum*

on the site of the Hayling Island temple, perhaps regarded as a thunder-bolt, and dedicated to the gods in the late Iron Age, or more probably in Roman times. Four pyramidal stones and a Bronze Age flint arrowhead came from the Romano-British cremation of a child at Gatcombe, Somerset. They were surely not toys, as the excavator suggested; they bring to mind the 'elf-shot' of folk-tale, or 'the right Elatrope', a small jadeite axe mounted in a sixteenth century English silver setting now in the British Museum. It is said to be 'the special stone to staunche blooding and good against poyson'. Such amulets were not confined to the lowest classes of society as this much later object shows but the beliefs embodied belong to very primitive and unsophisticated religious beliefs.[76] Such evidence has been collected by Dr. Anne Ross; our difficulty is to know when we can apply it to the recognisably Roman culture of Britain where, by its nature, we are led to consider only a relatively affluent society.

The archaeologist can reveal something of the way of life of those who lived below this level, and the thoughts and fears of some of the poorest members of society are perhaps reflected through the strange language of the inscribed leaden tablets, the *defixiones* from Bath, Uley and elsewhere. However, here the constraints of the cult and of the local scribes mean that these thoughts appear in a Roman guise.

A people without culture cannot have a history. The lowest classes, following the ways of life of their forebears, evade our scrutiny. But this would have remained true if we were writing about the Middle Ages. Enquiries like the Domesday Book, useful for purposes of assessing tax, did not touch on belief. Even Death, the great leveller, levelled the poor more than the rich, the non-Romanised more than the Romanised. Much of our evidence for funerary customs merely transposes the Roman love of display and competition in building and self-aggrandisement into another realm.

8 Religion and Burial Practice

Views about death were affected by religious attitudes in general. Even the most cursory study of literary and epigraphic evidence shows that there was no one Roman attitude to death, even though at times there was some uniformity in custom. The range is from almost total disbelief in anything after this life in the works of the Epicureans Caesar and Lucretius, or in the epitaph on a Wroxeter tombstone, proclaiming 'drink while your star still gives you time for life', through a cautious optimism at least in the survival of reputation, as Tacitus enunciated in his encomium on Agricola (*Agricola* 46), to the sublime hope of immortality expressed in Cicero's *Somnium Scipionis* (though elsewhere Cicero is more agnostic), or the Christian slogan on a bone casket-mount from York: *S[or]or Ave Vivas in Deo*, 'Sister, hail! Live in God!'.[1]

How the Other-World was Conceived

In very general terms we find ideas changing during the Roman period. In the late Republic and even the early Empire, cynicism and pessimism were more prevalent. Later, the impact of Neoplatonism, the cult of Bacchus, the Eastern mystery cults and Christianity made men and women more hopeful. Despite attempts to prove the contrary, the sudden spread of inhumation and of sarcophagi in the Antonine period does seem to correspond with a change of mood, an increased urge to look after or even venerate the body. The Lullingstone temple-tomb, the Holborough sarcophagus and various (?Christian) gypsum-burials are clear manifestations of this trend.[2] Alongside philosophic hopes and fears, there were traditional festivals devoted to ancestor worship and thus linking the living and the dead with a firm bond, especially the *Parentalia* in February and the *Rosalia* in May, when members of families feasted at the tombs or strewed them with roses, and a mythology of Hades, Dis and Charon's Fee, which provide a counterpart to such traditions. This is not the place for a full survey of burial rites in Roman Britain, a vast undertaking which fully deserves a volume on its own. However, burials and tombstones provide evidence for what people believed about their place in creation, relative to the supernatural world.

If we were to believe Caesar and other writers, the Celts and more particularly the priestly philosophers, the Druids, taught that the soul was immortal. It is most unlikely that the *Druids* were philosophers in any real sense, but it is almost certainly true that many of the Celts thought warriors who fell in battle were certain of rich rewards in the afterlife – and such beliefs made them fearless and bold. Archaeology shows us something of how the otherworld was conceived, at least by some, in the Arras-type graves of eastern Yorkshire and, much nearer Roman times, in the chieftain graves of Essex, Hertfordshire, Bedfordshire, Cambridgeshire and Kent – which indeed contained imported amphorae for wine (rather than oil or *garum* (fish sauce)?), Italian drinking vessels in pottery, glass and silver and bronzes (**94**). In addition there were fire-dogs for the roasting of meat, the remains of food (corresponding to the Celtic warrior's 'Champion's portion') and even board games. This series of graves continued into Roman times; one of the latest Welwyn-type tombs, that from Standfordbury, Bedfordshire, is probably of Flavian date.[3]

The same 'Belgic' beliefs in the other-world feast are manifested in two late first-century cremations from Winchester. One of the graves was excavated intact, and the objects it contained included samian vessels, a bronze jug, a glass jug, an elegant shale trencher (imported from the Durotrigian region around Dorchester), a knife, a spoon, and as the owner was literate and very probably a scribe, two *styli* and a seal box. But the main emphasis is on providing a banquet for the dead, with a meal that included a young pig and poultry. The excavator states that 'what seems established is that the Grange Road burials are completely native in

94 Late Iron Age tomb group from Welwyn, Hertfordshire. *Reconstructed in British Museum*

character, even if Romanised in content, and show traces of ritual practices fundamental to Belgic culture, still in full force near the end of the first century AD'.[4] This is perhaps too simple a view; Roman rituals were not necessarily so very different from 'Belgic' ones, and there had been about a century of Roman influence on at least some of the Celtic peoples of Britain.

In Essex we may look first at the rich finds, including Roman figurines and a Roman pendant from the Lexden tumulus near Colchester, and then turn to the graves of the colonists, also very richly supplied with grave goods. Grave 3 in the West Cemetery of that *colonia* is especially interesting. It contained the cremation of a child, with whom was interred a bronze skillet for libations, glass decanters, flagons and cups of St Remy ware, and a remarkable series of figurines showing diners and various household slaves, all perhaps *sigillaria* given to the child during life at the Saturnalia.[5] There was also a clay bust representing the *imago* of the boy and perhaps considered to enshrine his personality; note how close Roman belief and Celtic belief were at this point – though the Roman image normally includes the shoulders and chest as well as the head. Other pipeclay busts, both male and female, from London, York and Brighton (**95**) show that this practice was widespread.[6]

The Bartlow Barrows, on the borders of Essex and Cambridgeshire, were constructed in accord with an Iron Age tradition, and there are indeed comparable examples from Belgium, but the grave goods are significantly richly Roman.

95 Pipeclay Busts of woman, from a Roman burial at Springfield Road Villa, Brighton. Heights of both c. 12.5 cm. *Brighton Museum*

Barrow II contained a coin of Hadrian (Charon's fee), glass vessels and a gold ring (the badge of high status). Barrow III was filled with an amazing assortment of objects including a patera, two flagons, a bronze lamp, a folding chair and a glass bottle containing wine mixed with honey – *mulsum*, the refreshing Roman aperitif.[7] Thus the grave goods comprise all that the owner could wish to have with him in another world, including the flagon and patera essential for ritual libations; it will be recalled that they are very often shown on altars (Chapter 6) and they are certainly frequent tomb finds – note the Winchester jug. This idea of life within the tomb is fully in accord with Roman ceremonial feasting at the *Parentalia* and other times.

Petronius indeed shows us Trimalchio entertaining Habinnas, the architect of his tomb, and pointing out (*Satyricon* 71) with faultless logic that it is inconsistent to spend money on earthly pleasures and not on the place where one is to spend much longer.[8] However much the sophisticated reader may smile, Trimalchio has the weight of traditional belief on his side. Some tombs in Italy had *triclinia* (dining rooms), funerary gardens and other amenities. Many of them were large and intended to be impressive landmarks beside the roads. Thus it would be hazardous to claim that any grave in Roman Britain is 'completely native' any more than that any other is 'completely Roman'. It is more useful to select from the great variety of grave goods examples which throw light on individual attitudes to death, being all the time aware that at times social custom may have been as strong a factor as belief in regulating what happened at the funeral and afterwards.

A tomb relief from Rome shows the death-bed of a member of the Haterii family. The corpse is prepared and lies in state before it is taken to a splendid new house, often in temple-form, that has been prepared for it. In the early Empire however, the body was first cremated either with grave goods or without them, the grave goods being placed in the tomb afterwards. The destruction of the physical body did not, of course, mean the obliteration of the personality of the deceased – far from it.

At the time of the burial, libations of wine were made to the shade of the deceased, and a set of bronze flagon and patera was frequently left in the graves of the wealthy, for example in the Bartlow Barrows and at Luton near Chatham in Kent.[9] Like temples, tombs were formally dedicated, and the phrase *sub ascia dedicatum*, 'dedicated under the mason's axe' (i.e. before the interment had taken place) is recorded on a tombstone from Chester.[10] For the *manes*, addressed on tombstones as deities – *Dis Manibus*, 'To the divine Shades', sacrifice was acceptable and, indeed, necessary. In Virgil's account of Aeneas' visit to the underworld, a text which must have been well known in Roman Britain, the spirits are aroused by a sacrifice (*Aeneid* VI, 236–63). Joan Alcock quotes Cicero (*De Legibus* II, 22), that it was essential to sacrifice a pig; dogs and cocks, especially if they were black in colour, were also appropriate – a tombstone from Sea Mills shows both, and hounds were sacrificed at Lankhills, Winchester.[11]

Shellfish such as oysters sometimes occur in graves, for instance at Chichester, and they might conceivably have had a symbolic significance as reminders of the sea over which the happy dead had to pass. However, they were much esteemed as food in Roman Britain; vast quantities were consumed at meals within the *temenos* of the Hayling Island temple for instance. Eggs are certainly significant, however, and have been found with burials at Colchester and York. Like pomegranates, they represent the renewal of life, and were a potent symbol of rebirth. They still are, and the bereaved at Jewish funerals, by long custom, still eat hard-boiled eggs.[12]

The idea was firmly engrained that spirits could also drink, and Titus Flaminius at Wroxeter was expressing very much a minority, Epicurean view that they could not. First there was the wake, the party at the burial, epitomised by the remains of a funerary feast at Holborough, Snodland, Kent, where the dried residue of resinated wine and oil were found with the primary burial. Second, the continuing feast in the grave is represented by the vast number of intact wine vessels recovered from burials. Sometimes the wine was spiced, and a vessel found in a grave at Litlington near Cambridge, previously identified as an incense-burner was in fact an infusor: the name *Indulcius* pricked out on it may be that of the deceased (**96**).[13]

Of course, some mourners were concerned that the needs of the dead continued to be met in due style. This was the purpose of the temple-tombs discussed below. A pipe-burial was a highly convenient means whereby the living could share a repast with the dead. At Caerleon a second-century cremation burial in a lead canister was provided with a lead pipe which rises to the ground surface. The arrangement above ground is exemplified by the 'funerary table' which must come from another Caerleon pipe-burial, although unfortunately this beautiful eighteenth-century find is now lost. It was a table-top shaped like a Doric capital, fluted at the base of the *echinus*. The support must have been a fluted drum. The two most interesting features of this *monoped* were its central piercing (running down, no doubt, to the pipe) and the carving on the top of the table representing Venus holding a dolphin (of which more will be said below). It may be supposed that at

96 Burial group including wine-infusor and shovel for ashes, from Litlington, Cambridgeshire. *Museum of Archaeology and Anthropology, Cambridge*

the *Parentalia* and on anniversaries of the death and perhaps, too, at other times, a meal was eaten by relatives and descendants around the table; wine was drunk and some was poured down the hole to the deceased. Another cremation which employs two *imbrices* placed together to serve as a channel for liquids was noted at a grave in the St Pancras cemetery, Chichester. This use of tile may point to much simpler arrangements above ground, and show that the practice was not confined to the wealthy. It is incidentally recorded with an inhumation in a lead coffin at Colchester, provided with a pipe, and may have been a reasonably common practice throughout the Roman period which has gone largely unnoticed, because the channel into the grave, and of course above it, has so often been lost.[14]

Apart from food, the physical environment of the dead was catered for by the provision of perfumes like myrrh and frankincense, recorded at Weston Turville in Buckinghamshire. Evergreen plants such as box (from Chesterford and one of the Bartlow Barrows in Essex, as well as from Roden Downs in Berkshire) not only kept the grave fresh and wholesome but also suggested that, like the evergreen, the dead would continue to live. This symbolism would be emphasised by the decking of graves with roses at the *Rosalia*, and also by rosette symbols on tombstones. Aurelia Aureliana holds a bouquet on her tombstone at Carlisle, an allusion to this late spring festival.[15]

Not only must the atmosphere of the grave be sweet. It must also be light, and this is suggested by the placing of lamps in the tomb. A bronze lamp was found in one of the Bartlow Barrows, but generally the lamps were pottery. There are many examples from graves, for instance at Colchester, Chichester, York, London and Puckeridge, Hertfordshire. As Joan Alcock points out, 'they made the dead feel at home in new and strange surroundings'.[16]

Although the bringing of gifts to the deceased, and the holding of celebrations at tombs, show continuing love and veneration on the side of the living and the belief that the dead sometimes dwelt as sentient beings in the grave, on the whole the Romans preferred to separate themselves from the *manes* of their forebears, often by means of a wall, or at least the *pomoerium* of a town. It was indeed against the law to bury within towns, and where this occurs, as in the case of two soldiers thrown into a pit in second-century Canterbury, we may suspect untoward happenings. The Younger Pliny tells a splendid ghost story about an unquiet grave in Athens (*Ep.* VII, 27) and upon the *Lemuria* (Ovid, *Fasti* V, 419ff) Roman householders throughout the Empire performed a midnight ritual to expel possible ghostly intruders. In the countryside it may have been harder to separate the dead from the living, except where walled cemeteries existed, as at Langley and Springhead in Kent. These walled cemeteries had an additional advantage in providing shelter for a funerary garden where roses and other appropriate flowers could be grown.[17]

Sometimes quite a different attitude to the dead is manifested; the dead person can have the status of a hero. He is quasi-divine and his presence is actively sought by the living. Such beliefs are found in various ancient cultures, including the Egyptian. There are, of course, also hero-tombs in the Greek world (including the 'temple' recently excavated at Lefkandi in Euboea, dating from around the beginning of the first millenium BC), while in Britain we may remark the possible sanctity of prehistoric barrows, for instance at Uley, where Hetty Pegler's Tump lies very near the Iron Age and Roman site.[18] Such attitudes were perhaps strengthened by the mystery cults which took the edge off death, and above all by

Christianity which invested the grave of the martyr or saint with great power and sanctity.[19]

These attitudes are to be seen in pre-Christian cults, for instance at the temple-tomb of Lullingstone (97), which was constructed in the style of a Romano-Celtic temple and certainly dedicated to the service of the dead. Here, two inhumations lay side by side with their heads to the north and feet to the south; thus not oriented and neither suggesting a staunch belief in the Sun cult nor in Christianity. A date of around AD 300 is probable. The deceased both lay in lead coffins; at least, one coffin was of lead – the other was removed in the late fourth century by tomb-robbers. The surviving coffin was ornamented with embossed pecten shells which, as we shall see, have an other-worldly significance, and the body was packed in gypsum, a feature intended to help in preservation which was certainly popular amongst fourth-century Christians, who believed in a bodily resurrection. Here, however, the grave goods – pottery and bronze flagons, glass bottles, knives and spoons and a bronze *Medusa* mask, as well as a gaming board complete with counters, which may be compared with the set in a pre-Roman

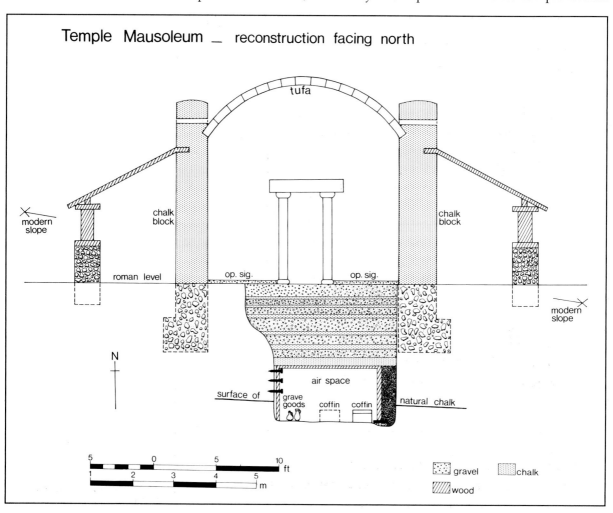

Temple Mausoleum — reconstruction facing north

Welwyn grave as well as with the near contemporary set from Lankhills – are surely indicative of a pagan rite.[20] Other temple-tombs may be suspected. It is possible that there was one at Great Tew, Oxfordshire, as David Smith has pointed out to me (although Donald Harden in the *VCH* records it as a hypocaust). The remains found in May 1810 and subsequently destroyed, consisted of a mosaic floor ornamented with 'urns and serpentine lines' above inhumations. A Roman bath representing the villa-house lay 'on the north of the temple'.[21]

Obviously, attitudes could vary. Cicero's *tempietto* erected for his beloved daughter Tullia (Cicero, *Ep. ad. Att.* 12, 36, 1) paid lip-service to the idea of deification also found in the *Somnium Scipionis*, but Cicero himself was too much of a stoic to believe it himself, at least with strong faith all the time. The owners of the Lullingstone mausoleum were surely convinced of an after-life, while Christians were so certain that the dead *indeed* lived and would be gloriously resurrected, that they were actually prepared to live at the gravesides of those whom they venerated. The Christian cult of St Alban which grew up around the martyr's tomb outside Verulamium marks a significant break with the past, because it

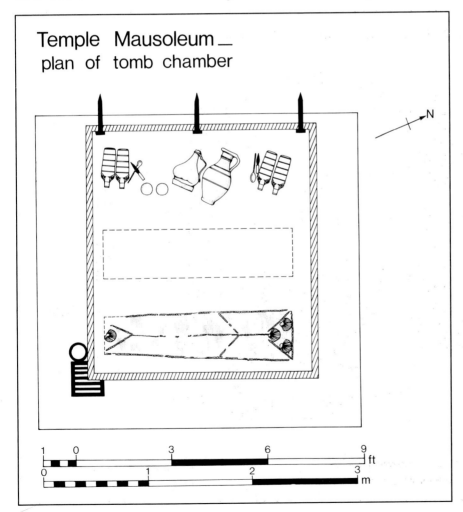

97 a & b The Temple-Mausoleum, Lullingstone Roman Villa.

98 Tombstone of Curatia Dinysia from Chester. Height 119 cm. *Grosvenor Museum, Chester*

completely ignores the boundaries between town and cemetery. In the Classical city only outcasts, lepers and lunatics would actually live in a cemetery.

Only a few of the images carved on tombs suggest the idea of the tomb as eternal home, and they are all ambiguous. The carving of a door upon a tombstone or the gable upon a sarcophagus implies that the grave is a house, and the common scene of the dead person reclining and feasting is suggestive of an idealised *Parentalia*. However, both themes are quite conventional and go back to pre-Roman times in the Hellenistic East. Joan Alcock has pointed to the contradiction that although 'the death of the body releases the spirit, yet the feeding of a dead body implies that the spirit is still imprisoned within its mortal form'. Equally contradictory is the presence of a shell-canopy, tritons and soul-birds which all belong to the conception of death as a journey to the other world on the fine grave stele of Curatia Dinysia at Chester, where the deceased is depicted reclining at a feast such as the *Parentalia* imagined as taking place beside or in the grave (**98**).[22]

Ravenous beasts epitomise the sudden approach of death – so apparent in the case of the lion from the Shorden Brae mausoleum near Corbridge (and also the famous Corbridge lion itself, clearly intended for a tomb), where the lion has seized its prey. Sphinxes, likewise harbingers of destruction, also represented the mystery of death. In addition, both lions and sphinxes were regarded as tomb-guardians; like Medusa heads they warded off the Evil Eye. This is very apparent on some early military tombstones like that of Rufus Sita at Gloucester and Longinus at Colchester, where two lions and a sphinx mount guard on the pediment. Medusa heads were not only shown on tombstones, but also appear on lead coffins, and as bone roundels and jet pendants sometimes buried with the dead.[23]

Despite the annual feasting at the tomb, it is doubtful whether many people believed – or feared – that they would spend eternity in a few yards of earth. '(Crito) was surety for me to the judges that I would remain (to stand trial), and you must be my surety to him that I shall not remain, but go away and depart.' So spoke Socrates at the end of Plato's great dialogue the *Phaedo*. Much of the evidence both from graves and gravestones in Roman Britain agrees with him, although the reference on a *stele* (written in Greek) from Brough-under-Stainmore to the soul of young Hermes of Commagene, 'winging his way to the land of the Cimmerians', and on a gravestone from Risingham to Flaminius Pansa going to a place where the ground is always frozen, make the other-world sound dark and forbidding. Even gloomier is the epitaph of a thirteen-year-old girl from York. 'The meagre ashes and the shade, empty semblance of the body' seek the mysterious *manes* who live in Acheron.[24]

However, it was clearly better even to go there than to wander for ever like the *Lemures*, and to haunt the living. The best known of all Roman funerary rites is the placing of a coin or coins with cremation or inhumation to pay the ferryman of the dead, Charon, or some other *chthonic* deity such as Mercury. It is of course possible that the vessels containing food may also have been intended as provisions before – or for – a journey.[25]

Hob-nailed boots, frequently discovered both with cremations and inhumations, are best explained as footwear for the deceased to walk to the underworld. Of course, in many instances, only the nails survive, and it has been suggested that on occasion a few nails were placed in tombs to stand for such shoes. A pair of purple shoes were found with a cremation from a rich grave in the walled cemetery at Springhead.[26] According to a widespread belief, it was not possible to walk to the other-world, for the simple reason that it lay *above* the earth or *across* Ocean. Images on funerary sculpture prove this, crescents and stars indicating the heavens and 'soul-birds' shown for instance on Curatia Dinysia's tombstone are suggestive of the actual flight of the soul. Sometimes the winds appear, and a stone head from York inscribed *D(is)M(anibus) C(onsecratum) E(st)* is thought to represent a wind-god. Of course, the winds were essential to ancient navigation, and might take their place alongside pecten-shells (*conchae*), incidentally also symbols of rebirth, dolphins and tritons as representative of the voyage of the soul over the sea to the Blessed Isles. Some people believed that the soul was purified by the elements of water and air and also fire – represented by the lions and torches ornamenting the Sittingbourne lead sarcophagus.[27] The concept of a journey, implying the continuation of active life, awakes the continuing need for divine help and protection. Many of the classical deities shrank from death, because it entailed pollution; even Artemis has to desert her beloved Hippolytus (Euripides, *Hippolytus* 1437f). However, before Christianity sundered the barriers between living and dead for ever, they had been breached in a number of ways.

Death and the Saviour-gods

Not only were there underworld deities such as Hades-Pluto, but other deities, like Bacchus, sometimes equated with Sabazios, Hermes-Mercury and Demeter were associated with the underworld, while heroes, notably Hercules and Orpheus, had passed the boundaries of living and dead and returned. The mysteries offered the formulae for eternal felicity. For instance, 'Thou shalt find to the left of the House of Hades a well-spring, and by the side thereof standing a white cypress. To this well-spring approach not near. But thou shalt find another by the Lake of Memory, cold water flowing forth, and there are Guardians before it. Say: "I am a child of Earth and of Starry Heaven, but my name is of Heaven alone. This ye know yourselves. And lo, I am parched with thirst and I perish. Give me quickly the cold water flowing forth from the Lake of Memory . . . ."' The text ends by promising felicity amongst the other heroes. The owner of the Piercebridge Orphic gem (Chapter 7) doubtless knew such passages.[28]

A rich array of mythological imagery on *stelae* and *sarcophagi* found around the Empire shows that the norm in the Empire was essentially optimistic.[29]

Amongst the deities attested in Britain, Venus has already been mentioned in connection with the Caerleon *Mensa Dolenda*, which as we have seen, in itself indicates a belief in life in the grave, while the iconography refers to the sea from which Venus was born and over which she presides. The dolphin she holds has a similar meaning to the shell and indicates the womb of rebirth. Pipe-clay statuettes of Venus have been found in graves at Verulamium, Carlisle and York, while others showing women suckling babies (*Dea Nutrix*), identifiable as Juno Lucina, a fertility goddess analogous to Venus, come from burials at Canterbury and Welwyn.[30] Minerva is also represented in funerary art on lead coffins from London and Milton-next-Sittingbourne, and on the bronze handle of an iron implement from the Ospringe cemetery, Kent. One of the few signet gems from a grave, the cremation of a soldier, merchant or smith shows Minerva. As signet-rings were usually passed on to one's heirs, it is possible that a strong factor in the Luce Sands cremation was that the gem would continue to have a use to the dead man; Minerva would stand by him as she had in the past by Hercules.[31]

Hercules was accessible to man both as a hero and a god, but in funerary contexts the fact that he had once been a man was probably of great importance: 'As I am so will you be', with the difference that it is a mighty god who calls, not a skeleton. The episode of Hercules rescuing Alcestis from the jaws of death is not recorded in the art of Roman Britain (though it is found in reliefs from a number of sites in Europe) but we do find him rescuing Hesione on a grave stone at Chester and a bronze statuette from an inhumation burial at York (now lost) showed him holding a dead serpent and an apple, an allusion to the myth of Hercules stealing the golden apples from the garden of the Hesperides. A figure of Hercules in white clay came from the same Colchester child's grave as the *sigillaria* showing diners and readers at a banquet.[32]

Preeminent amongst the saviour-gods was Bacchus (or Dionysos), who was envisaged as leading the dead to a life of triumph just as he had once rescued Ariadne on Naxos and carried her away with him to share the delights of the *thiasos*; truly he brought life to wandering men as the inscription below the London relief proclaims (**49**). A marble figurine of Bacchus was buried with one of the owners(?) of the Spoonley Wood villa (**84**), while the lead coffin from Holborough near Snodland, Kent, is ornamented with the figures of a maenad and a satyr (**99**). Here a large Y is shown on the lid of the coffin, which may be an Orphic symbol denoting moral choice in life. Pecten-shells, also included in the composition, symbolise the soul's journey to the Blessed Isles. Jocelyn Toynbee has noted of this coffin that 'once the interment had taken place, the decoration could have no effect on any living persons'. Thus the motifs were designed for the benefit of the dead and express the beliefs of the relatives who were 'if not members of a Bacchic sect, at least conversant with the common stock of doctrines and picture symbols of Bacchic other-worldly theology'.[33] It is of some interest that the second name of Curatia Dinysia on the tombstone at Chester (i.e. *Di(o)nysia*) proclaims a devotion to the deity, and that her tomb certainly expressed the idea of joyous survival after death. One of Bacchus' symbols was the wine-cup, and an elegant pottery *cantharus* found in a grave at York may well allude to him. So do the *canthari* on tombstones from Great Chesters and Chesterholm. While the majority of mosaics are not connected with graves, that at Great Tew may, as we have seen, have ornamented a tomb. Significantly, the device included a *cantharus*. Like the Christian Eucharistic chalice, the *cantharus* is suggestive of sacramental imbibing.[34]

Victory over death is presented with dramatic intensity on gravestones where the deceased appears as a hero riding down and slaying his adversary. Such scenes confined, in Roman times, to the stelae of auxiliary soldiers may be related to late classical monuments such as the Dexileos stele in Athens and to Hellenistic *gigantomachies*. In Britain, the bronze figurine from Martlesham, Suffolk depicted Mars Corotiacus riding over an enemy, while on a relief found at Stragglethorpe in Lincolnshire, a mounted Mars despatches a giant. Emperors are shown subduing their enemies in the same way, and from this idea of heroic victory it was but a short step to the idea of the Christian saint (St Michael or St George) fighting dragons.[35]

A recently discovered graffito on a pot from a grave at Dunstable, Bedfordshire, is a dedication by a guild of *dendrophori*, probably based on Verulamium. This

99 Lid of lead coffin from
Holborough, Kent. Length 106 cm.
Maidstone Museum

association of worshippers of Atys acted as a burial club. Pine-cones frequently encountered on gravestones may also refer to Atys, who died under a pine-tree, although we may note that the Bacchic *thyrsus* was itself tipped with a pine-cone, and furthermore, we have already seen that resinated wine was sometimes offered to the dead. Nevertheless, Eugenie Strong is probably right that the 'numerous examples of these pine or fir-cones in Britannia, from the crowning of graves' refer to Atys. On a Risingham tombstone, the pine-cone is associated with a cresent; at Carlisle, Aurelia Aureliana is flanked by cones, while Vitalis, whose name is in fact derived from *vita*, buried at Halton Chesters illustrates his faith in continuing life by also having a cone carved on his grave.[36]

Other deities may have been connected to the cult of the dead through religious guilds, all of which would, no doubt, have organised schemes for the proper burial of their members. Apart from the *dendrophori* of Atys, the *cultores* of Mercury at Birrens and the *Collegium Fabrorum* at Chichester, all the military units had associations which at the very least ensured proper rites for their members. In the army, membership of a burial-club was compulsory, and a deduction was made from pay to finance it. The difference between an ordinary army burial and that given by a more select fraternity was doubtless one of strict tradition versus enthusiasm. In death, as in life, official and unofficial observances must often have shaded off one into another.[37]

Petronius in his *Satyricon* presents the freedmen of Trimalchio's circle as intolerably morbid. It is likely that he was exaggerating to some degree, and there was certainly nothing corresponding to later Christian desires to be reminded of the physical facts of death. The body corrupted in the earth – the spirit had departed from it long before. Reminders of death or rather of the hope of immortality, are found ornamenting objects used in daily life (Bacchic parrots on spoons, and eggs carved on hairpins, for instance), while the busts of revered ancestors, such as the marble busts from Lullingstone, belonged as much to the home as to the tomb. Like the inscriptions upon tombstones or the commemoration of the daily lives of persons as various as a centurion at Colchester and a smith at York, these busts kept the memories of the dead fresh amongst the living and perhaps helped the dead too, wherever they were. Trimalchio (Petronius, *Satyricon* 71) said that the scenes upon his tomb would show him living after his death; not a very idealistic concept, but then he boasted that he had never heard a philosopher.[38]

The attitude of individual Romans to death gave rise to elevated thoughts, discernible to us both in iconography and burial practice. It also entailed the grossest superstition. Thus an amphora-burial excavated in Warwick Square, London, was carefully battened down with tiles and pot-lids to prevent the ghosts of the dead (**100**), evidently a mother and child, from walking. In the later Empire, corpses were often decapitated, probably to prevent ghosts from haunting the living – sometimes penal decapitation may be suspected, but the suggestion that ritual murder was practised in late Roman Winchester, men being offered to the infernal gods in order to ensure the fertility of notables, whose future life was in peril, is scarcely credible.[39] So much of our evidence for religion in Roman Britain concerns that literate, provincial-Roman society whose way of life was founded on contractual obligations, that when we find headless skeletons or the remains of small babies thrust down into the foundations of buildings (probably babies who

100 Late first-century cremation burial in Amphora, Warwick Square, London. *Museum of London*

had died in infancy) at Springhead, or the mad ravings of one of the more illiterate curse-tablets, we feel shocked by a way of thinking that is the antithesis of true *Romanitas*. Such manifestations of popular belief seem to have become increasingly common in the years of Roman Britain's decay in the late fourth and fifth centuries, despite the existence of the Christian Church, and such will be the theme of our last chapter (Chapter 10).

9 Religion and Politics

It will be apparent from our study of the Imperial cult that religion and politics were not easily divorced. The *Pax Deorum* provided divine protection for the State, just as the army provided material protection. The State could no more neglect the gods than it could neglect its fortifications. This chapter is however designed less as an illustration of unchanging factors in Roman life than as an illustration of the ways in which changing attitudes might affect even distant Britain. The ethos of the governing class in the early Roman period is splendidly evoked by Tacitus in the *Agricola*. At first sight this is not a source to tell us much about Roman attitudes to religion. Agricola fostered the building of *templa* in Britain just as he did *fora*. The reason was political, 'so that men, scattered and uncivilised and thus quick to take up arms, might be made accustomed by comfort to peace and *otium* (civilised retirement)' (*Agricola* 21). For himself, we know that he came under the influence of Greek philosophy at Massilia and had to be dissuaded from being too enthusiastic. Tacitus tells us that 'his soaring and ambitious spirit craved the beauty and splendour of high and exalted ideals' (*Agricola* 4). It is likely that Agricola shared the modified stoicism of his circle, and of the historian Tacitus. Fortitude, a sense of duty and of justice, a predisposition not to take matters to excess, a vague belief in deity and perhaps too in an afterlife — allowed the Roman to adopt an attitude of lofty magnanimity towards the cults of different regions, provided there was no clash with the best interests of the Empire.

The Druid 'Opposition'

Such clashes were essentially political rather than religious. In contrast to the Jews of Judaea whose 'Jealous God' made exclusive demands on the allegiance of his votaries, the Celts had no quarrel with the Roman system of multiple deities: They too were polytheists. All the same, there were two ways in which native aspirations clashed with the ideals of the Roman rulers. Both causes for conflict are associated with the Druids, who must be regarded as the intelligensia, holy men and priests of the Celts. The first was simply that they wanted independence. The second is that the Roman sense of order clashed with the inalienable rights of the tribes, the carrying of weapons and the sacrifice of human victims. It is easy to see that a Roman governor would be disturbed by breaches of the *Lex Iulia de vi publica*, and by slayings which to him were of course homicides. For the young Agricola, the tales of Druid excesses and the Boudican atrocities must have seemed a harsh contrast to the idealism of his philosophy.

The political power of the Druids was under threat in Gaul from the time of Augustus. The Elder Pliny tells us that the Senate had issued a decree in Tiberius' time, but says that the practice of their rites was carried on in Britain (*NH* xxx, 13). Suetonius (*Divus Claudius* xxv, 5) writes that Claudius 'utterly abolished the *cruel and inhuman* religion of the Druids among the Gauls'. The government presumably took action against the crueller aspects of celtic custom in Britain too, although its writ was at first confined to the south-east and did not include the client kingdoms or northern Britain. Suetonius Paullinus' rapid military advance into North Wales and Anglesey and the attempted absorption of the realm of the Iceni at the same time (AD 60/61) brought trouble. Tacitus does not directly implicate religion in Boudica's revolt except insofar as the Temple of the Deified Claudius was an affront to British pride, but it would not have been surprising if the remaining free Druids as a socio-religious elite were deeply involved in arousing the fighting spirit of their countrymen; further when Boudica's rebel army rampaged through Camulodunum, Verulamium and Londinium slaying everyone they met and when prisoners of war were put to death by order of the Queen, religious fanaticism may have played some part in justifying these atrocities: we are reminded of the Mahdist uprisings in the nineteenth-century Sudan.

The many skulls found in the London Walbrook are sometimes ascribed to this massacre (see Chapter 1), although recent research has shown that most are those of young adult males and not of the aged infirm and children we would have expected from Tacitus' narrative. Furthermore they show no sign of injury. Their presence in the stream does, however, suggest pre-Roman religious practice, and so some at least may be relics of the sack of London in AD 61. The bronze statue-head of the Emperor Claudius from the river Alde in Suffolk was presumably also a Boudican war trophy, which was either placed in flowing water as a votive dedication or thrown away to prevent its being found by the Romans in the hands of suspected rebels, after the failure of the uprising.[1]

The punitive Roman response to the Boudican revolt was not extended to native deities such as Andraste or against all sacred groves. A dedication from near Lincoln to Mars as 'king of the sacred grove' (*Rigonemetos*) shows that such groves continued to exist even near major Roman cities.[2] The official encouragement given to the building of temples by Agricola presumably extended to native cults which were thereby speedily Romanised. At Bath, the Flavian temple was built to a classical plan, but at Hayling Island in Cogidubnus' kingdom, the Roman structure was a stone version of the circular Iron Age shrine. As we have seen (chapter 3) an inscription from Hayling Island mentions a legionary, and thus shows how Romans made their peace with Celtic deities and transformed them into civilised Roman gods. Thus native religion survived and was even encouraged.

Stoic philosophy, predominant in the ruling circles at Rome until the end of the second century, fostered an attitude of toleration and symbiosis. Imperial influence on religion in Britain may sometimes be apparent, especially under Hadrian.

The Antonine attitude to Religion

The Imperial Peace was dependent on the skill of of the frontier armies and the strength of the *Limes*. Within the defences harmony prevailed between man and

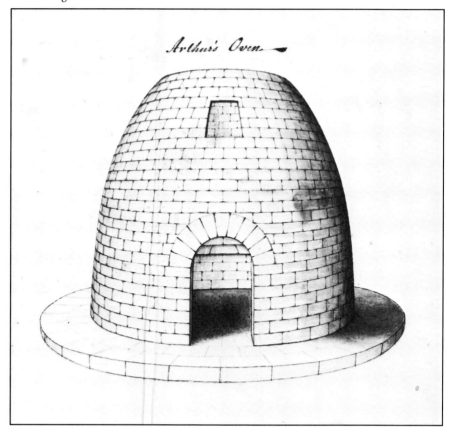

Arthur's Oven

man and between man and the gods; outside them there was only barbarism and chaos. Hadrian epitomised this with the Wall he built *divino pr(aecepto)*, in Britain.[3] Although there were sound military reasons for constructing such a frontier, its massive strength and stark, simple architecture probably had a symbolic message as well. Hadrian could not have had such a linear frontier constructed all around the Empire but he could well symbolise his world-view by selecting the shortest land frontier which was also the furthest from the Mediterranean and a place where, thanks to the gods, the barbarians had been defeated and scattered. They had rejected Roman civilisation and as a punishment they were to be shut out. In practice, as any Wall archaeologist and military historian will tell us, it was not to work like that but as a symbol it remained the grandest of all the city walls of the Empire. At the heart of the Empire Hadrian constructed other symbols of his ideals in his benefactions to Athens, the city which represented them before all others, and in his rebuilt Pantheon at Rome.

As we saw in Chapter 4, Antoninus Pius followed Hadrian's policies very closely. His building of a *Hadrianeum* at Rome with its embellishments of relief personifications of provinces, and the coins portraying provinces, in imitation of Hadrian's great provinces series, show as much. He was responsible for the Antonine Wall in Britain and very probably for the most remarkable temple or temple-like structure of Roman Britain to have survived into modern times. Arthur's O'on in the Carron Valley, north of Falkirk probably commemorated the

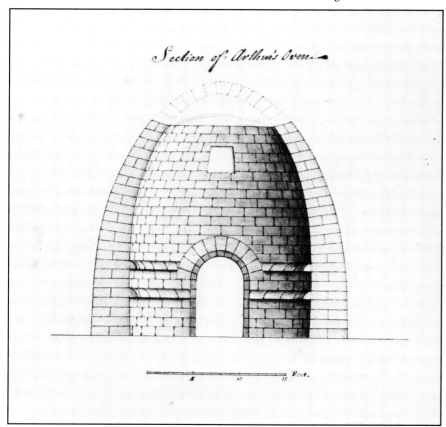

Section of Arthur's Oven

101 Arthur's O'on Stirlingshire; drawings in eighteenth century manuscript in Blair Castle, (dated between 1726 and 1743). *Royal Commission on the Ancient and Historical Monuments of Scotland*

construction of the Antonine Wall and although it was structurally rather different from the Pantheon, being constructed of mortared and dressed stone rather than of brick and concrete, and perhaps lacking a central *oculus* open to the heavens, the building may well have recalled the Hadrianic masterpiece to the travelled beholder. It contained a statue – we have a record of a bronze finger being found – but whether of Jupiter, Victory or some other deity is not known. Arthur's O'on was tragically demolished in 1743 in order to provide stone for the repair of a dam, but we have drawings by Stukeley, Gordon and others (101), while a replica was subsequently built in 1763 by Sir James Clerk and his architect-mason, John Baxter as a dove-cote on the stable-block of Penicuik House, Midlothian (109).[4]

The ideals held by Agricola and practised by Emperors from Nerva to Marcus Aurelius, are given their fullest expression in the *Meditations* that the last of these wrote for his son. The ruler and his deputies had a strong sense of duty; the Empire was in a sense a 'City of Zeus'. Undue enthusiasm was a bad thing, almost sacrilegious.

Commodus took no notice of what he was told by his father. Like Kaiser Wilhelm II he broke away from good parental influences. Spendthrift, cruel, obsessed by pleasure and sensation, he saw himself as the embodiment of Hercules and even of the Sun! Religious enthusiasm was, to our eyes at least, the most venial of his sins, but it was noted with disfavour. A gilded bronze statuette of Hercules from Birdoswald may conceivably depict Commodus in the guise of the god and hero (**102**). It is certainly of the right date and may have stood in a private shrine or even the *aedes* of a fort.[5] The idea that the great phallic hill figure, the Cerne Abbas Giant shows Commodus-Hercules is pleasing, but it is now believed that the figure is probably not Roman but comparatively recent (see Chapter 10) – and even if it were ancient there are other possibilities than Commodus-Hercules such as a Romano-British version of the Celtic god Dagda.

The Sun god had long been associated with the pretensions of rulers in the East. Nero had emulated them, and the Unconquered Sun, *Sol Invictus*, was favoured by Commodus. In so doing, he was the earthly representative of a celestial power, seen by all men from morning to night. An inscription set up by a detachment of the Sixth Legion under Calpurnius Agricola at Corbridge dates from before the time of Commodus, but the probable reason for its defacement was Commodus' advocacy of the cult, and the natural reaction to Commodus' enthusiasms after the tyrant's fall.[6]

The Severan Age and the third century

The presence of Hadrian in Britain merely reflected a prevailing ethos. When Septimius Severus came to Britain, he stayed longer, from 211 until his death in 214, and his influence (together with that of his wife Julia Domna) was all the more marked in that the Emperor himself epitomised an age of change. In one respect he was a traditionalist like Augustus and Hadrian, keen to nurture the gods of the State. Possibly of this time is the 'Screen of Gods', later dismantled and built into the fourth-century riverside wall at Blackfriars. The gods shown, Vulcan, Minerva, Mercury, Diana, are all thoroughly Roman. The monumental arch, ornamented with gods of the week, seasons, Minerva, Hercules and other deities also reflects a conservative taste.[7] There is a strong likelihood that if they are Severan, they come from a temple complex inaugurated as a result of Julia Domna's religious interests. Ralph Merrifield suggests that a relief showing four-seated women could represent the deceased and deified Julia Domna as a *Dea Nutrix* with the three Matres, but as she was certainly associated with a range of female deities in Donatianus' poem from Carvoran, the possibility that the relief is a compliment to the living Empress cannot be ruled out. Deification in one's lifetime is distinctly Hellenistic and Oriental and both Septimius Severus and Julia Domna were devotees of the Eastern cults. Two inscriptions from Blackfriars which may come from the same complex may be relevant here. One of them certainly records the restoration of a temple of Isis 'fallen down through age'. It dates from the mid-third century, so the temple outlasted the Severan age. The other altar also records the restoration of a temple fallen through age, though the deity is more doubtful. Mark Hassall has restored the name of the god as (I.O.)M., Jupiter Greatest and Best, but the spacing would equally allow (M.D.)M., 'the Great Mother of the Gods' i.e. Cybele, or (I.D.)M., 'the Great Goddess Isis'.[8] Julia Domna came from Emesa, where she was the daughter of the *Sacerdos Amplissimus Dei Solis Invicti Elagabali.* Her religious interests were wide. Donatianus' poem from Carvoran identifies her with *Dea Syria*, and Virgo (i.e. Juno) Caelestis, the North African tutelary deity.[9] In Northern Britain, the cult of Dea Brigantia, whatever the ultimate origin of the goddess, was undoubtedly linked to Severan syncretism in general and to Caelestis in particular.

102 Silver-gilt statuette of Hercules found near Birdoswald, Cumberland. Height 49 cm. *British Museum*

103 Relief showing Brigantia dedicated by the architect Amandus. From Birrens, Dumfriesshire. Height 92 cm. *National Museum of Antiquities of Scotland*

Norah Jolliffe rightly remarked that 'all the datable inscriptions of Brigantia's cult belong to the reigns of Severus and Caracalla, and must be interpreted against the background of the ideas and history of that period'.[10]

The only relief which certainly shows Brigantia comes from Birrens in southern Scotland (**103**). She is figured as Minerva, winged as a Victory, and with a mural crown which reveals her as a city (or provincial) *tyche*. Beside her, an *omphalos* or navel stone is paralleled by other sacred stones of Semitic deities, amongst them that of Julia Domna's native Elagabal. There is nothing at all here that belongs to Celtic religion. The truth would seem to be that the Severan division of Britain left Upper Britain with its capital at London in possession of the established symbol of the province *Britannia*. Lower Britain, most of which was Brigantian territory, was best symbolised by a new personification *Brigantia*. At least she had her origin in the area, although as we have seen there is little evidence of continued popularity, unless the female figure with mural crown on the fourth-century Brantingham mosaic is so identified (**104**).[11]

The political turbulence of the third century had little religious impact in Britain. It is at least easy to see how religion was viewed by the governing class by studying the impressive range of types on the Carausian coinage. Carausius 'paid the usual regard to the primary gods and goddesses – Apollo, Mars, Jupiter, Peace,

104 City-Tyche on a polychrome mosaic from Brantingham, Yorkshire. Height *c.* 120 cm. *Kingston upon Hull Museum*

Concord and Good Faith – which were essential parts of any ruler's propaganda'. Since Aurelian, indeed from even earlier times, Sol was important, but Carausius does not boast of association with Oriental deities in general. It would have been strange if he had, for unlike the Severans, he was a Western Celt, from Belgium. However, the only deity whose epithet is at all local is Hercules of Deutz (opposite Cologne), who came from the furthest edge of Carausius' sphere of influence. Propaganda, not sentiment, was at work here; the Genius of Britain and indeed Britannia herself welcoming the Emperor with the Virgilian phrase *Expectate Veni* certainly appealed rather to literate, wealthy *curiales* than to religious separatists.[12]

The Triumph of the Church

Traditional, official religion of this sort was threatened not by a recrudescence of nationalist cults such as Druidism but by Christianity. There was a strong political element in its arrival as a powerful force in Britain for the new faith was propagated by Constantine in the years after AD 312 and that Emperor had strong connections with the province and must have had a personal following there, both as the son of Constantius Chlorus who had defeated Allectus and re-united Britain to the central Empire and because his own reign had begun at York where he had been proclaimed in AD 306. Numismatic evidence suggests that he returned to Britain in 312 and 314, in other words both before and after his conversion.

For Constantine, Christianity was merely an extension and refinement of the Sun cult. He thought of himself as the comrade of the sun and his earlier coins bear the legend *Soli Invicto Comiti*. There were natural links between the veneration of a single, glorious sky-god and Christ, the single, divine saviour of mankind. The Sunday sabbath and the adoption of the birthday of the sun god for Christ's nativity (25 December) agrees with a conception of divine power that is evidently solar – as may be seen on a third-century vault mosaic from a tomb under St Peter's, depicting *Christus-Sol*.

In the later third century, the great promoter of the cult of the sun was L.Domitius Aurelianus (Aurelian), who ascended the Imperial throne in AD 270 and attributed his victory over Zenobia of Palmyra in 272 to the favour of Elagabal, the sun god of Emesa (*SHA Aurelian*, 25, 4). Aurelian did not repeat the excesses of Commodus or Elagabalus and his cult was thoroughly Roman and traditional in its practice. From 274 until the middle of the reign of Constantine, *Deus Sol Invictus* was recognised as the chief deity of the State and appears with great frequency on the coinage, including issues of the 'British Empire' and above all of Constantine, struck in Britain.

The most important find associated with the cult in Britain is a bronze cube with an intaglio device on each side. One of the six sides depicts the head of Sol together with the legend *Invictus Sol*. The style of cutting is late third century, and the object may be interpreted as the official stamp for lead seals on an Imperial Estate (**105**). In addition, as we have seen, the spread of orientation in burials is thought to begin before the establishment of Christianity, and could well be associated with the new cult which certainly fulfilled a deep, emotional need as well as being a reflection of State power.[13]

Christianity was not the only religion which had a natural affinity with the cult of *Sol Invictus*. Mithras was sometimes equated with the sun, and thus himself

105 (a & b) Bronze cube with intaglio device on each side, including one showing Sol Invictus from Kingscote, Gloucestershire. Each side *c.* 1.9 cm. *Corinium Museum*

acquired the epithet *Invictus*; elsewhere the two deities were separate but closely allied. An inscription dated to the early years of Constantine (307–8) before his conversion and when he had three other emperors as colleagues (Maximian, Galerius and Maxentius) together with a Caesar, Maximin, was found in the London Mithraeum. It is dedicated *deo Mithrae et Soli Invicto ab oriente ad occidentem*, 'to the god Mithras and the Unconquered Sun from the East to the West'.[14] The triumph of Christianity does not appear to have had a dramatic effect on other pagan cults but Mithraism was another matter. In 307 it was in high favour, but only half a dozen years later the Walbrook temple was sacked by a mob, probably of Christians. It is tempting to place this event around the time of Constantine's 314 *Adventus*. Mithraism was disseminating a heretical version of the sun cult (from a Christian point of view) and Christians have always been harsher on faiths which are near to their own such as the monotheistic creeds of Judaism and Islam than on those of total outsiders.[15]

The adherence of Constantine to Christianity may have appeared to be only a temporary aberration, especially in Britain where there can at first have been relatively few Christians, even if they were well enough organised to have a few bishops or (as we have just seen) to attack *mithraea*. Christianity continued to survive and to flourish because almost all the later emperors were fervent Christians and officially at least it was paganism that was practised on sufferance. In fact the roles were not exactly reversed, for the majority of the population remained pagan through most of the fourth century, if not longer. Certainly when Julian attempted to revive the fortunes of the pagan cult in 360, he would have found them still in a flourishing state throughout the North West provinces. In Britain this is implied by continuing activity at rural shrines such as those at Uley and Lydney Park and it is manifest in Lucius Septimius' restoration of a Jupiter column at Cirencester as well as in the blatant paganism of many of the mosaics in the country houses of the gentry.[16]

There may have been a shift towards Christianity at the end of the century. Written sources provide valuable evidence about both politics and religion in later Roman Britain and it is all by, and about, Christians. It is legitimate to wonder whether there is not an element of bias here, but it certainly suggests that the educated and literate were more and more likely to adopt what was now the official faith of the Roman world. Opposition is manifested through heresy, not paganism. Magnus Maximus left pagans alone, but he persecuted the Priscillianists with great ferocity and two of them, Instantius and Tiberianus, were exiled to Scilly (Sulpicius Severus II, 51, 3–4). The most troubling 'heresy' (for the authorities) of late Roman Britain was Pelagianism, certainly attested by Constantius in his account of St Germanus' visit to Britain in AD 429. The conflict between Augustine and Pelagius, of course involved more than a little local debate touching 'the obscure revolutions of fifth-century Britain'.[17] It would be wrong to see Pelagianism as being merely a British response to Christianity even though Pelagius was a Briton. There was a deep doctrinal conflict as to whether the individual could achieve salvation simply through his own right behaviour or had to wait upon God's *gratia* (grace). This theological dispute could have seemed relevant in a political situation where self-help was clearly more effective than waiting for forces to be despatched by a hard-pressed central Empire. Gildas, writing in the sixth century, shows us a Britain which, outside areas of Saxon control, is entirely Christian, though its rulers are often venial and unworthy (Chapter 10). This is surely an exaggeration though it does suggest that the aristocracy of tribal chieftains was by now largely converted. His book reveals that religious pressures on rulers could be as important as political influence on religion.

10 Adaptation and Change: Pagans and Christians in Late Antiquity

'I know that there were two religions,' replied Yorick, 'one – for the vulgar, and the other for the learned, but I think one Love might have served both of them very well.' Laurence Sterne, *Tristram Shandy*, Book VIII, Ch. 33.

When we write or think about the old religious order, it is tempting to see it as a monolithic system, blind or backward-looking, and utterly resistant to change. Such a view would have found a ready response amongst early Christians like Arnobius of Sica (Chapter 7). Gildas, in the passage with which this book began, mentions 'the devilish monstrosities of my land, numerous almost as those that plagued Egypt, some of which we can see today, stark as ever, inside or outside deserted city walls; outlines still ugly, faces still grim' (Gildas, *De Excid. Brit* 4, 3).

Piety could easily be represented as blindness or superstition. Such an attitude may be seen in the Middle Ages towards Judaism (the Synagogue is personified as a blindfolded woman, while the Church (*Ecclesia*) is blessed with sight).[1] Sectarian attitudes, for instance, of Roman Catholics towards Protestants, and *vice versa*, tell a regrettably similar story in more recent times.

Pagans, Gentiles, and Christians

One of the names given to pagans, *pagani* (i.e. dwellers in *pagi*), which may be translated as 'backwoodsmen', is significant. A less emotive word, *gentilis*, is employed by someone, presumably a pagan, writing out a curse to Sulis Minerva at Bath. It implies an ordinary person as opposed to the specially designated *Christianus*. The distinction sounds as though it was originally made by a Christian, but evidently it did not have overtones too emotive for a pagan to employ.[2] Greek speakers – for instance the Emperor Julian – used the term 'Hellene' to mean not just an exponent of Greek culture, but of Greek religion. It was a term used with pride to designate the guardian of a tradition.

For the early Christian, believing in a *new* covenant and in God 'making all things new', the Graeco-Roman tradition was less significant. Such a sense of the past takes time to develop. In many ways modern man finds it easier to sympathise with these Christians, for he himself uses the names of past cultures – 'Victorian', 'Medieval' and even 'Neolithic' – as terms of abuse. Against this sense of rootlessness, the fourth-century pagan grew up in a thousand-year tradition of continuously evolving religious institutions, and a dialogue between man and the gods which had developed from generation to generation. When we look at the words and works of the last pagans (or 'Hellenes') they have a truly moving power and dignity. Quintus Aurelius Symmachus' third *Relatio* presents Dea Roma supporting Symmachus' appeal to return the altar of Victoria to the Roman Senate House in these words: '... respect my length of years won for me by the dutiful observance of rite; let me continue to practise my ancient ceremonies, for I do not regret them. Let me live in my own way, for I am free. This worship of mine brought the whole world under the rule of my laws; these sacred rites drove back Hannibal from my walls and the Senones from the Capitol' (*Relatio* 3, 9).[3] The same feeling is evident in Lucius Septimius' restoration of the Jupiter column in Cirencester: *Signum et erectam prisca religione renovat.*[4] The *prisca religio*, the ancestral faith, has assumed the status of an entity, a faith, a church.

Professor Peter Brown (pre-eminent amongst others) has taught us not to think of Late Antiquity as a period of decline after the heyday of the Empire, but as a different kind of polity when men had different expectations from those of their ancestors. In other words, just as we would hardly expect our contemporaries to think or act in an identical way to people born at the time of the English Civil War, we have to be aware of the differences between the world of the Emperor Julian and that of his forebear Vespasian. Furthermore, if the temporal gap is wide, the religious divide between traditional polytheism and Christianity introduces new factors which can be equated with the chasm between Catholics and reformers in the sixteenth century and Cavaliers and Roundheads in the seventeenth century.

The apparent sharpness of the break was in practice much modified, bridged in very many cases by sentiment, family connections and culture. Violent revolution was exceptional, isolated and short-lived. Groups like the fanatic *Circumcelliones* of North Africa were feared and distrusted by all who valued the order of Roman society. The early fourth-century Christian(?) attack on the Walbrook Mithraeum (Chapter 9) was but one incident, probably aimed at Mithraism as such and not at paganism in general. The Mithraists were able to tidy the temple after the initial attack and bury their sacred sculptures, and within a short while the building was re-opened to pagan worship, but probably now as a temple of Liber-Bacchus.

The style of an inscription from Bath, telling us how a *locus religiosus* had been 'wrecked by insolent hands' and restored to the Virtue and *numen* of the Emperor by G Severius Emeritus, centurion in charge of the region, does not look Constantinian. It is probably much earlier, and in any case we know that the spring of Sulis Minerva continued strongly until the coin series ends in Britain, and probably even longer.[5]

Traditional society was resilient and strongly founded. Unfortunately, literary and epigraphic evidence which has a bearing on it, as far as Roman Britain is concerned, is sparse in the extreme. If there were British equivalents to the great Vettius Praetextatus (Urban Prefect AD 367–8; Praetorian Prefect AD 384), who listed his public offices only *after* his priesthoods, or of Attius Patera, Ausonius' friend whose family was intimately connected with the priesthood of Apollo-Belenus at Bayeux, and prided itself – by a strange irony – on Druidic descent, we have to turn to the visual arts, to those mosaics, frescoes, marble sculpture and the architectural evidence of cult rooms which reveal the personal beliefs of aristocrats on their estates, and *curiales* (often the same people?) in the towns.

Private Religious Cults in Late Antiquity

We have already seen (in Chapter 7) that some mosaic floors may be Christian. The

Hinton St Mary pavement is surely the floor of a house-church or chapel. Such house-churches are an accepted feature of Christian archaeology and are in no way controversial. It is not unreasonable to suppose that if Christians had special rooms for worship so did pagans – apart from *Lararia*, which were merely hallway shrines. Recent excavations at Littlecote, Wiltshire by Bryn Walters has led to the rediscovery of a triconch-chamber floored with a distinctive mosaic. The chamber is linked to a bath-house and stands away from the main Littlecote villa at a low-lying spot by the river. While detailed interpretation of the floor will be open to question, there has been reluctance and even hostility to the view that we have here any more than an elegant summer *triclinium*.[6]

The critics of the theory that the Littlecote building is a shrine have, however, perhaps unwittingly, said something valuable about the nature of much late Roman paganism at a period when public manifestations of polytheism risked persecution. Temple treasures were liable to confiscation from the time of Constantine until that of Julian and again from AD 391 in the reign of Theodosius.[7] It is clear that public temples survived in Britain, and their cults even flourished strongly at Lydney Park, Uley and probably Bath, amongst many other shrines, but it is almost certain that they had lost most of their plate and other treasures, as well as their estates. At Thetford, the late Roman treasure comes from a shrine, ultimately the successor to an Iron Age and early Roman structure, but as it will appear, the spoons seem to belong to a private religious dining club or *collegium* which had its headquarters there. Wealthy patrons wisely concentrated not on embellishing public shrines but private chapels, where there was greater safety from the law.

Just as Christian worship centred around the Eucharist, late Roman paganism was concerned with companionship within the group and the common sacred meal. Naturally, we must be careful not to interpret every representation of a deity or of a mythological scene as proof of pagan cult practices. Some were demonstrably not so intended, but the border between culture and religion was murky and much disputed. It was an area where Christians could still be won back to the old ways or pagans beguiled into thinking that Christianity was not as revolutionary as they had feared.

In the early Roman period, Olympian myth and religion could be used decoratively with few overtones. Christianity changed that. The Emperor Julian forbade Christians to touch the classics, because they had come to be regarded as holy works. The Christians had Mark and Luke; the pagans had Homer, the Greek tragedies, Virgil and Ovid. In a contest based on literary merit there is no doubt which group had the finer library. Even St Jerome felt the beguiling pull of Cicero. A significant passage in the work of Theodoret, Bishop of Cyrrhus, attacks 'the shamelessness of people who even now affect Greek ways'. He mentions paintings of Europa seated on the back of a bull – a theme incidentally represented in mosaic on the floor of the Lullingstone villa *triclinium* – as well as images of Aphrodite, Dionysos, Pan, satyrs, Ganymede and the eagle, and Leda with the swan. 'If you say that the poets have invented false myths,' he asks, 'why do you allow statue makers, carvers and painters to perpetuate the lie by means of their craft?'[8] We have to admit that often we do not know whether we are dealing with pagans or with Christians of Graeco-Roman culture such as Ausonius. The theme of Ganymede was used by Ausonius in an epigram on a youth called Glaucius

(Ausonius XIX, *epigram* 62). It was the subject of a fourth-century statuary group from the House of the Greek Charioteers at Carthage, as well as in Britain on a mosaic at Bignor (**85**). The story had amorous overtones, but was essentially connected with immortality.

The best contender for a pagan cult room attached to a Roman villa in Britain is that at Littlecote mentioned above. The central theme is Apollo equated with Orpheus, accompanied by Orpheus' regular attribute of a fox but surrounded by personifications of the seasons (riding upon animals) which belong with Apollo. Heads of Sol in the apses also refer to Apollo, but the Sun's rays project almost to the edges of the panel and may also be interpreted as pecten shells, recalling the belief in the voyage of the soul over the sea to the Blessed Isles. The other section of the mosaic is mainly geometric, but a panel with sea-panthers again evokes the marine *thiasos*, while a pair of facing panthers, one on each side of a chalice, is a well-known Bacchic device. The mystery at Littlecote seems to have exploited the close relationship between Bacchus, Orpheus and Apollo, and to have been connected with salvation. What lifts the Littlecote floor beyond the range of formal images is its setting and the design of the building. The building, if a *triclinium*, was a dining-room of a very special sort.

A villa which deserves renewed study for its remarkable series of mosaic floors is that of Brading on the Isle of Wight.[9] Its owner seems to have been a man with strong theosophical interests to which the term *Gnostic*, with its implication of hidden knowledge, might be legitimately applied. One room has a floor showing Orpheus and the beasts; another contains amongst other scenes a panel depicting Iao, whose representation on amulets is discussed in Chapter 5. This mosaic is at least a century and a half later than them (dating from the mid-fourth century). The god is shown beside a house with a ladder leading up to its door. Presumably this is an allegory of the straight and narrow ways of God leading to the security of the heavens. On the left of the house two griffins prowl, representing the demons encompassing man and threatening to destroy him (**106**). This room is too small to be a cult room, but the main hall of the villa and the apsidal chamber beyond it could have been so used. The central motif in the hall is a wheel-shaped device with the gorgon-head at its hub. Each of the four quadrants around it displays a myth; one of them is that of Lycurgus and Ambrosia, which is the theme of a famous late Roman *diatreton* (cage-cup) in the British Museum, as well as being figured on an earlier Bacchic column from Cirencester. It informs us that Bacchus looks after his votaries; Ambrosia, on praying to the god for release from her evil pursuer Lycurgus, was metamorphosed into a vine which strangled him. Another quadrant shows Triptolemos accepting seed-corn from the goddess Demeter.

Both these scenes of acceptance are balanced by scenes of rejection. Paris rejects the affections of the nymph Oenone, thus fatefully creating the circumstance whereby he was free to abduct Helen and precipitate the disaster of the Trojan War. The fourth scene shows a female figure fleeing from a pursuer. She may be Daphne, pursued by Apollo. If so, the artist has not shown the former's metamorphosis into a bush. Fleeing from a god is not, of course, the same thing as fleeing from the enemy of a god. Christians were forever pointing out the immorality of the pagan deities, but late Roman pagans saw the myths in symbolic terms. Indeed, such symbolic interpretations go back much earlier. A woman in the fresco of the cult-room of the Villa of the Mysteries outside Pompeii flees from

Bacchus. She is identified by Karl Lehmann as a personification of Ignorance.[10] A threshold from the hall into the apsidal chamber is dominated by the figure of an astronomer-astrologer. He was an important figure at a time when religious people were looking up to friends of God, Holy Men, to interpret the divine world for them. He could penetrate beyond this sublunary world and interpret divine will to men. Entering the chamber with its central *exedra*, we notice that there seems to have been a geometric border running around it, no doubt to take benches. Unfortunately, the mosaics are much damaged or missing, but one mythological theme is Perseus rescuing Andromeda, symbolising salvation from evil, as scenes of rescue or abduction usually do. Other mythological schemes in mosaic may well reflect cult; Reinhard Stupperich in reconsidering some aspects of Romano-British mosaic sees the careful classicism of much of this art as possibly a deliberate reflection of the fourth-century Pagan Renaissance.[11]

Urban sites have left us much less. The Walbrook Mithraeum continued to be used for pagan worship in the fourth century, but was probably rededicated as a

106 Polychrome mosaic showing various figures including the god Iao. Brading Villa, Isle of Wight, *in situ*

Bacchic *schola*. The sculptural group of that god with his thiasos, dedicated *Hominibus Bagis Bitam* may be as late as the fourth century in date and was certainly used then. Two torsos of satyrs (?) also belong to this phase. A so-called Mithraeum beside the baths at Leicester certainly in use down to the later fourth century has yielded a sculpted torso, which may be Bacchic, and is possibly a similar *schola*.[12] We may compare the shrine of Liber Pater in the forum at Cosa, also evidently the meeting place for a Bacchic society.[13] A sherd of pottery from the London temple ornamented with a frog in relief and similar fragments from Cosa with applique serpents and a lizard might be related to Bacchus' near relation *Sabazios*.

There is one other possible purpose-built pagan urban shrine in Britain, used in late antiquity. This is the Silchester 'Church', whose Christian use, as pointed out to me by Anthony King, is often assumed but certainly not proven. It is not a great urban basilica analogous to the cemetery churches of St Peter or St John Lateran, and essentially belongs to the tradition of the *schola*.[14] A mosaic floor in Germany casts some light on the mystery central to such a fraternity and also on cult practice. The Kornmarkt mosaic at Trier may be the floor of a religious meeting-place.[15] The identity of the cult is not known, but a scene showing Leda (*Lyda*) with a bird on a column – it should be a swan but looks more like an eagle – is labelled *Iobis*, 'of Jupiter'. There was evidently a place in this mystery for the effects of this union between God and mortal. Castor and Pollux (*Polus*) were born from eggs as divine saviours, while Helen of Troy (*Aelena*) was the cause of disasters, as the presence of Agamemnon, the Greek leader in the War shows. This is comparable to the myth scenes on the Littlecote and Brading floors. The other scene on the Kornmarkt pavement depicts not a myth but a scene of ritual, reminiscent of the painted cult scenes in the Capua Mithraeum frescos. Here a standing figure labelled 'Quodvoldeus' receives offerings(?) from a man walking towards him, *Felixsomedix*, and a kneeling figure, *Andegasipone*. Andegasus and Felix were members of the cult, and are shown in roundels and ellipses around the scene. Felix, Parecorius and Eusebius hold dishes above their heads containing fish and other food. Andegasus, Calemor, Theodulus and Florus are depicted with cult vessels. Two women, Criscentia and Eleni dance. It has been suggested that this represents a *Collegium Castorum* engaged in its celebration.[15]

The name of the cult is less important than its nature, and here we find a remarkable parallel in Britain when we come to examine the nature and purpose of the Thetford treasure.[17] This group of objects consists of silver spoons and gold jewellery, the latter in large part found in a shale casket. The circumstances of finding were such that any trace of a building (a temple where they might have been hidden) has been lost. The nearby presence of a much earlier Late Iron Age sacred site may be significant. As stated above, the treasure was probably used in the Thetford temple, although it is not its public plate (which would no longer have existed). Some of the spoons in the treasure are inscribed with the names of the individuals to whom they belong: three men – Agrestius, Auspicius and Restitutus – and three women – Silviola, Ingenua and Primigenia. It is probable that these were leading members of the *collegium* (or guild) of Faunus. Its mysteries were connected with that god, a very ancient Latin deity named on many of the other spoons, where he is equated with a range of Celtic gods (**107**). It is of some interest that all these spoons are said to be the property of Faunus, just as those others mentioned above belonged to votaries. Thus men and the god met together

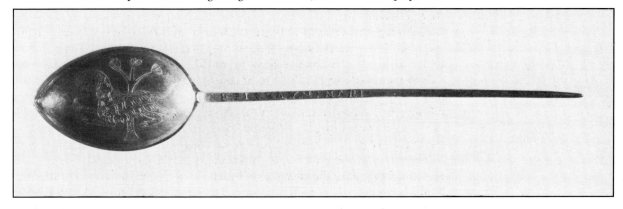

on equal terms, presumably at a feast where the god's image was displayed (*lectisternium*). Although there are of course no major figural representations or long inscriptions, enough remains to suggest the nature of the cult. Silviola is ultimately derived from *silva*, a forest; Agrestius is formed from *agrestis*, a countryman, and Ingenua means indigenous and freeborn. Faunus himself was a vegetation god, the denizen of wild places, equated in mythology with the Greek Pan (and his Celtic epithets are presumably those of similar but local rustic deities). His head appears on one of the gold rings, while another ring displays two woodpeckers on its shoulders, the birds reminding us that *Picus* (the woodpecker) was the father of Faunus (**108**). A gold buckle shows a satyr on its plate, and one spoon is ornamented on the bowl with a panther and another with a Triton, bringing to mind the Bacchic land thiasos and the marine thiasos of Neptune. The very presence of spoons and wine (?) strainers is suggestive of the feast, and it is clear that there was an element of ecstatic abandonment in the ceremonies easily equated with the rites of Bacchus. Probably the god Faunus was connected with the *Lupercalia* (15 February), but had a little feast on the Tiber Island two days earlier (13 February). However, he was also venerated in Italy on 5 December. Shortly after that was the great winter rejoicing of the Saturnalia (17–23 December), and this may explain why one of the spoons is inscribed *Deo Fauni Saternio*. The happy worship of Faunus was certainly Saturnian in its intensity and a further link may be seen in the fact that Picus' father was Saturn.[18]

It may be suggested on the evidence of the treasure, that the temple at Thetford was used by a religious fraternity in the fourth century, consisting of members of the local gentry – the class of people who lived in country houses like that beside the Littlecote cult-room. The Thetford treasure (with the Kornmarkt mosaic at Trier) demonstrates that feasting was an essential part of later Roman mystery. The Celtic equivalents to Faunus and the earlier shrine demonstrated that such a community often had traditional roots.

Although the pagan temples in the countryside were frequented during the fourth century and even later, there is little sign of wealth. Apart from Thetford, the best evidence for upper-class patronage is at Lydney, where a fine mosaic was laid, probably in the period between the accession of Julian and the death of Valentinian, when pressures on paganism were less intense (**58**). Objects of little intrinsic value continued to be bestowed on public temples, and at Bath and Carrawburgh, for instance, coins were tossed into sacred springs. A silver figurine

107 Silver gilt spoon with inscription *Dei Favni Nari* – (Property) of the god Faunus Narius, from Thetford, Norfolk. Length 18 cm. *British Museum*

108 Gold ring with woodpeckers on the shoulders. From Thetford, Norfolk. Internal diameter 1.8 × 1.4 cm. Each woodpecker is *c.* 1 cm in length. *British Museum*

of Tarvos Trigaranos and a marble statuette of Bacchus may have been given to the temple at Maiden Castle above Dorchester in the later fourth century, but this cannot be proved.[19]

The Last Days of Pagan Roman Britain

The process of Christianisation was a slow one, but the fact remains that the Thetford treasure (deposited in the last twenty years of the fourth century) is the last more or less dated group of pagan material in Britain which we can hope to interpret from the standpoint of conventional paganism. Dark Age documents are far harder to understand and are entirely Christian, while jewellery and other metalwork are once again basically Celtic, that is, curvilinear and non-representational. It seems clear that a large proportion of British society, however materially impoverished, was Christian and that this was true as early as St Germanus' first visit in AD 429. A century later, Gildas rails at unworthy and wicked rulers, but he does not imply that they were pagans. Ancient errors, the veneration of idols, belong for him to a very distant past.

But paganism did not vanish overnight; indeed popular cults still remained in Gaul much nearer to the centre of Mediterranean culture in the sixth century, although St Martin had begun the work of felling sacred trees and destroying temples in central Gaul in the fourth century (Sulpicius Severus, *Vita Martin*, 13–15). Gregory of Tours records that the people dwelling around Autun dragged around an image of Cybele on a cart until St Simplicius destroyed it (*Liber in Gloria Confessorum*, 76), while Wulfolaic the Lombard adopted the approach of St Simeon Stylites in the East by destroying a statue of Diana in a shrine near Trier, and then setting up a column on the spot where he sat, the visible 'Friend of God' (*Hist. Franc.* VIII, 15).

Stone images were presumably venerated in Britain too. Stone idols, as we have seen, are mentioned by Gildas, and in the Life of St Samson of Dol, the saint finds a crowd of pagans venerating a sacred stone in the area of Trigg, North Cornwall (1. 50). This he de-paganised by carving the Chi-Rho upon it with his own pocket knife. Dumnonia was never properly Romanised and the stone may have been a prehistoric *menhir*. Standing stones kept their sanctity and I vividly remember being forbidden to photograph a Christianised menhir by an old Breton lady.[20] The great prehistoric monolith at Rudston, Yorkshire stands next to the church, originally built on the spot in order to divert the religious veneration by pagan countrymen from it to Christ.

The peasant nature of surviving paganism in eastern Britain, would have aided symbiosis with Saxon heathenism. Evidence for *interpretatio Saxonica* is admittedly slight except at Yeavering in Bernicia, where an important British site seems to have continued under Anglo-Saxon overlordship. Archaeological evidence was found for sacrificial rituals, a temple structure of timber and a 'theatre' ultimately based on Romano-British models. There are non-Germanic elements amongst the regalia from Sutton Hoo, and the sceptre with its ornamentation of heads and a bronze figure of a stag has been assigned to Celtic south Scotland.[21]

In southern Britain, the funerary rite of decapitating corpses is, as we have seen, pagan in origin, but it occurs not only in the Late Roman Lankhills cemetery, Winchester but also at the seventh-century (early Christian-Saxon) Winnall cemetery nearby.[22] The significance of this continuing burial rite is uncertain. Custom may have been as important as faith.

The treatment of sculpture on pagan sites and the Dark Age history of these sites themselves are important. The fourth-century temple at West Hill, Uley was replaced by other buildings, one of which may have been a church. For the most part the altars and sculptures were disregarded, but the head of Mercury was carefully deposited in a cist of stone slabs. Either it was an object of superstitious veneration with the power to help living men, like the head of Bran in a famous Mabinogion legend, or it was regarded as representing a dangerous, primeval power which needed to be hidden away. At an earlier period, two portrait busts had been stowed away in the cellar of the Lullingstone villa and offerings had been laid out before them. Here, too, we do not know whether there were pagans at Lullingstone at this time or whether the self-same people who worshipped in the house church were indulging in a spiritual insurance policy by invoking the Genii of the place.[23]

It may be difficult for us, with our tastes firmly attuned to classical art from the time of the Renaissance, to understand how some fine Roman bronzes and sculpture could have been cut up to provide talismans with which to counter evil powers, or how magnificent works of Roman art could have been destroyed by early Christian 'saints', but the sub-Roman West was impoverished and dangerous.

Fear stalked the streets of the towns, often deserted and overgrown with weeds, and the even emptier countryside; fear of violence, of disease, of demons and of the unknown. However much of a Roman provincial with the attitudes of a Roman, a man's father, grandfather or great-grandfather may have been his descendant's world view had shrunk away from that of a cosmopolitan Roman citizen to that of an impoverished inhabitant of a distant country which, viewed from the Mediterranean, was a half-mythical abode of ghosts. Paganism crumbled into little more than superstition, but it is difficult without art and written sources to give a precise date to its end. In the fourth century, many of the shrines were in good working order, and possibly religious activity of a non-Christian kind continued in some of them through the fifth and even the sixth centuries. Some of this may have been partially revived from earlier 'Celtic' practices, transmitted through the primitive beliefs of the submerged peasantry and by influences from un-Romanised upland areas. However, in assessing the skull-cult from the shrine at Cadbury, Congresbury and the carefully preserved skulls at Wroxeter (see Chapter 1), we should not forget that human beings do acquire savage urges with lightning speed when ordered society collapses (as William Golding reveals in fiction in his terrifying *Lord of the Flies*). In any case the last stages of Pagans Hill, Canington and Cadbury, Congresbury can hardly be called Romano-British.[24]

Evidence for later Christianity is much better. At first sight this is surprising, for Christianity was an Oriental cult initially, with votaries drawn from amongst the most sophisticated and Roman (or Greek) groups in society. First, the Church was remarkably centralised and organised with a structure mirroring that of the secular world of the Empire. It was highly adaptable, as the emergence of a monastic tradition alongside the diocesan organisation shows. Secondly, it was the State Religion, and insofar as the Roman State could play a part (however feeble) in outlying areas of the Empire, the Church had some backing. Indeed, the State was frequently well served by churchmen whose power and influence were considerable; examples are men like Sidonius Apollinaris, Bishop of Clermont Ferrand, defender at one and the same time of his diocese and of *Romanitas*. In Britain, St Germanus of Auxerre gave military encouragement against the Saxons (Constantius *Vita Germani* XII). Finally, and perhaps most important, Christianity had become a religion of Holy Men and Holy Places; the burials of saints outside towns were *foci* of spiritual power. St Patrick and St Samson are examples of such men; St Albans outside Verulamium was such a place, an important martyrium continuing from Roman times into the Dark Ages and beyond. To it St Germanus came, as many were to come after him, in order to venerate the saint.[25]

In dealing with non-Christian religious sites, holy men could attempt to destroy their sanctity or convert it by replacing the temple with a church. The well-known instructions of Gregory the Great to Abbot Mellitus in AD 601, that idols in temples were to be destroyed but the buildings aspersed with holy water and Christian altars set up in them (Bede, *Eccles. Hist.* 1.30) seems to have been common practice for a long time, to judge from the Christianisation of the Chedworth spring (as early as the fourth century). Furthermore, churches were probably built on temple land at Witham in Essex, Icklingham in Suffolk and West Hill, Uley in Gloucestershire amongst other places during the late fourth and fifth centuries AD.[26] Such a use of pagan sanctuaries may, on occasion, have provided a spur to future development in the Middle Ages. Geography and sanctity together encouraged the survival of villas or rather villa-churches as the bases for new settlements. The beginning of such a process is apparent at Lullingstone and also nearby at Eccles, the place-name meaning a church and suggestive of the continuation of the use of a chapel beyond the life-span of the villa itself. Bath (*Aquae Sulis*) became Christian but remained a religious and healing centre with a curative spring in which men bathed 'wholly naked with every garment cast off' in the Middle Ages, to the great offence of King Henry VI amongst others.[27] The break in continuity there, implied in that moving poem *The Ruin*, may not have been as complete as once appeared, to judge from the number of post-Roman floor levels which have been recorded in recent excavations.

The ancient cults only survived through the Middle Ages through the media of superstition and folklore; spirits still inhabited fountains and wells; men and women still had recourse to magic and used amulets. The inarticulate substratum of these beliefs no doubt consisted of confused elements from Norse, Anglo-Saxon, Romano-British, Celtic and even earlier peoples, and it is hard to unravel them. Stories of phantom horsemen in the Chilterns and elsewhere invoke Celtic rider-gods, and the strangely antlered dancers of Abbots Bromley seem to be celebrating

109 Dovecote over stables at Penicuick House built by Sir James Clerk. It is based on Arthur's O'on (plate 101)

the fecundity of the Earth and its god Cernunnos. But we do not really know how these survivals truly relate to the religion of ancient Britain. It is appropriate to end this chapter and the book with a mystery – if it is right to call the Cerne Abbas giant a mystery. It is an enormous figure cut into the chalk of a Dorset hillside, and it certainly shows an ithyphallic Hercules. It could be a Roman period figure, but it is nowhere recorded before the eighteenth century. As it would not survive without regular scouring, it is surprising that if it is so old it has escaped medieval record.[28] I am inclined to follow those who believe that it dates from the seventeenth century, at a time when interest in the past of Britain was being fully awakened, and foremost amongst this interest was a desire to know about the old gods of the land but the problem of its origin is by no means settled.

The revival of interest in the classical past and of the gods of Greece and Rome is another story. The stable-block at Penicuik House was constructed in 1763, as we have seen (Chapter 9) with a replica of Arthur's O'on upon it (**109**). At Stourhead, West Wycombe and Stowe (for example)[29] temples were erected as a nostalgic evocation of deities which the owners of these estates knew from ancient authors, though they would hardly have been prepared to defend the presence of Bacchus, Pan, Venus, Diana or Apollo before their chaplains. Yet these gods and goddesses had once inhabited the land of Britain. They had transformed the barbarous spirit of the Celtic gods, and moved their votaries to delight in the arts of peace, by commissioning statues and silver plate and also by composing decorous inscriptions and even poetry in their honour.[30]

Abbreviations

A.N.R.W.   *Aufstieg und Niedergang der Römischen Welt* (Berlin and New York)
Ant. J.   The Antiquaries Journal
Arch. Ael.   Archaeologia Aeliana
Arch. Cant.   Archaeologia Cantiana
Arch. Journ.   The Archaeological Journal
B.A.R.   British Archaeological Reports
B.B.C.S.   Bulletin of the Board of Celtic Studies
B.J.   Bonner Jahrbücher
B.N.J.   British Numismatic Journal
C.I.L.   *Corpus Inscriptionum Latinarum*
Jähr. R.G.Z.M.   Jährbuch des Römisch-Germanischen Zentralmuseums Mainz
J.B.A.A.   Journal of the British Archaeological Association
J.R.S.   Journal of Roman Studies
L.I.M.C.   *Lexicon Iconographicum Mythologiae Classicae*
M.A.A.R.   Memoirs of the American Academy at Rome
P.B.S.R   Papers of the British School at Rome
P.P.S.   Proceedings of the Prehistoric Society
P.S.A.S.   Proceedings of the Society of Antiquaries of Scotland
R.C.H.M Eburacum   *Royal Commission on Historical Monuments, Roman York* (London, 1962)
R.I.B.   R G Collingwood and R P Wright, *The Roman Inscription of Britain I* (Oxford, 1965)
S.A.C.   Sussex Archaeological Collections
Y.A.J.   Yorkshire Archaeological Journal

Bibliography

Alcock, J P 1965. 'Celtic water cults in Roman Britain', *Arch. Journ.* CXII, 1–12.

Alcock, J P 1980. 'Classical religious belief and burial practice in Roman Britain'. *Arch. Journ.* CXXXVII, 50–85.

Alföldi, A 1949. 'The bronze mace from Willingham Fen, Cambridgeshire', *J.R.S.* XXXIX, 19–22.

Allen, D 1958. 'Belgic coins as illustrations of life in the late pre-Roman Iron Age of Britain', *P.P.S.* XXIV, 43–63.

Allen, D 1964–68. 'Celtic coins from the Romano-British Temple at Harlow, Essex', *B.N.J.* XXXII (1964), 1–6; XXXVI (1967), 1–7; XXXVII (1968), 1–6.

Ambrose, T and Henig, M 1980. 'A new Roman Rider-relief from Stragglethorpe, Lincolnshire', *Britannia* XI, 135–8.

Amy, R, Duval, P-M, Formigé, J, Hatt, J J, Piganiol, A, Picard, Ch and Picard, G-Ch 1962. *L'Arc d'Orange* XV supp. to *Gallia* (Paris).

ApSimon, A M 1965. 'The Roman Temple on Brean Down, Somerset', *Proc. Bristol Spel. Soc.* X, 195–258.

Ashby, T 1902. 'Excavations at Caerwent, Monmouthshire, on the site of the Romano-British city of Venta Silurum, in 1901', *Archaeologia* LVIII, 119–52.

Atkinson, R J C and Piggott, S 1955. 'The Torrs Chamfrein', *Archaeologia* XCVI, 197–235.

Austen, P S and Breeze, D J 1979. 'A New Inscription from Chesters on Hadrian's Wall', *Arch. Ael*[5]. VII, 114–26.

Babelon, E 1916. *Le Trésor d'Argenterie de Berthouville près Bernay* (Paris).

Barker, P. c. 1981. *Wroxeter Roman city. Excavations 1966–1980* (D.O.E. London).

Barrett, A A 1977. 'A Virgilian scene from the Frampton Roman villa, Dorset', *Ant. J.* LVII, 312–4.

Barrett, A A 1978. 'Knowledge of the literary classics in Roman Britain', *Britannia* IX, 307–13.

Bastet, F L 1979. *Beeld in relief* (Leiden).

Batteley, J 1711. *Antiquitates Rutupinae* (Oxford).

Batteley, J 1774. *The Antiquities of Richborough and Reculver* (London).

Bauchhenss, G and Noelke, P 1981. *Die Iupitersäulen in den Germanischen Provinzen* (Cologne and Bonn).

Beard, M 1980. 'A British dedication from the City of Rome', *Britannia* XI, 313–4.

Becatti, G 1961. *Scavi di Ostia. Mosaici e Pavimenti Marmorei* (Rome).

Bedwin, O 1980. 'Excavations at Chanctonbury Ring, Wiston, West Sussex 1977', *Britannia* XI, 173–222.

Bedwin, O 1981. 'Excavations at Lancing Down, West Sussex 1980', *S.A.C.* CXIX, 37–55

Bell, H I, Martin, V, Turner, E G, Van Berchem, D. *The Abinnaeus Archive. Papers of a Roman officer in the reign of Constantius II* (Oxford).

Bettey, J H 1981. 'The Cerne Abbas Giant: the documentary evidence', *Antiquity* LV, 118–21

Biddle, M 1967. 'Two Flavian burials from Grange Road, Winchester', *Ant. J.* XLVII, 224–50

Bird, J, Chapman, H and Clark, J 1978. *Collectanea Londiniensia. Studies in London archaeology and history presented to Ralph Merrifield* (London and Middlesex Archaeological Society: Special Paper No. 2).

Birley, A R 1979. *The people of Roman Britain* (London).

Birley, A R 1981. *The Fasti of Roman Britain* (Oxford).

Birley, E 1974. 'Cohors I Tungrorum and the Oracle of the Clarian Apollo', *Chiron* 4, 511–13.

Birley, E 1978. 'The religion of the Roman army, 1895–1977',*A.N.R.W.* 16.2, 1506–1541.

Blagg, T F C 1979. 'The votive column from the Roman temple precinct at Springhead', *Arch. Cant.* XCV, 223–9.

Blagg, T F C 1980. 'The sculptured stones' in Hill, C, Millet, M and Blagg, T F C. *The Roman Riverside Wall and Monumental Arch in London* (London and Middlesex Archaeological Society: Special Paper No. 3), 124–209.

Blagg, T F C 1982. 'Roman Kent' in Leach, P E (ed.), *Archaeology in Kent to AD 1500* (London), 51–60.

Bogaers, J.E 1979. 'King Cogidubnus in Chichester' Another Reading of *R.I.B.* 91', *Britannia* x, 243–54.

Bonner, C 1950. *Studies in Magical Amulets* (Ann Arbor).

Boon, G C 1972. *Isca. The Roman Legionary Fortress at Caerleon, Mon.* Third edition (Cardiff).

Boon, G C 1973. 'Sarapis and Tutela: A Silchester Coincidence', *Britannia* IV, 107–14.

Boon, G C 1973a. 'Mensa Dolenda – a Caerleon Discovery of 1774', *B.B.C.S.* xxv, 346–58.

Boon, G C 1973b. 'Genius and Lar in Celtic Britain', *Jahr. R.G.Z.M* xx, 265–9.

Boon, G C 1974. *Silchester: The Roman Town of Calleva Second ed.,* (Newton Abbot).

Boon, G C 1976. 'Clement of Alexandria, Wookey Hole and the Corycian Cave', *Proc. Bristol Spel. Soc.* XIX, 131–40.

Boon, G C 1978. 'A Romano-British Wooden Carving from Llanio', *B.B.C.S.* XXVII, 619–24.

Boon, G C 1981. 'Vessels of Egyptian Alabaster from Caerwent and Silchester', *B.B.C.S.* XXIX, 354–6.

Boon, G C 1980. 'A richly inlaid strigil from the fortress baths, Caerleon', *Ant. J.* LX, 333–7.

Boon, G C 1982. 'A coin with the head of the Cernunnos', *Seaby Coin and Medal Bulletin* no. 769 (Sept. 1982), 276–82.

Boon, G C 1982a. 'Roman Alabaster Jars from Trier and Cologne', *B.B.C.S.* XXIX, 847–9.

Borlase, W *Antiquities, historical and monumental of the County of Cornwall* (London).

Boucher, S 1976. *Recherches sur les Bronzes Figurés de Gaule Pré-Romaine et Romaine* (Ecole Française de Rome).

Bowman, A K 1974. 'Roman military records from Vindolanda', *Britannia* v, 360–73.

Bradford, J S P and Goodchild, R G 1939. 'Excavations at Frilford, Berks.', *Oxoniensia* IV, 1–70.

Bradford Welles, C, Fink, R O and Gilliam, J F 1959. 'The Feriale Duranum' in *The Excavations at Dura-Europos. Final Report V. Part 1: The Parchments and Papyri*, 191–212 (New Haven).

Bradley, R 1982. 'The destruction of wealth in later prehistory', *Man.* XVII, 108–22.

Bradshaw, J 1980. 'A Bronze Amulet from Boughton Aluph', *Arch. Cant.* XCVI, 394–6.

Branigan, K 1972. 'An unusual Romano-British cremation burial', *Ant. J.* LII, 185–6.

Branigan, K 1976. *The Roman Villa in South-West England* (Bradford-on-Avon).

Breeze, D J and Ritchie, N G 1980. 'A Roman Burial at High Torrs, Luce Sands, Wigtownshire', *Trans. Dumfriesshire and Galloway N H and Ant. Soc.* LV, 77–85.

Brewer, J N 1813. *The beauties of England and Wales XII. pt. II: Oxfordshire* (London).

Brown, P 1968. 'Pelagius and his supporters: Aims and Environment', *Journ. of Theol. Studies* N.S. XIX, 93–114 Reprinted in *Religion and Society in the Age of St Augustine* (London, 1972), 183–207.

Brown, P 1977. *Relics and Social Status in the Age of Gregory of Tours* Stenton Lecture 1976 (Reading); reprinted in *Society and the Holy in Late Antiquity* (London, 1982), 222–50.

Brown, P 1978. *The Making of Late Antiquity* (Cambridge, Mass.).

Brown, P 1981 *The Cult of the Saints* (Chicago and London).

Bruce-Mitford, R 1978. *The Sutton Hoo Ship-Burial II: Arms, Armour and Regalia* (London).

Bruun, P M 1966. *The Roman Imperial Coinage VII. Constantine and Licinius AD 313–337* (London).

Burkert, W 1966. 'Greek Tragedy and Sacrificial Ritual', *Greek, Roman and Byzantine Studies* VII, 87–121.

Burl, A 1979. *Prehistoric Avebury* (Yale).

Bushe-Foxe, J P 1913. *Excavations on the site of the Roman Town at Wroxeter, Shropshire, in 1912* (Society of Antiquaries of London).

Bushe-Fox, J P 1949. *Fourth Report on the Excavations of the Roman Fort at Richborough, Kent* (Society of Antiquaries of London).

Butcher, S A 1977. 'Enamels from Roman Britain' in Apted, M R, Gilyard-Beer, R and Saunders, A D, *Ancient Monuments and their Interpretation. Essays presented to A J Taylor*, 41–69 (London).

Carson, R A G and O'Kelly, C 1977. 'A Catalogue of the Roman Coins from Newgrange, Co. Meath, and notes on the coins and related finds', *Proc. Royal Irish Academy* LXXVII, 35–55.

Casey, J 1977. 'Tradition and Innovation in the Coinage of Carausius and Allectus' in Munby and Henig 1977, 217–29.

Casey, J 1978. 'Constantine the Great in Britain – the evidence of the coinage of the London mint AD 312–314' in Bird, Chapman and Clark 1978, 179–93.

Chadwick, N K 1966. *The Druids* (Cardiff).

Chapman, H 1974. 'Letters from Roman London', *The London Archaeologist* II no. 7, 173–6.

Charlesworth, D 1961. 'Roman jewellery found in Northumberland and Durham', *Arch. Ael*[4]. XXXIX, 1–36.

Charlesworth, D 1977. 'A Roman gold ear-ring from Birdoswald', *Ant. J.* LVII, 323.

Clarke, G 1979. *The Roman Cemetery at Lankhills*, Winchester Studies 3 (Oxford).

Clarke, G 1982. 'The Roman Villa at Woodchester', *Britannia* XIII, 197–228.

Clayton, J 1880. 'Description of Roman Remains discovered near to Procolitia, a station on the Wall of Hadrian', *Arch. Ael*[2]. VIII, 1–49.

Cocks, A H 1921. 'A Romano-British Homestead in the Hambleden Valley, Bucks', *Archaeologia* LXXI, 141–98.

Collins-Clinton, J. 1977, *A Late Antique Shrine of Liber Pater at Cosa* (Leiden).

Collis, J R 1970. 'Excavations at Owslebury, Hants. A second interim report', *Ant. J.* L, 246–61.

Conlon, R F B 1973. 'Holbrooks' – An Iron Age and Romano-British Settlement (Part 1)' *Essex Journal*, VIII, 30–50.

Corder, P and Richmond, I A 1938. 'A Romano-British Interment, with Bucket and Sceptres from Brough, East Yorkshire', *Ant. J.* XVIII, 68–74.

Courteault, P 1921. 'An inscription recently found at Bordeaux', *J.R.S.* XI, 101–7.

Cristofani, M 1979. *The Etruscans. A new investigation* (London).

Crummy, P 1980. 'The Temples of Roman Colchester' in Rodwell 1980, 243–83.

Crummy, P 1982. 'The Roman Theatre at Colchester', *Britannia* XIII, 299–302.

Cumont, F 1896/99, *Textes et Monuments Figurés relatifs aux Mystères de Mithra* 2 vols. (Brussels).

Cumont, F 1949. *Lux Perpetua* (Paris).

Cunliffe, B W 1968. *Fifth Report on the Excavations of the Roman Fort at Richborough, Kent* (Society of Antiquaries of London).

Cunliffe, B W 1969. *Roman Bath* (Society of Antiquaries of London).

Cunliffe, B W 1971. *Excavations at Fishbourne 1961–1969* 2 vols. (Society of Antiquaries of London).

Cunliffe, B W 1976. 'The Romano-British village at Chalton, Hants', *Proc. Hants. Field Club* XXXIII, 45–67.

Cunliffe, B W 1978. *Iron Age Communities in Britain* Second edn. (London).

Cunliffe, B W 1980. 'The Excavation of the Roman Spring at Bath, 1979: A Preliminary Description', *Ant. J.* LX, 187–206.

Cunliffe, B W 1981. 'Danebury, Hampshire. Third Interim Report on the Excavations

1976–80', *Ant. J.* LXI, 238–54.

Cunliffe, B W and Fulford, M H 1982. *Corpus Signorum Imperii Romani: Great Britain 1.2. Bath and the rest of Wessex* (British Academy).

Curle, J 1911. *A Roman Frontier Post and its People. The Fort of Newstead in the Parish of Melrose* (Glasgow).

Daniels, C 1962. 'Mithras Saecularis, the Housesteads Mithraeum and a Fragment from Carrawburgh', *Arch. Ael*[4]. XL, 105–15.

Dodds, E R 1968. *Pagan and Christian in an age of anxiety* (Cambridge).

Down, A 1978. *Chichester Excavations* III (Chichester).

Down, A 1979. *Chichester Excavations* IV. *The Roman Villas at Chilgrove and Upmarden* (Chichester).

Down, A 1981. *Chichester Excavations* V (Chichester).

Down, A and Rule, M 1971. *Chichester Excavations* I (Chichester).

Downey, R, King, A and Soffe, G 1980. 'The Hayling Island Temple and Religious Connections across the Channel', in Rodwell 1980, 289–304.

Drury, P J 1973. 'Romano-British jet objects from Chelmsford', *Ant. J.* LIII, 272f.

Drury, P J 1980. 'Non-classical Religious Buildings in Iron Age and Roman Britain: A Review', in Rodwell 1980, 45–78.

Dudley, D 1967. 'Excavations in Nor'nour in the Isles of Scilly, 1962–6', *Arch. Journ.* CXXIV, 1–64.

Dunbabin, K M D 1978. *The Mosaics of Roman North Africa* (Oxford).

Dyson, S L 1971. 'Native Revolts in the Roman Empire', *Historia* XX, 239–74.

Eiden, H 1950. 'Spätrömisches Figurenmosaik am Kornmarkt in Trier', *Trierer Zeitschrift* XIX, 52–71.

Ellison, A 1978. *Excavations at West Hill, Uley: 1977. The Romano-British Temple*, CRAAGS occasional Papers No. 3 (Bristol).

Ellison, A 1980. 'Natives, Romans and Christians on West Hill, Uley: an Interim Report on the excavation of a Ritual Complex of the First Millenium AD' in Rodwell 1980, 305–28.

Ellison, A and Henig, M 1981. 'Head of Mercury from Uley, Gloucestershire', *Antiquity* LV, 43f.

Enright, M J 1983. 'The Sutton Hoo Whetstone Sceptre: a Study in Iconography and Cultural Milieu', *Anglo-Saxon England* XI, 119–34.

Ericksen, R T 1980. 'Syncretistic Symbolism and the Christian Roman mosaic at Hinton St Mary: A Closer Reading', *Proc. Dorset Nat. Hist. and Arch. Soc.* CII, 43–8.

Erim, K T 1982. 'A new relief showing Claudius and Britannia from Aphrodisias', *Britannia* XIII, 277–81.

Eschebach, H 1978. *Pompeji Erlebte antike Welt* (Leipzig).

Esperandieu, E 1913. *Recueil Général des Bas-Reliefs, Statues et Bustes de la Gaule Romaine V. Belgique-Première Partie* (Paris).

Etienne, R 1962. *Bordeaux Antique* (Bordeaux).

Evans, J 1922. *Magical Jewels of the Middle Ages and the Renaissance, particularly in England* (Oxford).

Faider-Feytmans, G 1980. 'Enseigne Romaine découverte à Flobecq (Hainault)', *Helinium* XX, 3–43.

Ferguson, J 1970. *The Religions of the Roman Empire* (London).

Field, N H 1981. 'A Romano-British Amulet from Bradford Down, Pamphill, Dorset', *Ant. J.* LXI, 307–9.

Finucane, R C 1977. *Miracles and Pilgrims. Popular Beliefs in Medieval England* (London).

Fishwick, D 1961. 'The Imperial Cult in Roman Britain', *Phoenix* XV, 159–73, 213–29.

Fishwick, D 1969. 'The Imperial *Numen* in Roman Britain', *J.R.S.* LIX, 76–91.

Fishwick, D 1978. 'The Development of Provincial Ruler Worship in the Western Roman Empire', *A.N.R.W.* 16.2, 1201–53.

Foerster, G 1980. 'A Cuirassed Bronze Statue of Hadrian from a Roman Fort near Beth

Shean (Scythopolis)', *The Israel Museum News* XVI, 107–10.

Forster, R H and Knowles, W H 1914. 'Corstopitum: Report on the Excavations in 1913', *Arch. Ael³*. XI, 278–310.

Fowles, J and Legg, R 1980. *John Aubrey's Monumenta Britannica: Parts One and Two* (Sherborne).

Fox, G E 1897. 'Uriconium', *Arch. Journ.* LIV, 123–73.

Frazer, Sir J G 1929. *The Fasti of Ovid edited with a Translation and Commentary* (London).

Frere, S S 1959. 'Excavations at Verulamium 1958. Fourth Interim Report', *Ant. J.* XXXIX, 1–18.

Frere, S S 1972. *Verulamium Excavations* I (Society of Antiquaries of London).

Frere, S S 1972a. 'A further note on the Caistor St Edmund intaglio', *Britannia* III, 295f.

Frere, S S 1975. 'The Silchester Church: The Excavation by Sir Ian Richmond in 1961', *Archaeologia* CV, 277–302.

Frere, S S 1982. 'The Bignor Villa', *Britannia* XIII, 135–95.

Frere, S S and St Joseph, J K 1974. 'The Roman Fortress at Longthorpe', *Britannia* V, 1–129.

Gage, J 1834. 'The Bartlow Hills, in the parish of Ashdon in Essex, with an account of Roman sepulchral relics recently discovered in the lesser Barrows', *Archaeologia* XXV, 1–23.

Gage, J 1837. 'The recent discovery of Roman sepulchral relics in one of the greater Barrows at Bartlow', *Archaeologia* XXVI, 300–17.

Gage, J 1842. 'An account of the final Excavations made at the Bartlow Hills', *Archaeologia* XXIX, 1–4.

Gardner, W and Savory, H N 1964. *Dinorben. A Hill-Fort occupied in Early Iron Age and Roman times* (Cardiff).

Gazda, E K 1981. 'A Marble Group of Ganymede and the Eagle from the Age of Augustine' in Humphrey, J H (ed.), *Excavations at Carthage* VI (Ann Arbor), 125–78.

Gilbert, H 1978. 'The Felmingham Hall Hoard, Norfolk', *B.B.C.S.* XXVIII, 159–87.

Gillam, J P and MacIvor, I 1954. 'The Temple of Mithras at Rudchester', *Arch. Ael⁴.* XXXII, 176–219.

Gillam, J P and Daniels, C M 1961. 'The Roman Mausoleum on Shorden Brae, Beaufront, Corbridge, Northumberland', *Arch. Ael⁴.* XXXIX, 37–61.

Ginsberg-Klar, M E 1981. 'The Archaeology of Musical Instruments in Germany during the Roman Period', *World Archaeology* XII, 313–20.

Godwin, H 1956. *The History of the British Flora* (London).

Goodburn, R 1972. *The Roman Villa, Chedworth* (National Trust, London).

Goodchild R and Kirk, J R 1954. 'The Romano-Celtic Temple at Woodeaton', *Oxoniensia* XIX, 15–37.

Goodenough, E R 1956. *Jewish Symbols in the Greco-Roman Period* V (New York).

Gose, E 1972. *Der Gallo-Römische Tempelbezirk im Altbachtal zu Trier* (Mainz).

Gray, A St George and Bulleid, A 1953. *The Meare Lake Village* II (Taunton).

Green, C J S 1977. 'The Significance of plaster burials for the recognition of Christian cemeteries' in Reece 1977, 46–57.

Green, C. W. 1965. 'A Romano-Celtic Temple at Bourton Grounds, Buckingham', *Records of Bucks.* XVII, 356–66.

Green, M J 1974. 'A Marble Cockerel from the Bradwell Roman Villa, Buckinghamshire', *Britannia* V, 381–3.

Green, M J 1975. 'Romano-British Non-Ceramic Model Objects in South-East Britain', *Arch. Journ.* CXXXII, 54–70.

Green, M J 1975a. *A Romano-British Ceremonial Bronze Object found near Peterborough* (Peterborough City Museum. Monograph No. 1).

Green, M J 1976. 'A Corpus of Religious Material from the Civilian Areas of Roman Britain', *B.A.R.* 24 (Oxford).

Green, M J 1977. 'Theriomorphism and the role of Divine Animals in Romano-British Cult Art', in Munby and Henig 1977, 297–326.

Green, M J 1978. 'Small cult objects from the military areas of Roman Britain', *B.A.R.* 52 (Oxford).

Green, M J 1979. 'The Worship of the Romano-Celtic Wheel-God in Britain seen in relation to Gaulish evidence', *Latomus* XXXVIII, 346–67.

Greenfield, E 1963. 'The Romano-British shrines at Brigstock, Northants', *Ant. J.* XLIII, 228–63.

Grimes, W F 1968. *The Excavation of Roman and Medieval London* (London).

Grimm, G 1969. *Die Zeugnisse Ägyptischer Religion und Kunstelmente im Römischen Deutschland* (Leiden).

Grinsell, L 1976. *Folklore of Prehistoric Sites in Britain* (Newton Abbot).

Grinsell, L 1980. 'The Cerne Abbas Giant 1764–1980', *Antiquity* LV, 29–33.

Hanfmann, C M A 1980. 'The Continuity of Classical Art: Culture, Myth and Faith', in Weitzmann, K (ed.), *Age of Spirituality: A Symposium* (New York), 75–99.

Harding, D W 1974. *The Iron Age in Lowland Britain* (London).

Harker, S 1980. 'Springhead. A brief Re-Appraisal' in Rodwell 1980, 285–8.

Harris, E and Harris, J R 1965. *The Oriental Cults in Roman Britain* (Leiden).

Harrison, J E 1903. *Prolegomena to the Study of Greek Religion* (Cambridge).

Hartley, B and Wacher, J 1983. *Rome and the Northern Provinces. Papers presented to Sheppard Frere* (Trowbridge).

Haselgrove, C 1979. 'The significance of coinage in pre-Conquest Britain' in Burnham, B C and Johnson, H B (eds.) 'Invasion and Response. The Case of Roman Britain', *B.A.R.* 73 (Oxford), 197–209.

Hassall, M W C 1977. 'Wingless Victories', in Munby and Henig 1977, 327–40.

Hassall, M W C 1980. 'Altars, Curses and other Epigraphic Evidence' in Rodwell 1980, 79–89.

Hassall, M W C 1980a. 'The Inscribed Altars' in Hill, Millett and Blagg 1980, 195–8.

Hassall, M W C and Tomlin, R S O 1977–1982. Roman Britain in 1976–1981: Inscriptions, *Britannia* VIII–XIII.

Hatt, J-J 1951. *La Tombe Gallo-Romaine* (Paris).

Helgeland, J 1978. 'Roman Army Religion', *A.N.R.W.* 16.2, 1470–1505.

Henig, M 1972. 'The Aesica Amulet and its Significance', *Arch. Ael*[4]. I, 282–7.

Henig, M 1974. 'A Coin of Tasciovanus', *Britannia* V, 374f.

Henig, M 1977. 'Death and the Maiden: Funerary Symbolism in Daily Life' in Munby and Henig 1977, 347–66.

Henig, M 1977a. 'Roman Gemstones: Figuretype and Adaptation' in Munby and Henig 1977, 341–6.

Henig, M 1977b. 'A Bronze Cube from Kingscote, Gloucestershire', *Ant. J.* LVII, 320f.

Henig, M 1978. 'A Corpus of Roman Engraved Gemstones from British Sites', *B.A.R.* 8 Second edition, (Oxford).

Henig, M 1978a. 'Some reflections of Greek Sculpture and painting in Roman art from London', in Bird, Chapman and Clark 1978, 109–23.

Henig, M 1979. 'Bronze Steelyard Weight from Roman Villa, Kingscote, Gloucestershire', *Ant. J.* LIX, 370f.

Henig, M 1979a. 'Late Antique Book Illustration and the Gallic Prefecture' in Hassall, M W C and Ireland, R I, 'De Rebus Bellicis', *B.A.R* Int. 63 (Oxford), 17–37.

Henig, M 1980. 'Art and Cult in the Temples of Roman Britain' in Rodwell 1980, 91–113.

Henig, M 1981. 'A Figure of Fortuna from Kingscote, Gloucestershire', *Ant. J.* LXI, 351–2.

Henig, M 1982. 'Seasonal Feasts in Roman Britain', *Oxford Journal of Archaeology* I, 213–23.

Henig, M 1983. (ed.) *A Handbook of Roman Art* (Oxford).

Henig, M 1983a. 'A Question of Standards', *Oxford Journal of Archaeology* II, 109–12.

Henig, M and Munby, J 1973. 'Three Bronze Figurines', *Oxoniensia* XXXVIII, 386f.

Henig, M and Nash, D 1982. 'Amminus and the Kingdom of Verica', *Oxford Journal of Archaeology* I, 243–6.

Hill, C, Millett, M and Blagg, T 1980. *The Roman Riverside Wall and Monumental Arch in London* (London and Middlesex Archaeological Society, Special Paper No. 3).

Hingley, R 1982. 'Recent Discoveries of the Roman Period at the Noah's Ark Inn, Frilford, South Oxfordshire', *Britannia* XIII, 305–9.

Hobley, B 1966–7. 'A Neronian-Vespasianic Military Site at "The Lunt", Baginton, Warwickshire', *Trans. Birmingham Arch. Soc.* LXXXIII, 65–129.

Home, G. 1924. *Roman York* (London).

Hondius-Crone, A 1955. *The Temple of Nehalennia at Domburg* (Amsterdam).

Hope-Taylor, B 1977. *Yeavering: an Anglo-British Centre of early Northumbria* (D.O.E. London).

Hornbostel, W 1973. *Sarapis: Studien zur Überlieferungsgeschichte den Erscheinungsformen und Wandlungen der Gestalt eines Gottes* (Leiden).

Horsley, J 1733. *Britannia Romana* (London).

Hubert, H and Mauss, M 1964. *Sacrifice. Its Nature and Function* (Chicago).

Hull, M R 1958. *Roman Colchester* (Society of Antiquaries of London).

Hunter, A G 1981. 'Building-Excavations at the Cross, Gloucester, 1960', *Trans. Bristol and Glouc. Arch. Soc.* XCIX, 79–107.

Hunter, M W C 1971. 'The Royal Society and the origins of British Archaeology II', *Antiquity* XLV, 187–92.

Huskinson, J 1974. Some Pagan Mythological figures and their significance in Early Christian Art', *P.B.S.R.* XLII, 68–97.

Inan, J and Rosenbaum, E 1966. *Roman and Early Byzantine Portrait Sculpture in Asia Minor* (London).

Jackson, K H 1964. *The Oldest Irish Tradition: A Window on the Iron Age* (Cambridge).

Jackson, K H 1971. *A Celtic Miscellany* Revised edition, (Harmondsworth).

Jacobsthal, P 1944. *Early Celtic Art* (Oxford).

Jarrett, M G 1976. *Maryport, Cumbria: A Roman Fort and its Garrison* (Kendal).

Jenkins, F 1958. 'The Cult of the Pseudo-Venus in Kent', *Arch. Cant.* LXXII, 60–76.

Jenkins, F 1978. 'Some interesting types of clay statuettes of the Roman period found in London' in Bird, Chapman and Clark 1978, 148–62.

Jessup, R F 1954. 'Excavation of a Roman Barrow at Holborough, Snodland', *Arch. Cant.* LXVIII, 1–61.

Jessup, R F 1970. 'A Roman bronze ceremonial axe from near Canterbury', *Ant. J.* L, 348–50.

Johns, C 1982. *Sex or Symbol. Erotic Images of Greece and Rome* (London).

Johns, C and Potter, T 1983. *The Thetford Treasure: Roman Jewellery and Silver* (London).

Johnson, A E 1975. 'Excavations at Bourton Grounds, Thornborough 1972–3', *Records of Bucks.* XX, 1–56.

Jolliffe, N 1941. 'Dea Brigantia', *Arch. Journ.* XCVIII, 36–61.

Jones, A H M 1973. *The Later Roman Empire 284–602* (Oxford).

Jones, R F J 1981. 'Cremation and Inhumation – Change in the Third Century', in King, A and Henig, M (eds.) 'The Roman West in the Third Century', *B.A.R.* 109 (Oxford), 15–19.

Jordan, D 1980. 'Two inscribed lead tablets from a well in the Athenian Kerameikos', *Mitteil des Deutschen Arch. Inst. Athenische Abteilung* XCV, 225–39.

Kater-Sibbes, G J F 1973. *Preliminary Catalogue of Sarapis Monuments* (Leiden).

Kelly, E and Dudley, C 1981. 'Two Romano-British Burials', *S.A.C.* CXIX, 65–88.

King, A 1983. 'The Roman Church at Silchester reconsidered', *Oxford Journal of Archaeology* II, 225–37.

Kirk, J R 1949. 'Bronzes from Woodeaton, Oxon.', *Oxoniensia* XIV, 1–45.

Kolling, A 1973. 'Römische Kastrierzangen', *Archäologisches Korrespondenzblatt* III, 353–7.

Künzl, E 1969. 'Der Augusteische Silbercalathus', *B.J.* CLXIX, 321–92.

Lambrechts, P 1954. *L'Exaltation de la Tête dans La Pensée et dans L'Art des Celtes* (Bruges).

Lang, M 1977. *Cure and Cult in Ancient Corinth. A Guide to the Asklepieion* (Princeton N.J.).

Lattimore, R 1962. *Themes in Greek and Latin Epitaphs* (Urbana, Illinois).

Laver, P 1927. 'The Excavation of a Tumulus at Lexden, Colchester', *Archaeologia* LXXVI, 241–54.

Layard, N F 1925. 'Bronze Crowns and a Bronze Head-dress from a Roman site at Cavenham Heath, Suffolk', *Ant. J.* V, 258–65.

Le Glay, M 1981. 'Abraxas', *L.I.M.C.* I, 2–7.

Lehmann, K 1962. 'Ignorance and Search in the Villa of the Mysteries', *J.R.S.* LII, 62–8.

Lewis, M J T 1965. *Temples in Roman Britain* (Cambridge).

Liversidge, J 1977. 'Roman Burials in the Cambridge Region', *Proc. Camb. Antiq. Soc.* LXVII, 11–38.

Liversidge, J, Smith, D J and Stead, I M 1962. 'Brantingham Roman Villa: Discoveries in 1962', *Britannia* IV, 84–106.

L'Orange, H P 1947. *Apotheosis in Ancient Portraiture* (Oslo).

Louis, R 1943. 'Les Fouilles des Fontaines-Salées en 1942', *Gallia* I, 27–70.

Lowther, A W G 1976. 'Romano-British Chimney-Pots and Finials', *Ant. J.* LVI, 35–48.

Lysons, S 1797. *An Account of Roman Antiquities discovered at Woodchester in the County of Gloucester* (London).

Lysons, S 1817. *Reliquiae Britannico Romanae* II (London).

MacDonald, M J 1979. 'Religion' in Clarke 1979, 404–33.

MacGregor, A 1976. *Finds from a Roman Sewer System and an adjacent building in Church Street* (York).

MacMullen, R 1981. *Paganism in the Roman Empire* (New Haven).

MacNeill, E 1926. 'On the Calendar of Coligny', *Eriu* X, 1–67.

Maiuri, A 1932. *La Casa del Menandro e il suo Tesoro di Argenteria* (Rome).

Maiuri, A 1953. *Roman Painting* (Geneva).

Mallory, J P 1982. 'The Sword of the Ulster Cycle' in Scott, B G (ed.), *Studies on Early Ireland. Essays in honour of M V Duignan* (Belfast), 99–114.

Manning, W H 1966. 'A group of Bronze Models from Sussex in the British Museum', *Ant. J.* XLVI, 50–9.

Marsden, P R V [1967]. *A Ship of the Roman Period from Blackfriars in the City of London* (London).

Marsden, P R V 1980. *Roman London* (London).

Marsh, G D 1979. 'Three 'theatre' masks from London', *Britannia* X, 263–5.

Marsh, G D and West, B 1981. 'Skullduggery in Roman London', *Trans. London and Middlesex Arch. Soc.* XXXII, 86–102.

Maxfield, V A 1981. *The Military decorations of the Roman Army* (London).

May, T 1930. *Catalogue of the Roman Pottery in the Colchester and Essex Museum* (Cambridge).

McCann, A M 1968. 'The Portraits of Septimius Severus (AD 193–211)', *M.A.A.R.* XXX.

McCarthy, M R, Padley, T G and Henig, M 1982. 'Excavations and Finds from the Lanes, Carlisle', *Britannia* XIII, 79–89.

McWhirr, A, Viner, L and Wells, W 1982. *Cirencester Excavations II Romano-British Cemeteries at Cirencester* (Cirencester).

Meaney, A L and Hawkes, S C 1970. *Two Anglo-Saxon Cemeteries at Winnall* (Society for Medieval Archaeology, Monograph No. 4, London).

Meates, Lieut-Col. G W 1979. *The Roman Villa at Lullingstone, Kent. 1. The Site* (Kent Arch. Soc. Monograph No. 1, Maidstone).

Merrifield, R 1954. 'The use of Bellarmines as Witch-Bottles', *Guildhall Misc.* III, 3–15.

Merrifield, R 1955. 'Witch-bottles and Magical Jugs', *Folklore* LXVI, 195–207.

Merrifield, R 1969. *Roman London* (London).

Merrifield, R 1977. 'Art and Religion in Roman London – An inquest on the sculptures of Londinium', in Munby and Henig, 375–406.

Merrifield, R 1980. 'The contribution to our knowledge of Roman London', in Hill, Millett and Blagg 1980, 200–206.

Mitard, P-H 1982. 'La Tête en Tôle de Bronze de Genainville (Val-d'Oise), *Gallia* XL, 1–33.

Moore, C N 1975. 'A Roman Phallic Carving from Long Bennington,, *Lincs. Hist. and Arch.* X, 58f.

Morris, J R 1968. 'The date of St Alban', *Herts. Arch.* I, 1–8.

Munby, J 1977. 'Art, Archaeology and Antiquaries', in Munby and Henig 1977, 415–32.

Munby, J and Henig, M 1977. 'Roman Life and Art in Britain', *B.A.R.* 41 (Oxford).

Murray, A S 1896. 'On a Bronze Statuette of Hercules', *Archaeologia* LV, 199–202.

Murray, Sister C 1981. 'Rebirth and Afterlife. A study of the transmutation of some pagan imagery in early Christian funerary art', *B.A.R.* int. ser. 100 (Oxford).

Nash, 1982. 'A Bath full of Coins', *The Ashmolean* 1, 16–17.

Needham, S 1979. 'Two Recent British Shield Finds and their Continental Parallels', *P.P.S.* XLV, 111–34.

Noll, R 1980. 'Das Inventar des Dolichenusheiligtums von Mauer an der Url (Noricum)', *Der Römische Limes in Österreich* XXX (Vienna).

Norman, A F 1971. 'Religion in Roman York', in Butler, R M (ed.), *Soldier and Civilian in Roman Yorkshire* (Leicester), 143–54.

North, J A 1976. 'Conservatism and Change in Roman Religion', *P.B.S.R.* XLIV, 1–12.

Nutton, V 1968. 'A Greek Doctor at Chester', *Journ. Chester Arch. Soc.* LV, 7–13.

Ogilvie, R M 1969. *The Romans and their Gods* (London).

O'Neil, H E and Toynbee, J M C 1958. 'Sculptures from a Romano-British well in Gloucestershire', *J.R.S.* XLVIII, 47–55.

Onians, R B 1951. *The Origins of European Thought about the Body, the Mind, the Soul, the World, Time and Fate* (Cambridge).

O'Rahilly, T F 1946. *Early Irish History and Mythology* (Dublin).

Orr, D G 1978. 'Roman Domestic Religion: The Evidence of the Household Shrines', *A.N.R.W.* 16.2, 1557–91.

Painter, K S 1971. 'A Roman gold ex-voto from Wroxeter, Shropshire', *Ant. J.* LI, 329–31.

Painter, K S 1977. *The Water Newton Early Christian Silver* (London).

Parke, H W 1967. *Greek Oracles* (London).

Parke, H W 1977. *Festivals of the Athenians* (London).

Partridge, C. 1981. *Skeleton Green. A Late Iron Age and Romano-British site* (Britannia Monograph No. 2, London).

Payne, G 1874. 'Roman coffins of lead from Bex Hill, Milton-next-Sittingbourne', *Arch. Cant.* IX, 164–73.

Penn, W S 1959. 'The Romano-British settlement at Springhead: Excavation of Temple I. Site C.1.', *Arch. Cant.* LXIII, 1–61.

Penn, W S 1960. 'Springhead. Temples III and IV', *Arch. Cant.* LXXIV, 113–40.

Penn, W S 1964. 'Springhead: The Temple Ditch Site', *Arch. Cant.* LXXIX, 170–89.

Percival, J 1976. *The Roman Villa* (London).

Perkins, D R J 1981. 'A Roman Bronze Head from Margate', *Arch. Cant.* XCVII, 307–11.

Petch, D F 1962. 'A Roman Inscription, Nettleham', *Lincs. Architect. and Archaeol. Soc.* N.S. IX, 94–7.

Peters, W J T 1963. *Landscape in Romano-Campanian Mural Painting* (Assen).

Phillips, E J 1972–4. 'The Roman distance slab from Bridgeness', *P.S.A.S.* CV, 176–82.

Phillips, E J 1976. 'A Roman Figured Capital in Cirencester', *J.B.A.A.* CXXIX, 35–41.

Phillips, E J 1976a. 'A Workshop of Roman Sculptors at Carlisle', *Britannia* VII, 101–8.

Phillips, E J 1977. *Corpus Signorum Imperii Romani, Great Britain 1.1 Corbridge. Hadrian's Wall East of the North Tyne* (British Academy).

Pitts, L F 1979. *Roman bronze figurines from the civitates of the Catuvellauni and Trinovantes*, B.A.R. 60 (Oxford).

Potter, T W 1981. 'The Roman Occupation of the Central Fenland', *Britannia* XII, 79–133.

Powell, T G E 1980. *The Celts* second edition (London).

Preisendanz, K 1928–41. *Papyri Graecae Magicae* (Leipzig).

Price, J E and Hilton Price, F G 1881. *A Description of the Remains of Roman Buildings at Morton, near Brading, Isle of Wight* (London).

Quet, M-H 1981. *La Mosaïque Cosmologique de Mérida* (Paris).

Rahtz, P 1982. 'Celtic Society in Somerset', *B.B.C.S.* XXX, 176–96.

Rahtz, P and Watts, L 1979. 'The end of Roman temples in the west of Britain', in Casey, J, 'The End of Roman Britain', *B.A.R.* 71 (Oxford).

Rashleigh, P 1803. 'Account of Antiquities discovered at Southfleet in Kent', *Archaeologia* XIV, 37–9 and 221–3.

Reece, R 1977 (ed.). 'Burial in the Roman World', *CBA Research Report No. 22* (London).

Reece, R 1977a. 'Burial in Latin literature: two examples' in *ibid.* 44f.

Richmond, I A 1943. 'Roman Legionaries at Corbridge, their Supply-base, Temples and Religious Cult', *Arch. Ael⁴.* XXI, 127–224.

Richmond, I A 1950. *Archaeology and the Afterlife in Pagan and Christian Imagery*, Riddell Memorial Lectures, University of Durham (Oxford).

Richmond, I A and Gillam, J P 1951. 'The Temple of Mithras at Carrawburgh', *Arch. Ael⁴.* XXIX, 1–92.

Rivet, A L F and Smith, C 1979. *The Place-Names of Roman Britain* (London).

Roach Smith, C 1840. 'On some Roman bronzes discovered in the bed of the Thames in January 1837', *Archaeologia* XXVIII, 38–46.

Robinson, H R 1975. *The Armour of Imperial Rome* (London).

Rodwell, W 1980 (ed.). 'Temples, Churches and Religion in Roman Britain', *B.A.R.* 77 (Oxford).

Rodwell, W 1982. 'The Origins of Wells Cathedral', *Antiquity* LVI, 215–8.

Rosenbaum, E 1960. *A Catalogue of Cyrenaican Portrait Sculpture* (London).

Ross, A 1967. *Pagan Celtic Britain* (London).

Ross, A 1968. 'Shafts, pits, wells – sanctuaries of the Belgic Britons', in Coles, J M and Simpson, D D A, (eds.) *Studies in Ancient Europe. Essays presented to Stuart Piggott* (Leicester).

Ross, A 1968a. 'A Celtic Intaglio from Caistor St Edmund', *Norf. Arch.* XXXIV, 263–71.

Ross, A 1972. 'A further note on the Caistor St Edmund intaglio', *Britannia* III, 293–5.

Ross, A 1979–80. 'A Pagan Celtic Shrine at Wall, Staffordshire', *Trans. South Staffs. Arch. and Hist. Soc.* XXI, 3–11.

Ross, A and Feachem, R 1976. 'Ritual Rubbish? The Newstead Pits' in Megaw, J V S (ed.), *To Illustrate the Monuments. Essays on Archaeology presented to Stuart Piggott* (London), 230–7.

Rostovtseff, M 1923. 'Commodus-Hercules in Britain', *J.R.S.* XIII, 91–109.

Ryan, M 1982. 'Some Archaeological Comments on the Occurrence and Use of Silver in pre-Viking Ireland', in Scott, B G (ed.), *Studies on Early Ireland. Essays in honour of M V Duignan* (Belfast), 45–80.

Salway, P 1981. *Roman Britain* (Oxford).

Schwertheim, E 1974. *Die Denkmäler Orientalischer Gottheiten im Römischen Deutschland* (Leiden).

Scullard, H H 1981. *Festivals and Ceremonies of the Roman Republic* (London).

Sena Chiesa, G 1966. *Gemme del Museo Nazionale di Aquileia* (Aquileia).

Siviero, R 1954. *Gli Ori e le Ambre del Museo Nazionale di Napoli* (Florence).

Smith, D J 1962. 'The Shrine of the Nymphs and the Genius Loci at Carrawburgh', *Arch. Ael⁴.* XL, 59–81.

Smith, D J 1969. 'The Mosaic Pavements', in Rivet, A L F, *The Roman Villa in Britain* (London) 71–125.

Smith, D J 1977. 'Mythological Figures and Scenes in Romano-British Mosaics' in Munby and Henig 1977, 105–93.

Speidel, M P 1978. *The Religion of Iuppiter Dolichenus in the Roman Army* (Leiden).

Speidel, M P and Dimitrova-Milčeva, A 1978. 'The Cult of the Genii in the Roman Army', *A.N.R.W.* 16.2, 1542–55.

Stead, I M 1967. 'A La Tène III Burial at Welwyn Garden City', *Archaeologia* CI, 1–62.

Stead, I M 1979. *The Arras Culture* (York).

Steer, K A 1958. 'Arthur's O'on: A lost shrine of Roman Britain', *Arch. Journ.* CXV, 99–110.

Steer, K A 1976. 'More Light on Arthur's O'on', *Glasgow Arch. Journ.* IV, 90–2

Stevenson, R B K 1967. 'A Roman-period cache of charms in Aberdeenshire', *Antiquity* XLI, 143–5.

Strickland, T J 1982. 'Chester: Excavations in the Princess Street/Hunter Street Area 1978–1982. A First Report on Discoveries of the Roman Period', *Journ. Chester Arch. Soc.* LXV, 5–24.

Strong, D 1976. *Roman Art* (Harmondsworth).

Strong, E 1911. 'The Exhibition Illustrative of the Provinces of the Roman Empire in the Baths of Diocletian at Rome', *J.R.S.* I, 1–49.

Stuart, P and Bogaers, J E 1971. *Deae Nehalenniae* (Middelburg and Leiden).

Stuart, P 1981. 'Ein Bacchischer Wagenaufsatz', *Oudheidkundige Mededelingen* LXII, 47–50.

Stupperich, R 1980. 'A Reconsideration of some fourth-century British mosaics', *Britannia* XI, 289–301.

Sturdy, D 1973. 'The Temple of Diana and the Devil's Quoits: Continuity, Persistence and Tradition' in Strong, D E (ed.), *Archaeological Theory and Practice* (London and New York), 27–43.

Sutherland, C H V 1958. 'The First British Empire', *Archaeology* XI, 6–12.

Sutherland, C H V 1967. *The Roman Imperial Coinage VI. From Diocletian's reform to the death of Maximinus* (London).

Swain, E J and Ling, R J 1981. 'The Kingscote Wall-Paintings', *Britannia* XII, 167–75.

Taylor, M V 1963. 'Statuettes of Horsemen and Horses and other Votive Objects from Brigstock, Northants', *Ant. J.* XLIII, 264–8.

Thomas, C 1961. 'The Animal Art of the Scottish Iron Age and its Origins', *Arch. Journ.* CXVIII, 14–64.

Thomas, C 1981. *Christianity in Roman Britain to AD 500* (London).

Thompson, D B 1973. *Ptolemaic Oinochoai and Portraits in Faience: Aspects of the Ruler Cult* (Oxford).

Thompson, F H 1970. 'Dodecahedrons Again', *Ant. J.* L, 93–6.

Thompson, F H 1976. 'The Excavation of the Roman Amphitheatre at Chester', *Archaeologia* CV, 127–239.

Todd, M 1966. 'Romano-British Mintages of Antoninus Pius', *Num. Chron*[7]. VI, 147–53.

Toynbee, J M C 1934. *The Hadrianic School* (Cambridge).

Toynbee, J M C 1962. *Art in Roman Britain* (London).

Toynbee, J M C 1964. *Art in Britain under the Romans* (Oxford).

Toynbee, J M C 1964a. 'A new Roman mosaic found in Dorset', *J.R.S.* LIV, 7–14.

Toynbee, J M C 1964b. 'The Christian Roman Mosaic, Hinton St Mary, Dorset', *Proc. Dorset Nat. Hist. and Arch. Soc.* LXXXV, 116–21.

Toynbee, J M C 1971. *Death and Burial in the Roman World* (London).

Toynbee, J M C 1976. 'Roman Sculpture in Gloucestershire', in McGrath, P and Cannon, J (eds.). *Essays in Bristol and Gloucestershire History* (Bristol), 62–100.

Toynbee, J M C 1977. 'Greek Myth in Roman Stone', *Latomus* XXXVI, 343–412.

Toynbee, J M C 1978. 'A Londinium Votive Leaf or Feather and its fellows', in Bird, Chapman and Clark 1978, 128–47.

Toynbee, J M C 1981. 'Apollo, Beasts and Seasons: Some thoughts on the Littlecote mosaic', *Britannia* XII, 1–5.

Toynbee, J M C and Ward-Perkins, J 1956. *The Shrine of St Peter and the Vatican Excavations* (London).

Turnbull, P 1982. 'A Romano-British Sculpture from Well, North Yorkshire', *Britannia* XIII, 323–5.

Turner, E G 1963. 'A Curse-Tablet from Nottinghamshire', *J.R.S.* LIII, 122–4.

Turner, R 1982. *Ivy Chimneys, Witham. An Interim Report.* Essex County Council, Occasional Paper No. 2 (Chelmsford).

Vermaseren, M J 1963. *Mithras, the Secret God* (London).

Vermaseren, M J 1977. *Cybele and Atys. The Myth and the Cult* (London).

Vermaseren, M J and van Essen, C C 1965. *The Excavations in the Mithraeum of the Church of Santa Prisca in Rome* (Leiden).

Vermeule, C C 1959. *The Goddess Roma in the Art of the Roman Empire* (Cambridge, Mass.).

Vertet, H 1961. 'A mould of the potter *Cettus* and a note on the club as a religious symbol', *Ant. J.* XLI, 233–5.

Vogel, L 1973. *The Column of Antoninus Pius* (Cambridge, Mass.).

Vollenweider, M L 1966. *Die Steinschndidekunst und Ihre Künstler in Spätrepublikanischer und Augusteischer Zeit* (Baden-Baden).

Wacher, J 1974. *The Towns of Roman Britain* (London).

Walters, H B 1911. *Catalogue of Jewellery, Greek, Etruscan and Roman, in the British Museum* (London).

Walters, H B 1921. *Catalogue of the Silver Plate, Greek, Etruscan and Roman, in the British Museum* (London).

Walters, V J 1974. *The Cult of Mithras in the Roman Provinces of Gaul* (Leiden).

Ward Fowler, W 1899. *The Roman Festivals of the period of the Republic* (London).

Wardman, A 1982. *Religion and Statecraft among the Romans* (London).

Ward-Perkins, J B 1981. *Roman Imperial Architecture* second edition (Harmondsworth).

Watkin, W T 1886. *Roman Cheshire* (Liverpool).

Webb, P H 1933. *The Roman Imperial Coinage V: part II* (London).

Webster, G 1966–7. 'A Pendant in the form of a Phallic Amulet', in Hobley 1966–7, 126–9.

Webster, G 1978. *Boudica. The British Revolt against Rome AD 60* (London).

Webster, G 1979. *The Roman Imperial Army of the First and Second Centuries AD.* Second edition (London).

Webster, G 1980. *The Roman Invasion of Britain* (London).

Webster, G 1981. *Rome against Caratacus* (London).

Webster, J 1973. 'A Bronze Incense-Container in the form of Bacchus from Carlisle', *Trans. Cumberland and Westmorland Arch. Soc.* N.S. LXXIII, 90–3.

Wedlake, W J 1982. *The Excavation of the Shrine of Apollo at Nettleton, Wiltshire, 1956–1971* (Society of Antiquaries of London).

Weinstock, S 1971. *Divus Julius* (Oxford).

West, S E 1976. 'The Romano-British Site at Icklingham', *East Anglian Archaeology* 3, 63–125.

Wheeler, H 1981. 'Two Roman Bronzes from Brigstock, Northamptonshire', *Ant. J.* LXI, 309–11.

Wheeler, R E M 1943. *Maiden Castle, Dorset* (Society of Antiquaries of London).

Wheeler, R E M 1962. 'Size and Baalbek', *Antiquity* XXXVI, 6–9.

Wheeler, R E M and Wheeler, T V 1932. *Report on the excavation of the prehistoric, Roman and post-Roman site in Lydney Park, Gloucestershire* (Society of Antiquaries of London).

Wheeler, R E M and Wheeler, T V 1946. *Verulamium: a Belgic and two Roman cities* (Society of Antiquaries of London).

Wickham, H 1874. 'Roman Remains from Luton, Chatham', *Arch. Cant.* IX, 174f.

Williams, G H and Delaney, C J 1982. 'A Celtic Head from Llandysul', *The Carmarthenshire Antiquary* XVIII, 9–15.

Witt, R E 1971. *Isis in the Graeco-Roman World* (London).

Woodfield, P 1978. 'Roman Architectural Masonry from Northamptonshire', *Northamptonshire Arch.* XIII, 67–86.

Wright, R P 1944–7. 'A Roman Shrine to Silvanus on Scargill Moor near Bowes', *Y.A.J.* XXXVI, 383–6.

Wright, R P 1957. 'Roman Britain in 1956: Inscriptions', *J.R.S.* XLVII, 226–34.

Wright, R P 1958. 'Roman Britain in 1957: Inscriptions', *J.R.S.* XLVIII, 150–5.

Wright, R P 1964. 'A Graeco-Egyptian amulet from a Romano-British site at Welwyn, Herts', *Ant. J.* XLIV, 143–6.

Wright, R P 1970. 'Roman Britain in 1969: Inscriptions', *Britannia* I, 305–15.

Wright, R P and Richmond, I A 1955. *The Roman Inscribed and Sculptured Stones in the Grosvenor Museum, Chester* (Chester).

Zaehner, R C 1961. *The Dawn and Twilight of Zoroastrianism* (London).

References

Prologue (pp. 12–14)

1 See R H Barrow, *Prefect and Emperor. The Relations of Symmachus AD 384* (Oxford, 1973) for text and translation of this speech
2 Thomas 1981
3 Bruun 1966, 46ff, 92ff *passim*.
4 As in *R.I.B.* 103 (Cirencester). See P Brown, 'The Last Pagan Emperor', in *Society and the Holy in Late Antiquity* (London, 1981), pp. 83–102, especially p. 94, on Julian's own attitude
5 Hassall and Tomlin 1982, 404–6, no. 7
6 Ross 1967; Green 1976, and many other papers
7 On which, see Lewis 1966, and various contributors to Rodwell 1980, especially that by D R Wilson
8 Trans. J C Rolfe (Loeb Classical Library)

1 The Celtic World (pp. 17–24)

1 Trans. M Winterbottom, *Gildas. The Ruin of Britain and other works* (London and Chichester 1978)
2 Rivet and Smith 1979, 493; *R.I.B.* 635; cf. Needham 1979 esp. 127–8 on the ritual deposition of Bronze Age metalwork in rivers, Cunliffe 1978, 323 for Iron Age. See Bradley 1982 on the practical motivation in the disposal of personal property.
3 Ross 1968. Richard Bradley points out to me that the famous Wilsford Shaft, Wiltshire, may be simply a Bronze Age well
4 Alcock 1965; Rivet and Smith 1979, 254–5
5 Petch 1962
6 Thomas 1961, 40; Green 1977
7 Henig 1974; Atkinson and Piggott's attempt to separate the horns and cap (1955) does not convince me
8 Jacobsthal 1944, 59
9 Boon 1982; also see Allen 1958, nos. 68–9; Henig 1980, 108 and pl. 5.III
10 Lambrechts 1954, on the Celtic head cult; see Onians 1951, 95ff on the head in Classical antiquity. The word *Imagines* was later used in addition for the Imperial portraits attached to Roman Standards
11 Burl 1979, 30, 244
12 Battely 1711, 77; cf. Hunter 1971, 190 and Munby in Munby and Henig 1977, 425
13 Chadwick 1966
14 H Usener (ed.), *M. Annaei Lucani Commentaria Bernensia* (1869), 30ff; cf. Lucan, *Pharsalia* I, 444–6
15 Harding 1974, 102
16 MacNeill 1926; Powell 1980, 145, 215f, pl. 98
17 Allen 1964–68; Cunliffe 1980, 190
18 Cunliffe 1978, 175–8
19 *Current Archaeology* VII, no. 10, March 1981, 294–7
20 O'Rahilly 1946, 121–4
21 Jackson 1971, 154
22 Ryan 1982; Mallory 1982. But still see Jackson 1964
23 Drury 1980, 45–55; Cunliffe 1981, 246–9 is tentative, but favours a religious interpretation; Bedwin 1981
24 Ellison 1980, 306
25 M W C Hassall in *ibid*, 327. Fig. 15.8 Defixiones 3 and 4
26 *R.I.B.* 91
27 Cunliffe 1978, 323. I am grateful to Malcolm Bird for information on the Tiv
28 as Haselgrove 1979, 203
29 Cunliffe 1978, 316; on Danebury, *id.* 1981, 252
30 Cocks 1921, 150
31 Green 1965; Johnson 1975, esp. p. 29 on an inhumation near the site. References I owe to Anthony King
32 Marsh and West 1981; Barker c.1981, 15. Also see West 1976, 68–9 and Ross and Feachem 1976 for skulls in pits

2 The Roman Gods (pp. 25–35)

1 Webster 1980
2 *R.I.B.* 663, citing Diodorus XVII, 104
3 H Stern, *Le Calendrier de 354* (Paris, 1953)
4 Barrett 1978, 312, says that after Virgil, Ovid was 'undoubtedly the most popular of the Roman poets throughout the Empire'
5 Bradford Welles, Fink and Gilliam 1959

6 Scullard 1981, 193f

7 *ibid.* 76–8

8 Bradford Welles, Fink and Gilliam 1959, 199

9 Scullard 1981, 102f

10 The *Feriale Duranum* gives the date as January 3rd; see Bradford Welles, Fink and Gilliam 1959, 197f

11 *R.I.B.* 1215 (Risingham); 1694 (Chesterholm)

12 Scullard 1981, 97–100

13 Frazer 1929, iii 374

14 *R.I.B.* 1270; see Hassall 1980, 82; Henig 1982, 214

15 Toynbee 1962, 149–50, no. 54 pl. 60

16 Scullard 1981, 108–10

17 *ibid.* 110f

18 *ibid.* 118f

19 G. Webster in Hobley 1966–7, 126–9; Johns 1982, 73–4

20 Scullard 1981, 120f

21 *ibid.* 122

22 *ibid.* 124f

23 *ibid.* 149f

24 *ibid.* 166f

25 *ibid.* 159f

26 *ibid.* 177f

27 *ibid.* 205–7

28 North 1976

29 Ogilvie 1969, 25–8

30 Hassall 1980, 80

31 Turner 1963

32 Hubert and Mauss 1964, 33–5; Burkert 1966, 87ff

33 Parke 1977, 162–7

34 Cristofani 1979, 96–8

35 *C.I.L.* XIII, 6765 (Mainz); Cunliffe 1969, 189, no. 1.60

36 Hubert and Mauss 1964, 40f

37 e.g. that by Artemidorus, cf. R J White, *The Interpretation of Dreams: Oneirocritica by Artemidorus, translation and commentary* (Park Ridge, N.J. 1975)

38 Parke 1967

39 Vermaseren 1977, 38ff

3 The Romanisation of The Celtic Cults
(pp. 36–67)

1 MacMullen 1981, 118

2 Salway 1981, 678–9

3 on temples see Lewis 1965

4 Downey, King and Soffe 1980

5 Hassall and Tomlin 1981, 369 no. 3

6 Wheeler 1962

7 Blagg 1979; also Woodfield 1978, 68–9 fig. 5, for example from Ringstead, Northants

8 see *V.C.H. Berkshire* I, 283 and IV, 544; Grinsell 1976, 52; Hull 1958, 267–9; Hingley 1982, 309; Wheeler and Wheeler 1936, 123–33; Crummy 1982; Blagg 1982, 53–3; Henig 1982, 219

9 Marsh 1979; Henig 1982, 219; *Britannia* XIII (1982), 371–2

10 see MacMullen 1981, 1–48, a chapter entitled 'Perceptible'

11 *ibid.*, especially 13, 41

12 *ibid.*, 36–9, on parties

13 A Barratt in Webster 1981, 124–30 places his reign in the Claudio-Neronian period. There is a suggestion that the Fishbourne 'proto-palace' was his, but the Flavian palace is assigned perhaps to his heirs. See also Henig and Nash 1982 on the early Romanisation of Chichester

14 see Rivet and Smith 1979, 255–6 on the name *Sulis*; Alcock 1965 on Water-cults

15 Cunliffe 1969; 1980

16 The phrase actually used is *ad fontem deae Sulis*: see *Britannia* XII (1981), 375ff no. 9

17 *C.I.L.* XI, 1303, and in general 1292–1310 for other dedications from the site

18 *R.I.B.* 1526, 1527

19 *R.I.B.* 1534, 1522–35 for other dedications. On the site, see Clayton 1880

20 Smith 1962

21 *R.I.B.* 1228. On dreams, see MacMullen 1981, 60

22 *R.I.B.* 460

23 Strong 1976, pl. 33

24 Ross 1967, 205

25 *R.I.B.* 151, 105

26 Hassall and Tomlin 1977, 426–7 no. 4

27 *R.I.B.* 88

28 *R.I.B.* 653

29 Hassall and Tomlin 1979, 339–41 no. 1

30 Merrifield 1977, 383–7

31 *id.* 1965, 294 no. 350, pls. 88, 89; *id.* 1977; Toynbee 1978; Blagg 1980, 169–71, no. 34

32 Charlesworth 1961, 3, 4, 24 no. 1; Walters 1921, 46–7 no. 183

33 Hondius-Crone 1955; Stuart and Bogaers 1971

34 Hassall and Tomlin 1977, 430f, no. 18; Stuart and Bogaers 1971, no. 45

35 *ibid.* no. 6

36 see Etienne 1962, 173, for correct reading

37 rings: *R.C.H.M. Eburacum*, 133 and pl. 65; Barkway plaques: *R.I.B.* 219, 218

38 *V.C.H. Hertfordshire* IV, 149–50 and pl. X

39 Ambrose and Henig 1980; *V.C.H. Suffolk* I, 312; *R.I.B.* 213

40 Taylor 1963; Wheeler 1980; Rostovtseff 1923, 94 and pl. IV; *V.C.H. Cambridgeshire* VII, 84–5, pl. XIV A

41 Toynbee 1962, 131 no. 16, pl. 17; *R.I.B.* 274

42 Walters 1921, 59–64

43 Petch 1962; on the name of the dedicator, see Birley 1979, 143

44 *R.I.B.* 305, 307

45 *R.I.B.* 616, 617

46 Wheeler and Wheeler 1932; *R.I.B.* 307. Hound-figurines and hounds on votive plaques have

recently been found at a site in north west
Clwyd, and these may indicate that Nodens
was worshipped in North Wales as well
(information from Glenys Lloyd-Morgan
and George Boon); MacMullen 1981, 61

47 Toynbee 1976, 92–4
48 Hassall and Tomlin 1979, 344 nos. 3 and 4
49 *R.I.B.* 2071, 1208
50 trans. W D Hooper (Loeb Classical Library)
51 trans. A M Harmon (Loeb Classical Library)
52 Ellison and Henig 1981
53 Toynbee 1964, 156 pl. XLa; *Britannia* III, 1972, 329–30
54 Hunter 1981, 91–99
55 *R.I.B.* 733, 732
56 *R.I.B.* 1041
57 *R.I.B.* 1329, 1327
58 *R.I.B.* 452; see Green 1979 on objects which can be associated with him
59 Rivet and Smith 1979, 493; *R.I.B.* 635, 1534
60 Ross 1979–80
61 Toynbee 1957, 461f no. 5
62 O'Neil and Toynbee 1958, 52, 3 nos. 4–6
63 Goodburn 1972, 27 pl. 10
64 Birley 1979, 107
65 *R.I.B.* 772–777, 887–889
66 Wheeler 1943, 75f; Henig and Munby 1973 (see now *Gallia* XXXVIII, 1980, 319–20 fig. 7 for parallels); on the Southbroom cache, see *Guide to the Antiquities of Roman Britain* (British Museum, 1964), 54 and pl. 16, wrongly described as 'barbaric'. The best general account of bronzes is Boucher 1976
67 *R.I.B.* 1120, 583
68 Ausonius cf. translation by H G Evelyn White (Loeb Classical Library)

4 The Roman State and Religious Practice (pp. 68–94)

1 There is an extensive literature: see Wardman 1982, who shows that the State cult arose from real needs and was constantly changing. We must avoid seeing it in terms which are too formal. On Britain: Fishwick 1961, 1969, 1972, 1978 provides most of the evidence
2 MacMullen 1981, 103, 110
3 Weinstock 1971, e.g. p. 164 on the title *Soter*
4 Dio Cassius LXXV, 5.3–5 on Pertinax; also Dio Cassius LXXVII, 5.3–4 on cremation of Severus in Britain; no mention of the eagle, but it is probable that the same ceremony took place. On apotheosis in art see L'Orange 1947 and Vogel 1973, 33–40
5 Crummy 1980, 243–250; Ward-Perkins 1981, 226f
6 Fishwick 1972; 1978, 1216–9
7 Beard 1980; Fishwick 1961, 167; Birley 1981, 433–4

8 *R.I.B.* 5, 21
9 Courteault 1921; Etienne 1962, 173–4; Hassall and Tomlin 1979, 345 no. 5
10 Wright, Hassall and Tomlin 1976, 378 no. 1; Hassall 1980a, 195–6
11 *R.I.B.* 678, 687
12 Fishwick 1969
13 e.g. *R.I.B.* 4 (London) and 1272 (High Rochester)
14 *R.I.B.* 235
15 *R.I.B.* 1330
16 respectively *R.I.B.* 1327, 949, 1576, 193, 274
17 Toynbee 1972, 124–5 nos. 2–5, especially no. 3
18 Cunliffe and Fulford 1982, nos. 90, 92
19 Toynbee 1962, 123 no. 1; *id.* 1964, 47 pl. IVa, b
20 Birley 1981, 75 and 269
21 *ibid.* 50, pl. VIa, b; Foerster 1980
22 Boon 1974, 119 pl. 34g and refs cited
23 on Constantine: Toynbee 1962, 125 no. 6; *id.* 1964, 55 pl. VII, b
24 *R.I.B.* 662–3; Norman 1971, 144
25 Vollenweider 1966
26 Toynbee 1964, 49 pl. Va, b; Webster 1978, 106–7 pl. 5
27 *R.I.B.* 2200
28 *R.I.B.* 1466
29 *R.I.B.* 845
30 *R.I.B.* 844
31 *R.I.B.* 1227
32 *R.I.B.* 191
33 *R.I.B.* 582
34 Hassall and Tomlin 1979, 346 no. 7; Austen and Breeze 1979, 116–8; Birley 1978, 1513–5
35 Thompson 1973
36 Fishwick 1961, 218; *R.I.B.* 1778, 1212
37 Henig 1980
38 Richmond 1950; *R.I.B.* 1051
39 *R.I.B.* 89, 91
40 Fishwick 1978, 1252
41 trans. H Rushton Fairclough (Loeb Classical Library)
42 *R.I.B.* 1270
43 *R.I.B.* 812, 840
44 Henig 1978
45 Turnbull 1982
46 Hassall 1977, and see also my article *Britannia* in *L.I.M.C.* (forthcoming); on Roma see Vermeule 1959; Henig 1978, 304, App. 130
47 Erim 1982
48 *R.I.B.* 643, 2195; Toynbee 1934, 53–65; Todd 1966
49 Jolliffe 1941
50 Boon 1973, 108; D J Smith in Liversidge, Smith and Stead 1973, 97f
51 *R.I.B.* 102 and, for instance, *R.I.B.* 90 (Chichester); *R.I.B.* 2175 (Auchendavy)
52 Turner 1963
53 Marsden 1980, 50–52; Wacher 1974, 207 and fig.

53; Hassall 1980a, 195–6; Chapman 1974, 175 no. 3
54 Boon 1974, 119f, pl. 34c
55 Cunliffe and Fulford 1982, 29 no. 107, pl. 28;
R.I.B. 89
56 Neptune and Minerva: see *R.I.B.* 91 and
Bogaers 1979; Bath pediment: see Cunliffe
and Fulford 1982, nos. 32–7; on the
importance of Poseidon in Athens see Parke
1977, 97–103
57 Thomas 1981, 48–50
58 *R.I.B.* 103; Wacher 1974, pl. 55
59 Boon 1958; Henig 1978, no. 103
60 Phillips 1972–4. Recent examination has
shown that the distance-slab was painted. See
J Close-Brooks, 'The Bridgeness Distance
Slab', *P.S.A.S.* CXI (1981), 519–21
61 Helgeland 1978, 148–88, citing 1487
62 Richmond 1961, 226f
63 MacMullen 1981, 80f (J Terentius) Matres:
R.I.B. 919–20, 1421, 2135; Antenociticus: *R.I.B.*
1328; Cocidius: *R.I.B.* 1872; Dolichenus: *R.I.B.*
895
64 *R.I.B.* 2174–7
65 *R.I.B.* 986–7; Birley 1978, 1531; Rivet and Smith
1979, 363
66 Richmond 1943
67 Helgeland 1978, 1495f; and on Maryport:
Jarrett 1976, 4ff
68 Ross and Feachem 1976. Compare the Jewish
practice of burying unwanted sacred writings
in a pit (*genizah*)
69 Bowman 1974, 365; Boon 1974, 66–8 (Silchester;
an example from High Rochester is cited);
Robinson 1975, especially 107ff
70 Henig 1983a
71 Speidel and Dimitrova-Milčeva 1978, 1547–9;
Helgeland 1978, 1473–8; cf. *R.I.B.* 451 (Genius
Signiferorum, Chester) and 1262 (Genius
Signorum, High Rochester)
72 Faider-Feytmans 1980
73 Richmond 1943, 163–4; Toynbee 1971, 63
74 Mars Victor: *R.I.B.* 1221–3 (Risingham); Mars
Militaris: *R.I.B.* 838 (Maryport); Mars Ultor:
R.I.B. 1132 (Corbridge); Mars Pater: *R.I.B.* 1901
(Birdoswald)
75 Mars Cocidius: *R.I.B.* 602 (Lancaster), 1955–6
(Bankshead Milecastle between Birdoswald
and Castlesteads) and 1872 (Birdoswald); Mars
Camulus: *R.I.B.* 2166 (Bar Hill); Mars
Thincsus: *R.I.B.* 1593 (Housesteads); see
especially Birley 1978, 1523–32 on acceptable
local cults
76 Minerva: *R.I.B.* 429 (*actarius* at Caernarvon),
1134 (*librarius* at Corbridge); Watkins 1886,
197–200 (Chester shrine); Silvanus: *R.I.B.* 1905
(*venatores* at Birdoswald); on Hercules see
Richmond 1943, 171–3; Fortuna Augusta:

R.I.B. 1778 (Carvoran) and Fortuna Redux:
R.I.B. 445 (Chester); on the Genii, see Speidel
and Dimitrova-Milčeva 1978

5 Mithraism and the Other Eastern Religions (pp. 95–127)

1 Nutton 1968. Strickland 1982, suggests that
they probably came from the *valetudinarium*
(hospital) rather than the *praetorium*
2 Birley 1981, 248–50
3 On Britain, Harris and Harris 1965; Germany:
Grimm 1969, also Schwertheim 1974; Gaul:
Mithraic evidence assembled in Walters 1974
4 R Kipling, *Puck of Pook's Hill* (1906); John
Cowper Powys, *Porius* (1951)
5 Harris and Harris 1965, 1–54. The only new
evidence is a dubious Mithraeum at
Leicester; see Wacher 1974, 354f
6 Vermaseren 1963, 30–32, 144–6; Richmond and
Gillam 1951; 1ff; Smith 1962, 59ff
(Carrawburgh); Daniels 1962, 105ff
(Housesteads); Gose 1972, esp. 110–17 (Trier)
7 Vermaseren 1963, 144–6
8 Dodds 1968
9 Daniels 1962; Quet 1981
10 Vermaseren and Van Essen 1965 (for texts
from the Santa Prisca Mithraeum); Cumont
1896 (collecting together literary texts)
11 *R.I.B.* 1601
12 Harris and Harris 1965, 22 pl. V i; Richmond
and Gillam 1951; *R.I.B.* 1546
13 Wheeler and Wheeler 1936, 221 pl. LXVI
14 *R.I.B.* 641
15 Norman 1971, 149
16 Vermaseren 1963, 123–4 pls. opp. 160, 161
17 Daniels 1962, 111, but see Harris and Harris 1965,
34 n.6
18 Daniels, *loc. cit.*
19 *R.I.B.* 1599; Harris and Harris 1965, 35
20 *R.I.B.* 1600
21 Harris and Harris 1965, 26 and pl. VI; see also
Gillam and MacIvor 1964, 206–8
22 Vermaseren and Van Essen 1965, 134–5 pls.
CIV, CV
23 *R.I.B.* 3; Harris and Harris 1965, 7–8 pl. II and 33
24 *ibid.*, 3–38
25 Richmond and Gillam 1951, 84–5 no. 3. Grimes
1968, 114; Gillam and MacIvor 1954, 214–5 nos.
1–3
26 *ibid.* 215 no. 4; Richmond and Gillam 1951,
84–7, no. 1; Harris and Harris 1965, 34
27 Remains of feasts: M I Platt in Richmond and
Gillam 1951, 91; Grimes 1968, 113–4. On the
relief see Cumont 1899, 175 fig. 10
28 Cumont 1896, 7f
29 Richmond and Gillam 1951, 19 and pl. VI A
30 Toynbee 1963

31 On infusors: Boon 1974, 235, 351 no. 55; Liversidge 1977, 30f; spiced wine: see Apicius, *The Roman Cookery Book* ed. B Flower and E Rosenbaum (London, 1961), pp. 43ff; on resemblance of Mithraic infusor to Roman measures, see Harris and Harris 1965, 14 n.7

32 Zaehner 1961, 90–94; 115f

33 Cumont 1896, 39f

34 Vermaseren and Van Essen 1965, 217–21

35 *R.I.B.* 1; Merrifield 1977; Gazda 1981, 167 n.58

36 Ferguson 1970, 122

37 Vermaseren 1965, 145

38 Maxfield 1981

39 respectively: *R.I.B.* 1272, 1268, 1265

40 *R.I.B.*1583 and perhaps 1577

41 Lewis 1965, 99–107, figs. 100–104; Grimes 1968, 92–117

42 Centurions: cf. *R.I.B.* 322(?), 1398, 1600; *Beneficiarius consularis: R.I.B.* 1599; a legionary *Emeritus: R.I.B.* 3; *praefecti: R.I.B.* 1395, 1396, 1397(?), 1544–1546, 1992, 1993; a *tribunus: R.I.B.* 1272. Only Herion at Housesteads (*R.I.B.* 1601) is certainly outside the upper ranks of society

43 Richmond 1943, 171–3

44 Casey 1978. The last approximately dated monument is an inscription of AD 307–8, *R.I.B.* 4; Merrifield 1977, 375–82

45 Richmond and Gillam 1951, 41–3

46 Vermaseren 1977, 138–9

47 *ibid.* 96ff; Kolling 1973. Chichester, A Down, *Ant. J.* LXII, 1982, 368–9

48 *ibid.* 356f; Harris and Harris 1965, 109–12

49 Roach Smith 1840, 40–44, pl. VIII

50 Merrifield 1977, 398–9 is fairly circumspect on this identification, but Atys was sometimes figured as a huntsman in myth

51 Vermaseren 1977, 44, 115; Hassall and Tomlin 1980, 406f no. 7; Lewis 1965, 96; *J.R.S.* LIII (1963), 138 and pl. XVI, 4

52 Vermaseren 1977, 101–7, 131–7

53 MacMullen 1981, 114–8

54 Harris and Harris 1965, 79–80; see also G Marsh, *Trans. London and Middlesex Arch. Soc.* XXX (1979) p. 129 n.27

55 Boon, *Ant. J.* LXII (1982) 356. On libations, reputedly of Nile water, see Witt 1971, 61, 92

56 Hassall 1980a, 196–8 no. 2

57 Harris and Harris 1965, 80f. The seated goddess illustrated in Henig 1978a, 117 fig. 8 was correctly re-interpreted as Isis by Dr M L Vollenweider (pers. com.). For Harpokrates as Lord of All see Witt 1971, 210–21

58 on the temple: Harris and Harris 1965, 75–6; *R.C.H.M. Eburacum,* 53–4; see Birley 1981, 263–5. The date might be as early as the 170's or as late as the 190's

59 Boon 1973. Alabaster jars, *id.* 1981; 1982a

60 Thompson 1976, 195f, fig. 28 no. 41; Kirk 1949, 38 no. 1 (fig. 8 no. 7); Wright 1970, 305 no. 1; Gilbert 1978, 165 no 5; Kater-Sibbes 1973, 159 no. 829; Faider-Feytmans 1980

61 Wright, 1964; see Chapter 7

62 The chanting of vowels: see Demetrius, *De Elocutione* (translated by W. Rhys Roberts, Cambridge 1902) 71; on salvation: MacMullen 1981, 53 is over-sceptical here. The whole tenor of Egyptian religion was related to the After Life

63 On Isis: see Witt 1971, passim; Apuleius' passage, translated by W Adlington (Loeb Classical Library); on polyonomy: see Witt 1971, 102–3; MacMullen 1981, 90f; For the '*unique*' claims of Sarapis see *ibid.* 53f; Hornbostel 1973, 396

64 Cunliffe and Fulford 1982, no. 29; Fox 1897, 169–70 pl. V; Phillips 1976; Walters 1921, 48–51 nos. 188–94

65 As a saviour god, see Cunliffe and Fulford 1982, no. 3; Toynbee 1962, 128–9 no. 12 pl. 34; *R.I.B.* 1; on the silver plaque see J Hall, *Ant. J.* LXII, 1982, 363–5 on the mosaic see Smith 1977, 109

66 Richmond 1943, 194; Harris and Harris 1965, 56f

67 *ibid.* 57–9; *R.I.B.* 1131

68 e.g. *R.I.B.* 916 (*In honorem domus divinae*) Old Penrith; 1452 (*Pro Salute Augustorum Nostrorum*) Chesters; 1330 (*Pro Salute Imperatoris Caesaris Titi Aeli Hadriani*) Benwell

69 Toynbee 1978; Noll 1980, 52–76

70 MacMullen 1981, 61

71 Speidel 1978, 72–5

72 MacDonald 1979, 425–6, cited by Thomas 1981, 233; Scullard 1981, 207

73 Thomas 1981

74 see exhibition catalogue, *In the Image of Man. The Indian perception of the Universe through 2000 years of painting and sculpture* (London, 1982)

75 Thomas, 1981, 48

76 Eriksen 1980, 46; on the mosaic, *ibid.* passim and splendid earlier accounts, Toynbee 1964a, b; on the Vatican Sol, see Toynbee and Ward Perkins 1956, 116f pl. 32

77 Examples of the epithet *Invictus*-Silvanus: *R.I.B.* 1041 (Bollihope common); Hercules: *R.I.B.* 1215 (Risingham); Sol: *R.I.B.* 1137 (Corbridge); applied to Mithras, e.g. *R.I.B.* 1272 (High Rochester), *R.I.B.* 1395–7 (Rudchester). For Lullingstone labarum, see Toynbee 1964, 224f, pl. LV

78 Huskinson 1974, 73; Hanfmann 1980, 85–7; Eriksen 1980, 47

79 *ibid.* 45–60, citing Dunbabin 1978, 192–3

80 Smith 1977, 107 no. 3

81 Smith 1977, 146

82 Witt 1971, 269–81, especially 273, 281

83 Henig 1978 no. 361

84 Vermaseren 1977, 116–9

85 Thomas 1981, 116–7 (citing *R.I.B.* 307) also 121

86 see Eusebius, *Hist. Eccl.* VIII, 13, 13; Morris 1968; Thomas 1981, 48; Salway 1981, 713 believes it possible that Constantius was so pro-Christian that the attacks on mithraea may have occurred as early as 296 though elsewhere, *ibid.* 340, he states that a mild persecution of Christians could have been the moment at which the Water Newton hoard was buried

87 MacMullen 1981, 127–8

88 Thomas 1981, 170–80; Grimes 1968, 184; on Wells, see Rodwell 1982 – but the structure might very well be post-Roman

89 Rivet and Smith 1979, 49f, for relevant text from *Acta Concilii Arelatensis*

6 Religion in Britain: Cult and Social Function (pp. 128–167)

1 W Stukeley, *Itinerarium Curiosum* Centuria II (London) 1776, 51

2 Wheeler and Wheeler 1932, 86 no. 100; Thompson 1970 (*Dodecahedra*); Charlesworth 1977, 49–51; Henig in Bedwin 1980, 216f no. 114; Butcher 1977, 49–51 (stands)

3 see Cunliffe 1969, 27–8, 185–6; Cunliffe and Fulford 1982, nos. 29–31

4 As Phillips 1977, nos. 49, 105, 182; Cunliffe and Fulford 1982, no. 106, cf. Horsley 1733, 191

5 Green 1976, 220 and pl. XXV g; Wedlake 1982, 226–8, fig. 98 no. 31

6 Jessup 1970; Green 1975, figs. 2–3

7 Downey, King and Soffe 1980, 294; Ellison 1982, 312; also see Greenfield 1963, 261; inf. Norwich Castle Museum

8 A Phillips 1977, nos. 182, 184, 186, 198, 221; Cunliffe and Fulford 1982, no. 106; Penn 1959, 24 and pl. V, c and d; Horsley 1733, 191–1

9 Borlase 1769, 316–8 pl. XXVIII, fig. 1; Cunliffe 1980, 201 pl. XVIII; Toynbee 1962, 172–3, pl. 129 no. 109; Smith 1974, 30 no. 34

10 Painter 1977, 12–13 no. 5

11 Babelon 1916

12 Toynbee 1964, 322, pl. LXXIII b; Green 1976, 212 and pl. XXIV a; see above Chapter 5 n.51 for a probable hand of Atys from Sawbench temple nearby. Also see Chapter 5 for Isis jug

13 Johns and Potter 1983; Painter 1977, 13 no. 7

14 Toynbee 1963; *id.* 1964, 315–7; on the *Haoma* rite see Zaehner 1961, 38, 88–91, 317–8

15 Babelon 1916; Eiden 1950

16 Wheeler and Wheeler 1936, 190f; see May 1933, 144

17 Birley 1979, 122–3

18 *R.I.B.* 155; Cunliffe 1969, 28, 189

19 Wheeler and Wheeler 1932, 103; Hassall 1980, 82; *R.I.B.* 627

20 *R.I.B.* 2065

21 *R.I.B.* 1129

22 see MacMullen 1981, 11, on the provision of experts at sanctuary sites

23 Phillips 1972–4, 177 pl 9c; Smith 1962, 80f; Toynbee 1962, 149 no. 50, pl 53

24 Rosenbaum 1960, 42 no. 14 pl. XIV; Inan and Rosenbaum 1966, 124 no. 143, pl. LXXXV, 1, 2

25 Layard 1925; Toynbee 1964, 338–9; *id.* 1962, 178 no. 128 pl. 139; see Henig 1980, 103. Gilbert 1978, 170–4; *J.R.S.* LII (1963) 138 and pl. XVI, 6; for the head-dresses and other ornaments worn by *galli* see Ferguson 1970, pl 5 and Vermaseren 1977, 97 and pl. 68

26 Layard 1925, pl. xxviii

27 Webster 1973; Forster and Knowles 1014, 300 fig. 11; Home 1924, pl. opp. 130. Information from Valerie Hutchinson. While all these are too small to be temple incense-burners, the burning of incense is well attested and two clay examples have been discovered in Coventina's well, Carrawburgh; *R.I.B.* 1530, 1531 (our illustration 73)

28 on music, see Ginsberg-Klar 1981. Gilbert 1978, 180–1 just failed to recognise the nature of the Felmingham Hall hemispheres

29 Faider-Feytmans 1980; *R.I.B.* 658; Henig 1978 no. 357; *id.* 1983a

30 Corder and Richmond 1938; C M Johns in Potter 1981, 101–4

31 M. Henig, *Britannia* xix (1988), 364–6

32 Boon 1978

33 Hayling Island: G Soffe (pers. com.). It is double-headed. Chalton: see Henig in Cunliffe 1976, 62f no. 4, where the late Roman date proposed is probably incorrect

34 Bruce-Mitford 1978, 310–60; Enright 1983

35 Amy et al 1962, 86 and pl. 44; Alföldi 1949, 19; Norwich Castle Museum (Fitch Colln). Gilbert 1978; Green 1977

36 Gardner and Savory, 68–70, 138–41; Green 1975a

37 Boon 1972, 67f, fig. 39; Henig 1983a

38 Temples: *R.I.B.* 91, 658, 1988; also see Hassall and Tomlin 1977, 430 no. 18; Arches; Petch 1961; Blagg 1980, Jupiter columns are collected by Bauchenss and Noelke 1981, especially 505–7 for Britain; Blagg 1979; Woodfield 1978, 92 no. 18; Henig 1983, colour plate 13 (Lillebonne mosaic) and ill. 112 (Berthouville plate); mosaics: Wheeler and Wheeler 1932; Penn 1959, 21, 23 pl. III

39 on betels, see Alföldi 1949, 19; Künzl 1969, 348–58; Vertet 1961. See Stuart 1981 on a similar

object from Bacharach which may have been from a cult vehicle. Stuart does not, however, think that the Willingham Fen example is a cart-fitting

40 Mitard 1982 discusses parallels from Gaul (cf. n. 58 below for the tin mask from Bath, which is of course much less accomplished in style)

42 *R.I.B.* 2059

42 *R.I.B.* 323 (Caerleon); for the rest, see further below

43 Hassall and Tomlin 1979 no. 3; Wright 1957, 150; Hassall and Tomlin 1982, 404–6 no. 7, which mentions the striking reminiscence to the words of St Paul: 'there is neither bond nor free, there is neither male nor female ...' (*Gal.* 3, 38)

44 Hassall and Tomlin 1981, 372–5 no. 8; *id.* 1979 no. 3; *R.I.B.* 306

45 Hassall and Tomlin 1979, 341–2 no. 2

46 Wright 1968, 150

47 Turner 1963

48 Hassall and Tomlin 1982, 408–9 no. 9

49 Wright and Hassall 1973, 325

50 see note 43

51 Bell, Martin, Turner and Van Berchem 1962, 99–118

52 Toynbee 1978; Noll 1980, 52–76

53 Toynbee 1978; Wedlake 1982, 143–5 and frontispiece; *Britannia* x (1979), 309 and pl. XV A

54 *R.I.B.* 215

55 Henig 1979a, 24

56 *R.I.B.* 191, 194, 195, 305, 219

57 *R.I.B.* 313, 274

58 Wacher 1975, 287 pl. 54; Mitard 1982, especially 31–3 no. 14

59 Kirk 1949, 45 nos. 30–32 Fig. 9 no. 11; Goodchild and Kirk 1964, 28 nos. 1–5, Fig. 10 and pl. III c (Woodeaton); Wheeler and Wheeler 1932, 102, no. 8, pl. XXXIV (Lydney); Conlon 1973, 37 and Fig. 4 (Harlow)

60 Taylor 1963; Wheeler 1981; Henig in Ellison 1978, 37f; *id.*, 1980, 322; Wheeler and Wheeler 1932, 40, 89; Kirk 1949, 30f; Henig and Munby 1973; Boon 1973; picture of Lamyatt Beacon cache in *J.R.S.* LI (1961) pl. XX, Mars, Hercules, Minerva, Mercury and a Genius

61 on models, see Green 1975; Manning 1966; Hubert and Mauss 1964, 12

62 Wheeler 1981, 310 and pl. L

63 Butcher 1977, 49–51, 54–6

64 Jenkins 1958; *id.* in Penn 1959, 55ff fig. 12; also in Dudley 1967, 19f, pl. IV b; Wheeler and Wheeler 1936, 190f; Penn 1960, 126f fig. 8.17; Ellison 1978, 40; Wedlake 138–42; *R.I.B.* 1530, 1531

65 Henig 1980, 101–2

66 Hassall 1980, 84; see Charlesworth 1961, 24 no.

1; *R.C.H.M. Eburacum*, 133 nos. 140, 141. Mr Jack Ogden informs me of other 'Tot' rings from eastern Britain; R P Wright in Collis 1970, 257–9 on ostentatious gifts as a means of acquiring prestige, see Bradley 1982

67 see Cunliffe 1980, 201 (breasts); Painter 1971 and Barker c. 1981, 16 (eyes); Wheeler and Wheeler 1932, 24 no. 121; Penn 1964, 173 pl. 1.B; Green 1976, 220 (limbs); on Corinth see Lang 1977; on Forêt de la Halatte, see Espérandieu 1913, 126–43

68 *R.I.B.* 1426; see Hassall 1980, 81

69 Parke 1967, 137–41

70 Birley 1974

71 *R.I.B.* 1228, 1791

72 Apuleius' *Metamorphoses* XI, 5; see J Gwyn Griffiths, *The Isis Book* (Leiden, 1975), 75 and commentary

73 *R.I.B.*1778 (dated AD 136–8)

74 *R.I.B.* 153; Cunliffe 1969, 198 no. 4.3

75 *R.I.B.* 1024

76 e.g. *R.I.B.* 587, 1131

77 F H Thompson 1976, 168–9, and note by R P Wright p. 184; for the *defixio*, which is anonymous, see *R.I.B.* 323

78 Finucane 1977

79 Julian Munby points out this remarkable dream to me. See F Tupper and M B Ogle, *Master Walter Map's Book 'De Nugis Curialium'* (London, 1924), 291

80 Finucane 1977, 92–5

81 Brown 1981, 69ff

82 *ibid.* 106ff

83 Turner 1963, 122

84 Bastet 1979, 33–4 pl. 21 a–d

85 see Brown 1978, 41–5

86 as Alan Wardman points out (Wardman 1982, 10), a temple had to be inaugurated – *i.e.* marked out by augury. Small, private foundations were not legally temples

87 Wheeler and Wheeler 1936, 113–20; on lamp chimneys, see Lowther 1976, 35–6, 48

88 On London (Walbrook) see Merrifield 1969, 92 and 168ff; Marsden 1980, 74–5. On Springhead see Harker 1980; Salway 1981, 596. The Altbachtal is published by Gose 1972

89 On Bath in general, see Cunliffe 1969; on the spring, *id.* 1980. On coal see G Webster, 'A Note on the use of coal in Roman Britain', *Ant. J.* xxxv (1955) 199–217. Salway, 1981, 515 n. 1, makes the interesting suggestion that freedmen were sometimes sent by their *patroni* 'as proxies to set up a dedication at the healing shrine'. The coins, see Nash 1982 for an interim statement, not followed up by Walker in Cunliffe 1988. For Fontaines Salée see Louis 1943

90 Ellison 1980

91 Wedlake 1982, 16

92 Wheeler and Wheeler 1932

93 Percival 1976, 155, 214 no. 39

94 C H V Sutherland in Bradford and
Goodchild 1939, 49–53, 61–5; Hingley 1982

95 Carson and O'Kelly 1977, especially 42, 49

96 Bedwin 1981; ApSimon 1965

97 Toynbee 1976, 92, 88f, 81

98 Hull 1958, 236–40 pl. XXXVIII; Richmond and
Wright 1948–51; Wright 1944–7

99 Boon 1972, 100 (Caerleon) – also see *R.I.B.* 323
on *defixio* from amphitheatre; Thompson
1976, 166–70 (Chester)

100 Boon 1974, 58, 172

101 *R.I.B.* 247, 270; Hassall in Down 1981, 101 and
pl. 13; Hassall and Tomlin 1981, 384 no. 36

102 *R.I.B.* 2102–3 (Birrens), 1327–9 (Benwell); on
Corbridge, see Richmond 1943, 132–4

103 cf. *R.I.B.* 6–7 (London) and 221 (Clothall,
Herts.)

104 Jordan 1980

105 *R.I.B.* 6, 154, 221; Scullard 1981, 75

106 Sterne, *Tristram Shandy* Book III, Ch. XI;
Merrifield 1954; *id.* 1955

107 Webster 1966–7, 126–9; Scullard 1981, 118f

108 *ibid.* 91; Moore 1975; on phalli in general, now
see Johns 1982

7 Religion and Superstition in The Home and in Daily Life (pp. 168–189)

1 see the sacred images scattered through
sacro-idyllic landscape painting. Peters 1963

2 '*Querolus* sive *Aulularia*' ed. G Ranstrand
(Göteborg, 1951), 5ff

3 Scullard 1981, 58–60; Curle 1911, 283

4 Boon 1973b; *id.* 1974, 160–4; Frere 1972, 57–60;
Orr 1978, 1589f

5 Bushe-Fox 1949, 133–5 no. 158, pl. XLI; Smith
1962, 80f, pl. XI, 1; Boon 1973; Pitts 1979, 67f;
Gilbert 1978, 164–5

6 A R Millard, unpublished interim report on
1956 season

7 Onians 1951, 95–122

8 Meates 1979, 21, 36

9 Toynbee in Cunliffe 1971, II, 156–7; Ashby 1902,
148 fig. 6; Ross 1967, 88 and *passim*, Williams and
Delaney 1982

10 Maiuri 1932, 98–106, figs. 47–9

11 Orr 1978, 1572–5. The Verulamium pot is
illustrated in Society of Antiquaries of
London MS 720, p. 164, and I am grateful to
the librarian Mr John Hopkins for pointing it
out to me, see Cunliffe 1968, 107 no. 246 for
other examples and references

12 Frere 1972, 105f, 140–4; McParke, Bulmer and
Rutter 1980, 24

13 Green 1974; Lysons 1797, 10–11,
pls. XXXVI–XXXIX; Clarke 1982, 207–9;
Branigan 1976, 63–4, pls. 26, 27

14 Toynbee in Down 1979, 181–3; G Speake, *Ant. J.*
LXII 1982, 377–9; Henig 1981; *id.* in Frere 1982,
193f; Cunliffe and Fulford 1982, no. 96

15 Marsden [1967], 37

16 Henig 1982, 218

17 Toynbee 1964, 221; Meates 1979, 33f

18 Goodburn 1972, 24; Thomas 1981, 219–20

19 Smith 1977, 120 no. 49, 141 no. 52

20 Scullard 1981, 17

21 Frere 1959, 12 pl. IVb

22 *R.I.B.* 325; Scullard 1981, 79–80; Henig 1982, 214

23 Scullard 1981, 124–5

24 on Silvanus: *R.I.B.* 181 (Keynsham); also
Goodburn 1972, 27

25 Boon 1976. G E McCracken, *Arnobius of Sicca.
The case against the Pagans* (Westminster,
Maryland, 1949)

26 Henig 1978, *passim*; on death, see Henig 1977

27 on mythology, Smith 1977. Valerie
Hutchinson has assembled a very impressive
corpus of material from Britain associated
with Bacchus

28 Smith 1969, 82

29 Toynbee 1964, 276–7; Smith 1977, 107 no. 3;
R.I.B. 292; cf. Maiuri 1953, 115, for skeleton of
butler on Pompeian mosaic

30 Smith 1977, 108–10

31 Cunliffe 1971, I, 163–5; Toynbee 1974, 276

32 *ibid.* 250f

33 Barrett 1977

34 Wheeler and Wheeler 1932, 65–6, 102 pl. XIX;
Eschebach 1978, 311 pl. 204, Smith 1977, 134 no.
104

35 *id.*, 134 no. 100, 135 no. 107

36 Swain and Ling 1981; however, compare pl.
XI B with Lehmann 1953, fig. 27 and pp. 52–4
(Lehmann's interpretation is controversial,
but I find it convincing)

37 Toynbee 1964, 241–46

38 For myths on mosaics, see Smith 1977

39 as funerary images, cf. Toynbee 1971, 165, 173

40 Smith 1977, 118–9; the Ostian mosaic: Becatti
1961, pl. LXXII, 42; for *antefixa*, see Hull 1958,
pl. XXX B, and Toynbee 1964, 429–31

41 Thomas 1981, 101

42 Toynbee 1964, 95; Boon 1974, 292, fig. 34, 7;
Bushe-Fox 1949, 135 no. 159

43 Henig 1979

44 Batteley 1774, 116; Boon 1980

45 Henig 1977

46 Murray 1981, 23

47 Henig 1977, 116, 248f, nos. 493; *id.* 1980, 93–4 pl. 5.1

48 on the Carlisle gem, see McCarthy, Padley
and Henig 1982, 84. For others, see Henig 1978,

72–4, 77f

49 *ibid.* 77.

50 *ibid.* 68–86

51 *ibid.* 104f

52 Compare Hassall 1977 with Henig 1978, 195 no. 77, 222 no. 302, 305 no. App. 140; also Toynbee 1962, 157 no. 80, pl. 77 with Henig 1978, 294–5, no. App. 79 and 303–4 no. App. 129. For eagle and standard gems, see Henig 1978, 270f nos. 705–7; and the High Rochester inscriptions dedicated to the standards, *R.I.B.* 1262, 1263

53 Henig 1978, 88

54 *ibid.*; *R.I.B.* 1783, 1124, 1129, 1171

55 Kater-Sibbes 1973, 160 no. 836, for this interpretation which I now accept. See Henig 1978, no. 358 and McCann 1968, 183 pl. xcii j, for the view that it shows Septimius Severus with his sons Caracalla and Geta as Serapis and the Dioscuri respectively. On the Chesterholm gem, see Henig 1977a and Henig 1978 no. App. 148

56 Henig 1972; *id.* 1978, 95, 231 no. 366. The titles Sabaoth and Abrasax both appear on a gem from the Thetford treasure; see Hassall and Tomlin 1982. On the type, see Le Glay 1981

57 Henig 1978, nos. 359 (also G Boon, *Ant. J.* LXII (1982)), 356, 33, 103 and App. 214; also *id.* 1977b

58 Henig 1978, nos. 361–2; Thomas 1981, 130–2

59 Henig 1978, 106

60 Information from Mr P R Scott

61 Sena Chiesa 1966, 79; *id.* 1978, 41

62 Henig 1978, 100f

63 Ross 1968a; *id.* 1972 and Frere 1972a for inconclusive discussion of this gem

64 Field 1981. For prehistoric bronze belt-links, see Gray and Bulleid 1953, 216–7 and pl. XLVI, nos. E103 and E163

65 on jet, see Toynbee 1974, 363ff; Drury 1973

66 Bushe-Fox 1913, 30f no. 27; *id.* 1949, 128 no. 111. I am grateful to the local archaeological unit for information on the Milton Keynes amulet

67 on rings, see Henig 1978, 278 nos. 765–6; bronze, Webster 1966–7; Fowles and Legg 1980, 388f, 506f; Bradshaw 1980; Perkins 1981; Down 1978, 296f no. 49; antler, *ibid.* 314f no. 208; Frere and St Joseph 1974, 59–71. Dr Hugh Chapman kindly informs me of an example from London with rivets in place. For general accounts of phalli, see Turnbull in *Bull. Inst. of Arch.* 15, 1978 and Johns 1982

68 Jenkins 1978, 159f no. 13; Sun and moon on jewellery from Italy: Siviero 1954, 54 no. 168, pls. 138–9; as a motif in the East: Goodenough 1956; on jewellery from Britain, see Charlesworth 1961, 21, 34–5 nos. 1–3: for explanation as Taranis, Green 1979

69 Charlesworth 1977; On Thetford see Johns and Potter 1983

70 useful articles in I Singer (ed.), *Jewish Encyclopaedia* (New York and London 1901–6) especially L Blau on *Amulets*, P M Casanowicz on the *Mezuzah*, L Blau and E G Hirsch on *Phylacteries*; for Amulets and amulet cases from Britain see MacGregor 1976, 10f no. 72; *R.I.B.* 436, 706; Wright 1970, 305 no. 1. On material elsewhere, see Walters 1911, 377–82 nos. 3150–3157, and Preisendanz 1928–41

71 Henig in McCarthy, Padley and Henig 1982, 88f

72 see Evans 1922

73 Bonner 1950 is still the best general introduction

74 see Hassall and Tomlin 1982, 421–2

75 Wright 1964; Wheeler and Wheeler 1936, 221f and pl. LXVI a

76 Carson and O'Kelly 1977; Stevenson 1967; Laver 1927, 250 (pl. LX, fig. 3). Information R Downey, A King and G Soffe; Branigan 1972; Evans 1922, 175 pl. IV

8 Religion and Burial Practice
(pp. 190–205)

1 *R.I.B.* 292; Richmond 1950, 1–24; *R.C.H.M. Eburacum*, 73

2 I follow Toynbee, 1971, 40f, rather than Jones 1981

3 Stead 1979; *id.* 1967

4 Biddle 1967, especially 248

5 Laver 1927; May 1930, 251–3 pl. LXXV; Hull 1952, 251; see Henig 1982, 214

6 Alcock 1980, 53; Jenkins 1978, 160–1; *R.C.H.M. Eburacum*, 69, pl. 31; Kelly and Dudley 1981, 83f

7 Gage 1834, 1–23; 1836, 300–17; on the tradition, see Jessup 1959

8 Reece 1977a, 44

9 Gage 1834, 8; *id.* 1836, 303; *id.* 1842, 3; Wickham 1874; Jessup 1959, 27f

10 *R.I.B.* 491; Hatt 1951, 85–107

11 Lattimore 1962, 90ff; Alcock 1980, 63; MacDonald 1979, 421–3; *R.I.B.* 137

12 Down and Rule 1971, 103, Burial Group 127, cup C; Alcock 1980, 56

13 *R.I.B.* 292; Jessup 1954, 12; *id.* 1959, 21; Liversidge 1977, 30f; see Boon 1974, 351 no. 55

14 Wheeler 1929; Boon 1973a; Down and Rule 1971, 72

15 Alcock 1980, 62; Godwin 1956, 181; Cumont 1949, 42ff; Phillips 1976a, 105 pl. XV

16 Alcock 1980, 60f; May 1930, 178–91; Down and Rule 1971, 71f; *R.C.H.M. Eburacum* 87 fig. 66; Marsden 1980, 76f; Partridge 1981, 272f

17 Jessup 1959, 11–32

18 M Popham, E Touloupa and L H Sackett,

'The hero of Lefkandi', *Antiquity* LVI (1982), 169–74; Ellison 1980, 305

19 Brown 1981, especially 69ff

20 Meates 1979, 122–32; Green, C J S, 1977; Stead 1967; Clarke 251–4, col. pl. 1b

21 Brewer 1813, 462–4

22 Alcock 1980, 64; Wright and Richmond 1955, no. 108; *R.I.B.* 562; also note other tombstones *ibid*. nos. 111–16

23 Lions: Gillam and Daniels 1961, 53, 55; Toynbee 1964, 114; Liversidge 1977, 19f. Sphinxes: Toynbee 1964, 112–3; *R.C.H.M. Eburacum* 131 no. 120. Both lions and sphinxes: *R.I.B.* 121, 201; Medusa: e.g. *R.I.B.* 295; see Meates 1979, 129. Jet Medusas from burials, *R.C.H.M. Eburacum*, 142

24 *R.I.B.* 758, 1253 (see Phillips 1977, 97f no. 98 for fuller reading), 684

25 Alcock 1980, 57–60, 66–73; Salway 1981, 704; MacDonald 1979, 409, 412–4, where it is suggested that jewellery was also given to the gods of the dead rather than as ornament for the deceased

26 *ibid*. 407; Rashleigh 1803, 222 pl. XXXIX; Salway 1981, 705

27 *R.C.H.M. Eburacum*, 132 no. 130; Cumont 1949, 208ff fig. 2 (stele from Walbersdorf); Payne 1874

28 For such formulae as these Orphic instructions in the gold *lamellae*, perhaps Hellenistic, from Petelia (and others elsewhere) see Harrison 1903, 660–74

29 Toynbee 1977

30 Boon 1973a, 358; Alcock 1980, 50f

31 *ibid*. 51; Breeze and Ritchie 1980, 78 no. 1

32 Toynbee 1977, 366–86 on the Labours in general, especially 384; *R.C.H.M. Eburacum*, 71; May 1930, 252 no. 1126

33 Branigan 1976, 64 pl. 27; Toynbee in Jessup 1954, 34–40; Cumont 1949, 278f

34 *R.C.H.M. Eburacum*, 86 no. f.xii fig. 66; *R.I.B.* 1745, 1714

35 Ambrose and Henig 1980; see Richmond 1950, 22–3

36 Hassall and Tomlin 1980, 406f no. 7; Strong 1911, 17; Phillips 1977, 99 no. 268, 95 no. 258; Alcock 1980, 54

37 Toynbee 1971, 54f; Webster 1979, 271f

38 Henig 1977; Meates 1979, pls. III, IV; Toynbee 1964, 59–63 pl. X; *ibid*. 185 pl. XLVI a; *R.C.H.M. Eburacum*, 128 no 96

39 Marsden 1980, 76; MacDonald 1979, 414–21 (who suggests ritual sacrifice); McWhirr, Viner and Wells 1982, 108–9, 194 (penal execution)

9 Religion and Politics (pp. 206–216)

1 Marsh and West 1981, esp. p. 97; Toynbee 1963, 123 no. 1, pl. 7; *id*. 1964, 46–8 pl. iv. See Dyson 1971, especially pp. 261ff on the psycho-religious nature of the Boudican revolt

2 Petch 1962 (Mars Rigonemetos)

3 *R.I.B.* 1051

4 Steer 1958; *id*. 1976

5 Murray 1896

6 *R.I.B.* 1137

7 Blagg 1980

8 Merrifield 1980; *R.I.B.* 1791; Hassall 1980a

9 *R.I.B.* 1971; and cf. *C.I.L.* XIII, 6671 (Mainz) Iuliae Augustae Caelesti Deae

10 Jolliffe 1941, 55. Originally she was probably the local eponymous goddess of the Brigantes

11 Toynbee 1962, 157 no. 80 pl. 77; Smith in Liversidge, Smith and Stead 1973, 92. Identification as *Brigantia* suggested by Henig in *L.I.M.C*

12 Sutherland 1958, 10; Webb 1933, 426ff. cf. also Casey 1977

13 on the seal see Henig 1977b; note the portrait head of Constantine from York: Toynbee 1962, 125 no. 6 pl. 12 and Thomas 1981, pl. 2; on coins see Sutherland 1967, 131ff; Bruun 1966, 97–106; Casey 1978

14 *R.I.B.* 4

15 Merrifield 1977, 376–8 pl. 171b; see Casey 1978

16 Excavations at Lydney (by P J Casey) have shown that much of the building is earlier than the Wheelers believed, probably late third and early fourth century but the cult certainly continued well into the second half of the century. cf. University of Durham/ University of Newcastle upon Tyne, *Archaeological Reports for 1980* (Durham 1981), 30–32; *R.I.B.* 102; Stupperich 1980

17 Brown 1968; on Pelagius also see Birley 1979, 134–56

10 Adaptation and Change: Pagans and Christians in Late Antiquity (pp. 217–228)

1 E Mâle, *L'Art Religieux du XIIIe siècle en France* Paris, 1902) 223–5 and fig. 83

2 Hassall and Tomlin 1982, 404–6 no. 7. See Chapter 6

3 trans. R H Barrow, *Prefect and Emperor. The Relationes of Symmachus AD 384* (Oxford, 1973), 41

4 *R.I.B.* 103

5 *R.I.B.* 152

6 on Bryn Walters' view, see *Current Archaeology* No. 80 (December 1981) 264–8. The theory, that this is a cult-room, has been criticised by Jocelyn Toynbee (1981) and by Roger Ling and Michael Insley, *Current Archaeology* No. 82 (May 1982), 350. I have defended Walters' interpretation in broad outline, *ibid*. No. 83 (August 1982) 375

7 Jones 1964, 938
8 *Ellenikon Therapeutike Pathematon* 3.79–84, cited by Gazda 1981, 167
9 Price and Hilton Price 1881
10 Lehmann 1962
11 Stupperich 1980, 301
12 see Gazda 1981, 167, note 58; Wacher 1974, 354–5
13 Collins-Clinton 1977
14 Frere 1975; see now King 1983
15 Eiden 1950
16 Hanfmann 1980, 89–90
17 Hassall and Tomlin 1981, 389–93; Johns and Potter 1983
18 Scullard 1981, 72, 76–8, 201; Henig 1982, 214–6
19 Wheeler 1943, 74ff
20 see Grinsell 1976, 16ff; Brittany (settled by Britons in post-Roman times) maintains many ancient customs; at one *Pardon* which I attended, as a child, a green bough was thrown down from a church tower, the remnant of some vegetation rite perhaps?
21 Hope-Taylor 1977, 265–6, 278–9; Enright 1983
22 Clarke 1979, 372–5; MacDonald 1979, 414–21; Meaney and Hawkes 1970, 30–32
23 Ellison 1980, 313f; Meates 1979, 39; Merrifield 1977, 397
24 see Wedlake 1982, 79–82 for re-use of a small part of the Nettleton temple (?Fifth century). Rahtz and Watts 1979, especially 199f, well at Cannington near Bridgwater;

25 Brown 1977; *id.* 1981
26 Turner 1982, 21–5 (Witham, Font), West 1976 (Icklingham, Font and Church); Uley (church) see n.23 above. Also note Thomas 1981, 218–9
27 J Gillingham, *The Wars of the Roses* (London, 1981), 54, citing John Blackman, the King's Chaplain
28 Grinsell 1980; Bettey 1981
29 There is a vast bibliography: see especially K Woodbridge, *Landscape and Antiquity: Aspects of English Culture at Stourhead 1718 to 1838* (Oxford, 1970), and his National Trust Guide, *The Stourhead Landscape* (London, 1982)
30 Rahtz and Watts 1979, 201f, on a black Wedgwood teapot lid with a female mourning figure on it, from the temple at Pagans Hill. The author would like to apologise for misleading a friend and the public in the matter of a similar lid from Levens Park (*Britannia* VI, 1975, 216–8). It came from a possible Roman temple site in an English seventeenth and eighteenth century park. The *Comparanda* assembled by Julian Munby are totally valid, and such considerations would have been well known in the eighteenth century when the lid was lost, or probably deliberately dedicated to Diana. See also Sturdy 1973, 32 fig. 3

Index